Making the Connections

Using internal communication to turn
strategy into action

Bill Quirke

Gower

© Bill Quirke 2000

Paperback edition published 2002

Published by
Gower Publishing Limited
Gower House
Croft Road
Aldershot
England Hampshire GU11 3HR

Gower
131 Main Street
Burlington, VT 05401–5600
USA

Bill Quirke has asserted his right under the Copyright, Designs and Patents Act 1988 to be identified as the author of this work.

British Library Cataloguing in Publication Data
Quirke, Bill, 1954 –
    Making the connections : using internal communication to
    turn strategy into action
    1. Communication in management 2. Communication in
    organizations 3. Information resources management
    4. Organizational change
    I. Title
    658.4'5

ISBN 0 566 08175 X [hbk]
ISBN 0 566 08517 8 [pbk]

Printed and bound in Great Britain by
MPG Books Ltd, Bodmin, Cornwall

Contents

List of figures

Preface

Making the connection

Companies know that communication with their people is important. They know that the energies and the enthusiasm of their employees need to point in the same direction. However, in the enthusiastic rush to plug together different components of communication best practice, many organizations are shortcircuiting their own efforts. There is no shortage of good intentions and no shortfall in professionalism and good ideas. However, the road to incoherence is paved with good communications. Often, internal communication is less than the sum of its parts, because those parts do not fit together effectively. Organizations concentrate on getting the right individual parts and then merely cobble them together – the recipe for Frankenstein's monster.

What's the problem?

Too often, those on the front line report that there are fatal disconnects between the business strategy and the communication strategy. There is no clear link between information that is sent to employees and what they are supposed to understand from it. The small detail, carefully crafted in the boardroom, makes no sense when it is divorced from its context. Meanwhile, companies are keen to find new technological approaches to communication that only exacerbate the problem.

Life is moving too fast to rely on the inadequate way we currently communicate in organizations. Today's best practice hero too easily becomes tomorrow's financial zero. Employees who thought their company was doing well and their future was secure can suddenly discover that events on the other side of the globe can put them out of a job.

In a world of tighter interdependencies, where fortunes are so closely linked, people need a better understanding of the connections. Internal communication has absorbed too well the lesson that the medium is the message. The message is often failing to get through because the medium eats the message. We need to move from the message and media business to that of creating meaning and understanding.

What needs to change

In an information age, internal communication is the core process which enables businesses to engage their people's intellectual and creative assets to produce value. Despite the increasing complexity of the world, people still want to know some simple truths about what is going on, and they want to be treated as if they matter.

We have to make two changes simultaneously – identify what is the intended business value in communicating and design a better process to deliver that value. We have to shift from seeing internal communication as a process of distribution, to using it as a process of conversion. Just as an assembly line worker converts, or adds value to, a component he receives from up the line, so we have to convert information we receive into meaning in order to make the right decisions.

The role of internal communication is to illuminate the connections between different pieces of information, to shine a light on the web of interdependencies and to show the links between one area and another. Its job is to provide the information to do the job, but to paint the bigger picture and to tell the fuller story that puts that information into context.

How this book will help

This book looks at what a successful business needs from its people, what gets in the way, and the role of communication in helping bridge the gap. It is designed to help companies link together the disparate components of their internal communication for a more effective result. It describes the why, the what and the how of internal communication – why business needs better communication to achieve its objectives, what internal communication needs to deliver to add value, and how organizations need to manage their communication for best results.

Its aims are fourfold:

- ■ to target communication on creating business value
- ■ to show how to plan communication for greater coherence
- ■ to argue for the importance of context in turning information into meaning
- ■ to push the importance of conversation to centre stage.

The book is organized into four Parts. Part I, 'Turning Communication to Advantage', shows how organizations need better communication to deliver results and how the management and practice of internal communication need to be improved in order to meet business's needs.

Part II, 'Talking Business', examines how good communication can produce greater value by addressing key issues at the top of business agendas. It focuses on the key concerns of chief executives – creating competitive differentiation, developing new markets and products, reducing cost, streamlining processes, restructuring and redefining the roles of the divisions and the corporate centre. It highlights how internal communication can help organizations achieve their strategic objectives by enabling employees to deliver a differentiating proposition to customers, making restructuring work, or increasing cross-business collaboration, and innovation.

Change is a significant feature of today's business world and Part III, 'Changing Communication' looks at how to use communication to make more effective change and how to create greater responsiveness and agility within the organization. It gives specific recommendations for communicating change, driving change initiatives and projects, promoting internal campaigns and sustaining greater responsiveness.

In terms of their internal communication, organizations first have to do the right thing by connecting communication strategy to their business strategy and, second, do things right – have efficient and effective processes. Part IV, 'Pulling it Together', shows how to structure and manage internal communication to deliver the business agenda and closely details the links in the communication chain.

Satellite broadcasts alienate the middle managers they were designed to inspire, and e-mail clutters and voicemail frustrates instead of helping. Face-to-face meetings force managers to undermine their own credibility by presenting irrelevant and tedious corporate information. Then, after all the effort and the investment involved in communicating, the finance director asks the inevitable question about the cost and value of internal communication.

As the quantity of information increases the quality decreases. Although employees are sent more and more pieces of the jigsaw, they are unable to put them together to form a coherent picture. Organizations indulge in 'flatpack communication' – sending out the components of the picture and relying on the recipient to assemble them, with the inevitable result that the end-product has a few screws loose or missing.

Why this happens

None of this is inevitable. Some simple links and connections can be made to ensure that communication helps, rather than hinders, the business. This book is about making those connections. It explains how businesses can use better internal communication to achieve differentiation from their competition, to improve their quality, customer service, and innovation, and to manage change more effectively. It shows how organizations need to use their best 'joined-up' communication if they want to be successful.

Bill Quirke

Acknowledgements

My thanks to Jane Lebeau for pulling this book together, to Rupert Cryer for his research and background work, and to Alyson Lamb and Richard Bloomfield for sharing their thinking.

BQ

Part I
Turning Communication to Advantage

Valuing communication

Business today faces a torrent of changes that redefines what is required of employees. Organizations are quickly discovering that they need more than simple compliance from their staff: they need – now more than ever – to engage their minds, creativity, energy and commitment. A business can only achieve its best when everyone's energies point in the same direction.

This changes not only the assumptions on which internal communication is based, but also the job it is intended to do. Traditionally, internal communication has focused on the announcement of management conclusions and the packaging of management thinking into messages for mass distribution to the 'troops'. However, its real place is at the leading edge of change. The value that it can add is immense – faster change, more flexibility and innovation, better quality decisions, better knowledge-sharing and a more motivated workforce. Although, as a whole, leaders believe in the power of communication, even leading companies fail to harness that power to deliver the necessary results. Internal communication is vital to success but must, first, be reinvented so that it can be used for strategic advantage through aligning attitudes, sharing knowledge and managing information.

The purpose of this chapter is to lay the foundation for the remainder of the book by highlighting the urgent need to improve communication, the business pay-off for doing so and the gap that needs to be closed between aspirations and day-to-day practice. It also makes the connection between the business issues that senior management see as priorities and the importance of good communication to achieving them. It describes how successful organizations see the value of internal communication and the distinctive way in which they treat it as a means to an end, and highlights those areas in which outdated approaches have created toxic complexity that must be reduced.

Trapped in a time warp

The problem is very simple – although success depends on a new approach to internal communication, organizations are spending all their time and effort on an outdated one. Failure to change in organizations is due to the disconnect between the communication that the business needs and the communication it receives. In other words, internal communication is trapped in a time warp. If cars had improved at the same rate as computers, says Bill Gates, we'd have $25 cars achieving 1000 miles to the gallon. But if cars had improved at the same rate as internal communication, we'd still be walking in front of them with a red flag!

The way in which organizations have approached communication has been based on applying outdated rules – with disappointing and frustrating results. Companies are falling into a vicious circle. By failing to make a strong enough connection between business strategy and internal communication, they then fail to plan and monitor progress appropriately. Finally they become increasingly frustrated by the failure of communication to deliver results. Although their expectations may have been low, their approach has not met them. Organizations have expected employees to know what is required. This is not enough, and organizations are short-changing themselves by not seeing communication through to the end – converting awareness into action. The real value of internal communication is to help deliver business ends by enabling employees to turn strategy into action. However, getting there means draining a swamp of communication confusion and complexity to create a path of coherence and consistency.

What is changing?

The job which internal communication has to do has changed because organizations are facing unprecedented pressures to deliver in a rapidly changing environment. Research consistently shows that senior managers have five principal concerns:

- creating competitive differentiation
- developing new markets and products
- reducing cost and streamlining processes
- restructuring, integrating an acquisition, making a merger work or divesting a non-core business
- redefining the roles of the corporate centre and the divisions.

Organizations are discovering that business challenges like these can all be affected by the clear targeting and management of internal communication. However, a 'one size fits all' approach will not work and internal communication needs to be aligned specifically with the organization's individual business strategy. Discussed below are four examples of how different strategies demand different internal communication approaches and how seriously successful companies take the role of internal communication.

Using internal communication to create competitive differentiation

Tesco, the UK supermarket chain, aims to create greater loyalty among its customers and to increase the average size of their shopping basket. One enjoyable personal contact with staff per trip, their research shows, can earn lifetime loyalty from a customer.

Tesco employs 150,000 staff in 560 stores who need to deliver this experience to its customers. Since personal contact plays such a key role in customer retention, employees must understand Tesco's brand promise. The job of internal communication is to create a deeper understanding of the brand promise among employees, and to help them translate it into specific actions for customers – opening up checkouts when queues get long, packing bags, helping shoppers take their shopping out to the car park and even providing jump leads when their car batteries go flat. Internal communication's value lies in helping differentiate Tesco from its competitors and creating higher customer loyalty for higher profitability.

In the world of professional services the big five accountancy and consulting firms are federations which share a name and a culture. Now they want to build distinctive brands. Ernst & Young, KPMG, Pricewaterhouse, Coopers and Andersen Consulting are spending significantly on building global brands. Their investment is aimed at differentiating themselves and reassuring their clients worldwide, who feel branding is increasingly important in helping them choose from whom to buy a service.

These firms sell a diverse set of sophisticated services worldwide, but global clients expect consistent delivery throughout the world, wherever offices are located. Global branding carries with it the promise of global consistency.

Professional service firms have to develop a portfolio of standard processes differentiated by strong brand values, thought leadership and the ability to develop solutions for clients. These ambitions demand not only better management of the knowledge and learning within the firm but also greater collaboration between employees. Creating value therefore demands that employees have an external focus, since it is knowledge of their clients' industry issues which demonstrates a real familiarity with the business and helps win contracts. The challenge is for employees to combine knowledge and understanding of the client's problems with the knowledge of the consultancy's worldwide capabilities that could help solve them.

Ernst & Young uses internal communication to help them do just that. Its role is to help create an organization which is increasingly comfortable with continuous change, has higher levels of staff retention, increased project efficiency and knowledge management, and thus greater client value.

Using internal communication to developing new products and markets

SmithKline Beecham (SB) is a successful company in a very successful sector, with spectacular growth figures. Within the consumer healthcare organization internal communication is clearly linked to creating shareholder value.

The company's strategy is to exploit its portfolio of brands as effectively as possible. To do that, SB Consumer Healthcare applies global processes with a local face in individual markets. The aim is to drive greater innovation and creativity across the business, to reduce costs and to reduce duplication by sharing services. They also aim to standardize processes where possible, because it makes it easier to improve them and focuses time and effort on innovation in new areas, rather than on reinventing wheels that exist elsewhere in the business.

To SB the importance of internal communication lies in helping develop a pan-European business in which managers from each country understand and support a European approach and have stronger local ownership of global processes.

Using internal communication to reduce cost and streamline processes

Unipart manufactures and distributes auto parts to car manufacturers and a large supply chain for the replacement market. In terms of quality and productivity it is now a world leader. It has three key objectives – remove cost and waste, improve productivity and deliver outstanding customer service.

Unipart's aim is for their 4000 employees to help achieve those objectives, as well as pursuing its core crusade of achieving 50 per cent more for 50 per cent less cost. Its key to achieving this is to target the supply chain. The organization recognizes that there is a close interdependence between the suppliers in the chain. If there are inefficiencies, duplication and waste in the supplier at the bottom of the chain, these are inevitably passed upwards. Waste is then multiplied at each successive link, saddling the ultimate customer with disproportionately high costs. Beating the competition therefore requires a much tighter management of the supply chain.

Unipart has developed its own approach to supply chain management which involves working in project teams with suppliers to identify the hidden cost of transactions which benefit nobody and eliminate them, thereby reducing cost and inconvenience to both parties. This approach is in stark contrast to the traditional one of using purchasing power to browbeat suppliers into offering better deals.

However, to make this partnership approach work, attitudes and behaviours needed to shift within the Unipart workforce; they had to understand and buy into the ethos of partnership and let go of the browbeating approach.

For Unipart the importance of internal communication lies in providing employees with the knowledge to do the job, the will to identify and make change, and the licence and permission to get on and do it.

All these organizations have adopted a similar approach to internal communication. They have approached it as a means to an end, rather than an end in itself, and they have:

- clearly identified their strategy
- made the connection between the strategy and the specific attitudes and behaviours they need from their people
- focused their communication on helping achieve those attitudes and behaviour

Using internal communication to gain people's support for the business strategy

Organizations are keen for their employees to understand the business strategy but, more importantly, they want their people to help turn this strategy into reality by providing excellent customer service, continuous improvement and innovation.

A company thrives by offering customers something different and more valuable than its competitors can. It has to ensure that its employees deliver on the promise it makes to customers and that employee values, loyalty and behaviour are all connected. Building an internal culture that creates unity and pride among employees acts as a competitive edge that is difficult for competitors to copy.

Indifference, however, can kill differentiation. Customers' satisfaction is affected by their experience of the entire organization's performance, so employee attitudes and behaviour are critical to retaining them. The *Journal of Marketing* cites the main reasons for customer defection as being employee-related. While only 9 per cent of customers are lured away by the competition, 68 per cent are turned away by an employee's indifferent attitude.

Providing a quality service or product to the customer and good communication are inextricably linked. Research shows that good internal communication fosters increased employee satisfaction. Better satisfaction reduces staff turnover, and higher staff retention is linked with higher customer satisfaction. Research carried out by the management consultancy, Bain and Co, reveals that satisfied customers are more likely to stay loyal, and that higher customer retention leads to higher profitability.

Organizations are eager to make the customer's voice heard within the organization, to challenge internal viewpoints, create a greater sense of commercialism and re-educate employees about customers' priorities. Yet, too often, the way in which they manage communication does not fit these aspirations but, instead, causes resistance and misunderstanding.

In one organization, senior management were frustrated at the failure of production workers to appreciate the true level of market competitiveness. While only 25 per cent of the board believed that customers were satisfied, nearly 50 per cent of first-line supervisors believed that they were satisfying customers. They then reassured their team members that everything was fine – defeating the board's efforts to sound a wake-up call to the workforce.

This disconnect between top management and those at the sharp end was due to a breakdown in the management chain and a failure to discuss information and educate people about its implications. This company is not alone: 80 per cent of companies reviewed by continuous improvement consultancy Peter Chadwick in the UK, France and Germany monitored customer satisfaction, but only 20 per cent made the information available below middle management. Information about customers and what they value is typically only circulated to 35 per cent of staff. Without such knowledge, how can those at the sharp end be expected to understand the customer and add value?

Scott
Zith

Innovation is crucial to strategy

Recent research by KPMG suggests that most of the UK's largest businesses believe innovation to be crucial in creating an enduring and successful strategy. Management seems convinced that successfully introducing new products and ideas can help even mature companies revive their fortunes. This is borne out by a PricewaterhouseCoopers study of 800 large companies. The most innovative 20 per cent had generated 75 per cent of their turnover from new products and services in the previous five years. The least effective 20 per cent gained only 10 per cent of their turnover in that way.

Today's pace of technological advance means that any gain in superior performance will be brief. Points of competitive differentiation – such as price, quality and distribution – are soon matched. No single innovation will yield a sustainable competitive advantage. The competitive advantage of companies such as General Electric grows out of the company's culture – a climate that fosters continual innovations and keeps searching for competitive advantage. The question marks that have recently appeared over M&S would have been unthinkable at almost any previous point in the company's history and show that no competitive advantage can be taken for granted. However, if you get the culture right, sustainable competitive advantage by innovation and other means can follow. Good internal communication is key to getting the culture right.

Continuous improvement

A KPMG study of a cross-section of 135 manufacturers worldwide over a 15-year period highlighted lack of quality as the single most important source of weakness in Western industry. It concluded that the most significant cost reductions are realized by improved cooperation and communication between the marketing and research and development departments. This approach leads to the reduction of waste through better process control, reduced engineering changes and improved product design. Creating this sort of continuous improvement requires better communication. Achieving a culture focused on continuous improvement requires well informed, and well educated employees.

Lack of attention to communication and involvement has undermined improvement programmes. Western manufacturing still lags behind due to the very limited success of its improvement programmes, most of which start with a bang, become bogged down and finally fizzle out. They fail principally because project leaders take too narrow and specialist a view and do not communicate with, and involve, enough other disciplines and departments – particularly the shopfloor.

All the changes described above involve people working with their colleagues. These people have to understand what's happening, deal with change, form new relationships, play by new rules and make new decisions faster and in cooperation with colleagues, all with one end in mind – creating greater value.

How can communication create value?

The managing director of one company said that although he had many business and people problems, he had, thankfully, no communication problems. Here was a man who took a limited view of what communication could do for him, but for whom the potential value of internal communication lay waiting. The first step to realizing its value is to expect it to have some.

Competition has forced companies to compete more fiercely and prompted consumers to ask for more for their money. To compete through greater innovation, better quality, cost-effectiveness and customer service, organizations need motivated and committed employees.

As things now stand, organizations are unlikely to achieve the objectives of engaging and informing their employees. There are two reasons for this. First, communication strategies are too often based on keeping people informed in a stable, 'jobs-for-life' hierarchical organization with a dominant market position. These are useless in a fast-changing, insecure organization fighting for market share and trying to innovate and develop new products. Second, organizations are not applying the lessons which they have learned in other areas of the business – that value is created through careful management of assets, efficiencies in supply chain management, applying a customer focus and continuous process improvement.

Communication is vital to creating value. Its importance lies in turning strategy into action. For strategies to succeed people need to understand what the strategy is, the context to the strategy and the rationale behind it. They need to know their own role and the specific actions they should take. Unfortunately, organizations often do not treat communication as a value-adding business discipline but as a branch of welfare, and, when necessary, a means of propaganda.

Internal communication is so critical to business success that it cannot be approached as a cottage industry, or left to 'gifted amateurs'.

Helping manage complexity

Flatter structures are devolving decision-making to lower levels in the organization, creating the need for more information to ensure high-quality decisions. Employees expect to be treated as adults and want to know the 'why' as well as the 'what' behind management decisions. All this means a geometric increase in the amount of information being circulated, and greater complexity and interdependence of information.

Change now means being in a state of almost constant flux. Winning organizations are those which are most fluid, anticipate change and adapt quickly. Businesses which are able to make constant changes both quickly and effectively are more competitive. This means that speed of change, learning and adaptation is key to competitive advantage. Speed of implementation is more important than brilliance of strategy. However, speeding up the change process is a tall order; in effect, organizations have to change the gearbox while keeping the car on the road. They have to win the support and participation of their employees, manage change while maintaining normal activities, and ensure that the changes they introduce stay in place. Effective internal communication facilitates change. Handled correctly, it makes implementation easier and faster, reduces resistance to change and gives clearer leadership.

Toxic communication

Although internal communication can provide greater value for organizations, there are some improvements which have to be made first.

Business leaders are failing to convey their objectives to their staff. Trust inside organizations is low, and some employees are happy to be ignorant of what is going on around them. While change is constant, it is communicated poorly, and information overload overwhelms limited employee 'brainspace'. Finally, organizations are confusing volume and value, and producing 'toxic communication' which consumes time while creating confusion.

Research among employees over the last ten years shows the impact of the disconnect between the thinking of the leaders and the attitudes of the led. Understanding what leads to success creates the motivation to achieve it; 84 per cent of employees who understand what makes their business successful want to help create that success, whereas only 46 per cent of those who don't understand share that feeling. When employees understand their overall role in the business, 91 per cent will work towards that success, but the number plummets to 23 per cent if they don't. The message is clear – employees who understand the big picture are more likely to play their part to help their company succeed.

To succeed, companies need employees who are clear about the overall direction and the part they need to play. They also need their employees to be willing to follow the lead and play their part. When it comes to being clear and willing, employees fall into four categories:

1   *Unclear what the strategy is, but willing to help.* 50 per cent of employees typically do not know what the strategy is and only 25 per cent ever get feedback on progress. This 25 per cent tends to be positioned near the top of the organization, so those on the front line, with customer contact, have the least idea. Willing, but unclear about direction, they are 'unguided missiles'. These represent the greatest opportunity for organizations. They have the good will towards the organization, and usually a desire for greater involvement. If people are a company's greatest asset, these people represent assets which are seriously underperforming.

   Employees rarely operate in a 'strategy vacuum'. Even when they are completely misguided or out-of-date, they usually believe that they have some idea of what's going on in the business and fill in the vacuum for themselves. In other words, a lack of direction from the leadership leaves these people to find their own way. At best, this robs the company of their true efforts; at worst, it turns them into 'unguided missiles'.

   When organizations are shifting strategy, responding to change in markets and competitors and looking for new ways of adding value, they are very likely to leave their employees behind. These employees

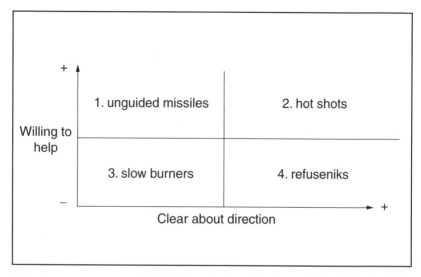

Figure 1.1   The different degrees of employees' clarity and willingness

will continue to pursue a vague notion of a strategy based on past glories and outdated definitions of value and service.

Companies move on and leave the employees responsible for delivering the promise behind. Employees who insist on providing Rolls Royce solutions to Mini problems are often working from a keen sense of heritage and pride based on their past product leadership. Their enthusiasm creates unnecessary cost, complexity and confusion.

2   *Clear and willing.* These employees know the company's direction, understand the broader context, know their part, and get feedback on both the company's progress and on their own performance. They are the 'hot shots', warming to the company's aspirations and fired up to help achieve them.

3   *Unclear and unwilling.* These employees are the 'slow burners' who are not sure where the company is heading, but drag their feet anyway. They are usually characterized as not knowing and not caring. However, they are in fact a mixture of sheep and goats – those who feel unmotivated because they lack a sense of direction and those who are happy to continue going their own way.

Companies tend to become fixated both with this group – because they are perceived not to care – and with the next group, the 'refuseniks', because they seem to actively oppose change. However, their real focus should be on group 1, who represent huge untapped potential, and on providing them clear goals and direction. Similarly, clearer direction will raise the motivation and desire to contribute of significant numbers of group 3.

4   *Clear but disagree.* People resist doing anything which violates their sense of professionalism. They may try to continue with an old strategy because they believe that it makes better sense. Where they disagree with the direction of the company, these 'refuseniks' may actively resist or undermine it.

Communication as a way of making connections

If companies want high performance, leaders must demonstrate the connection between individual and company success. There has to be a link between the leader, who can see what needs to be done, and the doers, who have their hands on the levers of change but who may not see the big picture. Communication should provide that link, connecting those who know what needs to change to those who have the power to make change happen. That applies equally to leaders setting the course for their people, as it does to people alerting their leaders to oncoming icebergs.

Making the connection means providing everyone with a shared understanding of the organization's strategic business issues and ensuring that they understand the 'whys' as well as the 'whats'. As reasonable as this sounds, that connection is not being made strongly or consistently enough.

A survey by Albert Karr of the chief executives of 164 large companies showed that most of them believed that personal communication increases workers' job satisfaction and commitment and results in improved earnings. However, most of the chief executives questioned also said that, because of other demands, they couldn't afford to give more time to communicating with their people.

A survey carried out by Forum Corporation found that 82 per cent of Fortune 50 executives believed that their corporate strategy is understood by 'everyone who needs to know'. This suggests that there is a limited number of people who need to know, and that the majority of employees are not among that number. A Louis Harris study concludes that 'less than a third of employees say management provides clear goals and direction', pointing to a large gap between perception and reality. Further evidence comes from Professor Robert Kelley of Carnegie Mellon University who found that nearly 70 per cent of the 400 corporate executives he asked believed that business leaders fail to adequately communicate their goals to employees.

In one professional services organization the managing director was genuinely convinced about the importance of communication and urged his senior managers to invest time in it. The business was run on time-sheets, and the only category to which communication time could be allocated was 'administration'. Each week the MD reviewed billable time and rebuked any manager with any but the most minimal administration time. Since those with reduced billable time were expected to lose their jobs, the unspoken messages given to senior managers was 'Internal communication is vital, but if I catch you doing it, you're fired'. This is not an unusual instance. Senior managers know that it is 'politically correct' to preach the importance of communication. The actual effectiveness of their communication can fall well short of their aspirations.

Trust is low

Employee attitude surveys typically show that most of the information employees receive is via the grapevine, and they have a healthy scepticism about the information they do receive through formal channels. Often they believe management has a hidden agenda, and feel that saying what they really think would be a career-limiting move. At the same time, managers think that they are good at communicating, are cynical about their leadership's ability and are overloaded with information they can make little sense of, but still won't share.

Ignorance is bliss

Employee research consistently shows that only 50 per cent of employees know where their companies are going or what they are trying to achieve. Despite this level of ignorance, managers think they are doing a good job in communicating. The lower you go down the organization – that is, closer to the customer – the business's objectives become less and less clear. Where people do know the objectives they rarely get feedback on progress, making the business's objectives academic and detached from day-to-day work.

Almost 100 per cent of employees are convinced that they themselves are already doing a good job and that they are helping their company reach its destination even when they don't know what that is. Where understanding of business strategy is restricted to a limited few senior managers, there is a disconnect between strategy and implementation.

The role of leadership in communication

Senior business leaders are under pressure. The stakes are high, both for the business and for them personally – between 35–50 per cent of CEOs are replaced within five years.

In today's turbulent environment, business needs leadership from managers – people who don't just execute the rules but understand the principle behind them, so they can deal with the changing demands of the business. Jack Welch, CEO of General Electric Company, recognizes this:

. . . yesterday's idea of the boss, who became the boss because he or she knew one more fact than the person working for them, is yesterday's manager. Tomorrow's person leads through a vision, a shared set of values, a shared objective.

Within organizations, structures are flatter, staff are more mobile and power and authority are vested in the person, not in the position. It is the job of leaders to navigate the inevitable turbulence of change. In today's world, business is driven by knowledge, networks and relationships.

A key issue for internal communication is building stronger relationships between management and staff, especially at times of change when the staff's trust in senior management usually declines. Also crucial is gaining the commitment from senior management to invest time in face-to-face communication, despite apparently always having more urgent things to do.

Communication is not the responsibility of a single charismatic leader, but of all managers. Peter Drucker estimated that '60 per cent of all management problems result from faulty communication'. Creating a customer- and quality-focused culture requires strong and clear leadership from a committed senior management, because lack of commitment is transparent and readily detected.

Poor communication of change

Employees report that they want to perform well at work, but are often prevented from doing so by a limited understanding of what is required. This is compounded by communication whose meaning is unclear and which does not specify what, if any, action is required, and by information which is poorly presented and difficult to use.

Management credibility and trust are assets under attack from confused and poorly integrated communication. Such complexity and confusion is being driven by competing communicators within the organization, by a proliferation of messages and a multiplicity of channels. A report by Synopsis which examined current practice in internal communication within 123 organizations in the UK, Europe and North America found that well intentioned communication is generating more heat than light, raising both senior management and employee frustrations and causing the considerable investment that organizations make in communication to evaporate. Senior management's frustration at the slow pace of change is matched by employees' frustration at information overload and the continuous waves of change initiatives. Employees' horizons and tolerance thresholds are sinking and their willingness to listen and engage is diminishing.

The speed of organizational change is hindered by:

- initiative indigestion – the number of initiatives exceed people's ability to digest change
- change initiatives that confuse employees and clamour for their time and attention
- a dissonance between the strategic thinking of senior leaders and the perceptions of those at the sharp end

■   a disconnect between the leaders and the change strategists and the
    professional communicators whose function is to facilitate change
    within the rest of the organization.

This failure to make communication clear and simple is creating resistance and contributing to the high failure rate of initiatives. The growing
volume of information competing for employees' attention is confusing
rather than helpful, and frustration with how communication is managed
is rising. A survey by Pitney Bowes (1998) revealed that 'communication
tools are being adopted by Fortune 1000 companies at a stunning pace,
with little sensitivity to cost or the overall effect of the communications
glut upon workers'.

Employee overload

Organizations are beginning to realize that information overkill is consuming precious time, creating mixed messages and exacerbating the
media onslaught on the individual. However, people in organizations do
not passively swallow all the information they receive. Because they only
have a limited capacity, they develop coping strategies to deal with
information overload – deleting e-mails unread, waiting until messages
are sent many times as a test of their urgency, or assuming that anything
really important will be repeated around the coffee machine.

The limit to communication is not the number of trees left standing
from which to make newsletters, but the extent to which people have
the capacity, inclination, time and goodwill to engage with the communicator. Getting a message through is easier if the sender has some positive
pre-existing relationship with the recipient. Relationship determines
meaning, and people's relationships are becoming increasingly stretched,
as their workload increases.

Employees' 'brainspace' – the time and attention they are willing to
give to messages aimed at them – is shrinking. Their capacity to process
the information they receive is also under attack. With more work being
done by fewer people, there is less time for chatting and for the social
interactions that used to diffuse communication around organizations.
An international engineering company that reduced its headcount and
closed the staff restaurant to save costs discovered that its employees'
understanding of the business direction plummeted.

As companies look more closely at using flexible workforces, using
telephone call centres, and mixing and matching full- and part-timers,
this erosion of understanding threatens to get worse. It is estimated that,
by 2003, 50 per cent of the workforce will be part-time, and 70 per
cent of those will be women. Part-timers may tend to see the job as only
a part of their lives and as something that has to fit in with other

commitments. They will be working short and irregular hours, and may rarely come together in one place as a group. Yet they will increasingly come to represent their company to the customer, and it is vital that they understand what's going on.

Confusing volume and value

Organizations are crippling themselves by distributing large amounts of meaningless information, and technology is exacerbating existing bad habits. Typically, confusion reigns between the volume of information being made available and its value. The information flow inside the typical company is increasing at about 2 per cent per month, yet a recent survey showed that 75 per cent of people were not getting the relevant information that they needed. Just over half said that technology had increased the quantity, but not the quality, of internal communication.

If raw information is not refined into meaning and relevance it threatens to become deadweight, as organizations capture and distribute more, but lower-quality, information. In one company this took the form of newsletters describing, in detail, the workings of the distribution process using words suitable for a graduate-level reading ability – despite the fact that the average reading level among employees was that of a nine-year-old.

People who do not understand what's happening do not feel in control of their own destiny. Failure to make communication simpler increases resistance to change initiatives. These can range from business process re-engineering, with a failure rate of around 70 per cent, to the 70 per cent of mergers which do not realize their promise due to human resource issues.

Summary

In a world of constant change, demanding quantum leaps in performance, communication can be a powerful means of making change happen. To do that it must be well managed. Continuing as it is, undisciplined and unmanaged, it will clutter the organization, spreading greater complexity and confusion. Poorly disciplined communication will prove a roadblock to the very change that's needed.

The traditional approach to internal communication is that of the production line, the most efficient communication at the lowest unit cost by exposing the greatest number of eyeballs, in the largest sized groups, to the greatest number of slides in the shortest amount of time. This may be efficient, but it certainly is not effective. While some organizations continue to view internal communication as the dissemination of information or messages, others are starting to use it as a key means of engaging and directing their people.

Having laid out all the problems, we are forced to ask 'Where's the solution?'. The following chapter lays out a model for the way forward, which subsequent chapters unpack in detail.

Improving internal
communication

In the restless quest for value, organizations will turn out every cupboard in the business to find underperforming assets, and to turn every asset they have to advantage. Increased competition, rapid product development cycles, faster innovation, more sophisticated supply partners and more demanding customers mean that sustainable advantage cannot depend on product brands and services alone. Companies must use all their assets, business processes and relationships to compete successfully.

In the information age an organization's assets include the knowledge and interrelationships of its people. Its business is to take the input of information, using the creative and intellectual assets of its people to process it in order to produce value. Internal communication is the core process by which business can create this value. However, managing communication as a core process will require the adoption of some established business principles.

This chapter describes an integrated approach which will turn communication to business advantage. It highlights the typical flaws in traditional approaches to communication and identifies some of the key elements of successful internal communication. It argues that to gain the greatest value from communication, the process must be better managed, and provides a framework for integrating communication more effectively. Finally, it shows how to reconnect disconnected communication links to form a virtuous circle of communication.

As organizations have reorganized their operations around greater customer focus, supply chain management, key processes and new definitions of added value, functional departments have reinvented themselves to redefine how they can be valuable to the business. During the 1990s traditional business functions were transformed as they sought to demonstrate the relevance of their role. Manufacturing has been reborn as logistics, order fulfilment and supply chain management. Purchasing has become the more strategic-sounding 'procurement and supplier partnership'. Born-again finance departments have transformed themselves from accounts and spreadsheet producers to providing management with information, interpretation and strategic options.

The principles that these shifts have in common is that they have focused on creating value, reducing complexity, reducing diversionary activity and duplication, increasing cooperation and managing end-to-end processes rather than just individual events. Their reinvention has been driven by the need to create greater customer and shareholder value.

Internal communication is about to join the party as a reinvented function which applies the same principles. This will be driven by companies demanding a better return from their investment in communication, and a realization that internal communication has a more significant task in the business. It will adopt the same value-focused disciplines found elsewhere in the organization, redefine the value it can bring and reinvent its processes and process management.

For an organization's communication to be a strategic tool, it must be able to help the organization connect to knowledge and information, integrate and share information, extract meaning from it, and turn information into decisions that add value. This demands internal communication that helps people convert information into action in a four-step process:

1   **Providing content**: providing people with data, information, ideas, concepts.

2   **Putting it in context**: people need to be able to process that information, and to make it relevant to their situation. They need to be able to put it into a context – to add a new piece to the jigsaw of what they already know.

   Putting information in context is important because meaning depends on shared context. Seeing the bigger picture also helps people navigate through information sources and communication channels. After all, if you know where you are trying to get to, and you know where you are, reading a map is easier.

3   **Having conversations**: people need to explore, test and understand the implications of what they are doing. This is best done through conversation – a process that enables them to develop a shared understanding through sharing views and perceptions.

4   **Gathering feedback**: ensuring that communication has been understood as intended, to see what has been added to it and what has resulted from it.

The problem is that organizations typically concentrate on the first element of this four-step process – delivering content and creating awareness – and not enough on the others. Their first step should be to shift from seeing communication as providing input to seeing it also as producing outcome. Without checking the outcome of communication – that the information has been received, that it has been understood correctly, how it has been interpreted and whether it has been translated into action – there is no true communication, just the distribution of information and the broadcasting of messages.

Managing communication as a cycle

While it is politically correct among senior managers to say that internal communication is important, several problems typically accompany such a claim. Business leaders do not give communication priority, and it is not seen as a key part of leadership. A vicious circle therefore turns into a downward spiral. For example, a lack of time invested in discussing strategy leads to a lack of understanding at all levels of the organization. Behaviours do not change so actions do not match the strategy, so frustration sets in and less time is invested in the right areas. Business priorities continue to squeeze out communication time and local management do not make communication a priority. The communication function is inadequately resourced, and there is insufficient business support for skills development. Finally, regular measurement and accountability are avoided, so there is no evidence of change or return on investment.

Meanwhile those who are keen to improve internal communication inside the organization become increasingly concerned. They want to link communication to the business strategy, but may have managers or internal clients who perceive communication as being largely about distributing newsletters. Communicators – that is, those whose primary job is to support communication within the organization – will see senior management commitment as crucial to building stronger relationship between the leaders and employees. They want senior managers to participate actively in internal communication, but managers may already feel they are committed enough.

Communicators understand that forward planning is critical to avoiding information overload, to making the best use of communication channels and to targeting information to the right people. However, simply getting the communication infrastructure in place to get the right information, to the right people, at the right time is often enough of a problem. Whether they can become involved in planning will depend on the perception and role of the internal communication department, and of them personally.

Almost all of them will want to develop a vibrant two-way communication process that adds value to the business. In this they will be hampered by a lack of time and by the apparent reluctance of senior management to buy in to two-way communication on matters which are important to staff.

Finally, they will yearn for valid measurement of internal communication, to help accelerate the rate of improvement, demonstrate the value they add and to defend their budgets in lean times. They will understand that the true cost of communication lies in the line manager and employee time it takes up, not in their production budgets. While they are there to support the line manager in fulfilling their duty to communicate, they will know that the best way to achieve a return on investment is to make managers accountable, and to measure them regularly. However, it may only be the communication department, not the managers who are held to account.

Their frustration will come from the fact that they see internal communication as something that can add value, while the rest of the business may not have woken up to this fact.

Many organizations have already improved their communication in a first wave of greater professionalism, better standards and consistency of presentation. This has taken them some distance toward their goals. Now they need to move to the second wave – using internal communication to create understanding that can be turned into valuable action. This requires better communication integration and management, greater involvement and dialogue, and creation of a greater shared sense of context.

While no company gets everything right, there are some simple reasons why some get it so wrong. At the heart of their failure is a series of broken connections in the communication circuit. Communication strategy is not connected to business strategy; measurement is not connected to business outcomes; face-to-face communication is not connected to creating understanding.

In most organizations different responsibilities are placed in different departments – planning in Strategy, internal communication in Corporate Affairs, measurement in Personnel – and are not integrated or connected to each other. This is like setting different builders to work in different parts of the house and hoping the end result will hang harmoniously together.

Organizations therefore first need to make the connections between departments that own parts of internal communication and then make the connections between the separate elements of internal communication that each department owns. The key is to view communication as a process and to manage it as a cycle. Based on work with leading companies over the last 15 years, and drawing on Synopsis' research into best practice in over 120 UK and US organizations, I outline below a framework for integrating communication more effectively.

An effective integrated communication framework

The framework is based on the principles of linkage and mutual reinforcement. Many organizations are doing good things in individual parts of their internal communication processes, but lose the benefit by not linking them together, or by leaving out a key part of the circuit so that communication does not flow as they expect. Problems in one part of the communication circuit show up as symptoms in a different area, in the same way that referred pain in the leg points to a problem in the back. For example, the team meeting process in an organization may constantly be reviewed in the face of continual complaints from employees. Yet despite continually retraining managers and team leaders to improve their interpersonal skills, they still fail to turn the sow's ear of poorly produced and irrelevant information into the silk purse of enthused and engaged employees. The root problem may be senior management's lack of planning as to what should be communicated, resulting in an output of boring corporate information that discourages local managers from holding meetings at all.

Clearly, to get a better return from their investment in internal communication, organizations need to form a virtuous circle of communication, comprising the following seven links (see Figure 2.1).

- Strategy
- Leadership
- Planning and prioritization
- Channel management
- Role of the internal communication function
- Face-to-face communication
- Impact measurement.

The first three links focus on doing the right thing, and making the connection between the business strategy and the communication strategy. The next four links focus on doing things right – having efficient and effective processes. When activity in all the links is managed and aligned, internal communication brings a real business pay-off.

While this framework is based on experience of the best internal communication practice in leading companies, it is not offered as a prescription of best practice. It is a *good* practice which has to be tailored to an organization's individual business needs to obtain the best fit. Organizations can make the mistake of 'cherry-picking' apparent 'best practices' and adopting them without considering their unique needs –

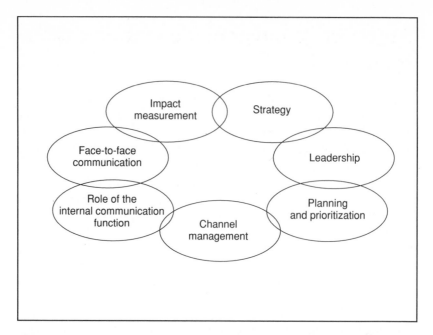

Figure 2.1   Making the connections to form a virtuous circle of communication

a strategy rather like taking someone else's medication just because it seems to do *them* good!

Thus, the challenge for internal communicators is twofold: to develop and implement best practice in each of these areas, and to link them together so they are mutually reinforcing.

Strategy

The purpose of internal communication is not just to keep employees happy. It should be business-focused and help employees understand the business's competitive strategy and how to deliver on it to produce profit.

There are three steps to achieving this. Organizations should clearly identify their strategy, identify the attitudes and behaviours they need from their people, and then target their communication towards helping achieve those attitudes and behaviours. The focus is on closing a performance gap – identifying the roadblocks to adding value and then using communication to help remove them.

Successful companies do not start to communicate when some change is needed, they already have the understanding of the bigger picture in place to allow for rapid response. Successful communicators forge strong links with those who drive strategy and change – the strategy, planning, marketing and IT functions.

Leadership

Leadership involves setting the agenda and then taking others with you. To do this effectively leaders have to communicate in a way that inspires others and builds a sense of commitment to shared goals.

Leaders may have different styles, ranging from big picture to small detail, and from entrepreneurial to controlling. Whatever their style, communication remains central to their leadership role, the critical success factors being:

- **Consistency of message.** The leadership team must be seen to be in agreement and consistent in purpose.
- **Clarity of purpose.** The top team should define the direction of the organization, state it clearly and simply, and then make sure it is distilled into a few unambiguous targets.
- **Clarity of principles.** People should understand the way in which their leader would apply the organization's values, so that they can make decisions on the ground according to these principles.
- **Focus.** Very few priorities should be set, and they should be emphasized repeatedly.

Successful leaders understand the importance of good communication and plan time to make themselves visible to their people. For example, Jim Burke, the CEO of Johnson & Johnson, spends 40 per cent of his time communicating the organization's credo. The fact that the board allocates time for communication sends a message to leaders at all levels that they too are expected to make such time available.

To have full impact on the organization, internal communication and its strategy must have the full endorsement of the board. This will make finances and resources for communication more readily available and keep communication on the board's agenda since they will want to see a return on investment.

Leaders need to sponsor and review the internal communication strategy and plan, and agree and stick to key messages. They should show the way by having specific communication targets which are publicly measured.

Business is complex, yet strategy needs to be simplified if it is to connect with those at the front line. Successful leadership is directly rooted in effective communication which is kept simple. This means presenting the case clearly, in a way that is compelling and allows people to take action. Too often, leaders create difficulties by communicating a million complicated things rather than a few simple, significant ones. Organizations should therefore be able to express plainly the business strategy in a one-page summary, with the top five priorities clearly described. There should be clear goals linked directly to the strategy of the business and a clear link to what the customer wants and needs. Performance information should be communicated as a series of simple 'Are we winning?' measures, not as a raft of ratios and percentages.

Planning and prioritization

The disconnection between leaders and their organization is reflected in the fact that, although 55 per cent of companies surveyed in the UK have board-level representation of internal communication, only one-third of boards actually approve the communication strategy and plan. To make matters worse, internal communicators are not being involved closely enough with the functions which typically plan and drive change – strategy and planning, marketing and IT.

Without planning, organizations cannot hope to manage people's reactions to change. Instead, they are forever 'catching up', so reducing the speed with which change can be brought about. If communicators do not have sufficient contact with those directing change in the business, they can be forced into setting the wrong priorities and end up announcing the 'what' of change rather than sharing the 'why'. Communication plans need to be reviewed quarterly to help the business respond quickly to change. Most communication plans tend to be set annually and are rarely revisited by the leadership team. Small wonder then that businesses struggle to make change happen; one of the most powerful weapons in the change armoury – communication – is firing blanks.

For example, the objective of most mega mergers is to increase market share while making substantial cost savings via economies of scale. Achieving economies of scale usually involves merging functions or organizations, creating savings by removing duplication of function and achieving operating efficiencies. The end result is fewer employees who then have to operate in new environments, role and locations. Achieving this involves the careful communication of redundancies, training, cultural change and relocation. However, although communicating to employees is a critical part of achieving the benefits of a merger, 75 per cent of acquirers reviewed in one survey had given the communication plan very little consideration before acquisition. As a result, staff do not receive information in a timely manner and become disaffected when they hear of key decisions through the grapevine. The outcome can be a host of 'people problems' that lead to poor productivity, lower employee commitment and, ultimately, a mass exodus of disgruntled employees.

From the leadership's viewpoint, therefore, failure to plan communication means failing to achieve the full benefits of the merger.

Plan change communication

Programmes of change are a fact of modern business life. Yet research shows that over a quarter of those managing change initiatives do not produce communication plans and, even where they do, they are rarely to a common format. Without a common format, it is that much harder to clearly perceive how and when different changes initiatives will affect people in the organization. This leads to change managers competing for communication time and resources, with the risk that change fails through initiative overload – too many changes hitting people too quickly. This may explain why employees keep seeing sudden, apparently unexpected and uncoordinated change, which only serves to increase their anxiety and frustration. It may also reinforce employees' perception that the management team does not have its collective act together.

Too few businesses involve their top team in approving the internal communication strategy and plan. Businesses may say they want their people to sing from the same songsheet, but they fail to ensure that the top team agrees the words – small wonder, then, that the result is a cacophony of mixed messages.

Organizations need to think ahead, show clear linkages between different initiatives and give people the bigger picture of change. Those leading change initiatives are risking failure by not planning communication and not coordinating it with other initiatives.

If communicators are to help the business achieve its objectives they must be involved earlier in the planning process and involve senior management in the planning. They need to ensure they focus on business objectives, not communication objectives, and identify issues from the employees' viewpoint, not just the organization's. Communicators can help by being explicit and specific about what decisions must be made and what people need to do differently. Changed behaviour is the desired outcome of communication – not awareness, consistent messages or the dissemination of data.

Developing an annual calendar of communication events and milestones, explicitly linked to the business plan, is a good first step. The focus should be on educating people about the rationale for change, rather than simply announcing conclusions. This will require involving communicators earlier in the planning, rather than at the end when implementation looms.

Channel management

Communication is about the transfer of meaning from person to person, not simply the passing on of messages. The more chaotic, new or interconnected change becomes, the more employees are forced to make choices and prioritize. Helping them find their way through the complexity of change depends on making information meaningful and highlighting its point. In order words, companies who want to create understanding need to make meaning not messages.

Employees' mental capacity to absorb and process information should be treated as a strategic resource. The business's success depends on employees being able to make sense of information and turn it into appropriate decisions for the overall good. The average professional worker receives 178 messages per day by fax and voicemail. In a world that automatically increases employees' information load by 2 per cent per month, communication *reducers*, not producers, are needed.

Communication channels must be better managed to manage the flow of information, reduce interruptions by irrelevant messages, and liberate employees' time and brain space. Equally, organizations need to target their audiences more closely and tailor messages more specifically to address recipients' concerns, so increasing their impact.

Reducing information overload requires organizations to adopt a more sophisticated approach to managing information and interaction. They need to shift from the 'oil refinery' model of communication, in which more and more messages are pumped down communication pipelines, towards a model of 'air traffic control', which has an overview of communication activities and plans and coordinates communication to avoid overload and communication collisions. This means that organizations will have to work harder to make communication simpler, translating 'management speak' into 'plain talking' which carries some meaning for recipients.

Supply partnerships are a well established policy in virtually every industrial sector. To become valuable, internal communication has to follow the same route. Internal communication needs to be treated as an end-to-end process, with reduced complexity, greater cooperation along the supply chain of information, with clear roles and accountabilities.

The role of the internal communication function

Most businesses want a great deal from their internal communication function, ranging from the strategic to the tactical. Internal communicators are typically overloaded and frustrated as they try to focus on the strategic, while having to devote most of their time to dealing with the tactical.

The obstacle to internal communication departments adding value is lack of access to decision-makers and being trapped in their internal customers' perception of them as messengers. This is made worse by their own narrow focus on internal communication objectives rather than business objectives.

For internal communication to deliver value it has to be located close to the heart of the business – somewhere it can support the ways in which value is created for customers and close to where the money is made.

Organizations also need to structure their communication department to match their organizational structure. In addition, to better manage communication, eliminate confusion and coordinate messages, they will have to reorganize the department itself. Communication professionals should be of a high standard, with the skills and experience to understand business strategy. Clearly, if part of their job is to express strategy in words that can be turned into action, it helps if they understand it first themselves. Furthermore, clarifying the role of the internal communications department forces the top team to clarify what it wants its internal communication to achieve. In so doing, the top team will realize that internal communication needs to be more than a production department.

Face-to-face communication

By distributing information in the belief that they are communicating, organizations are deluding themselves. They are confusing information with communication. The sharing and distribution of information is the first, but not the last, step in the communication process. Information can travel over wires. Communication happens between the ears.

Communication combines two strands – information and interaction. Information refers to the delivery and receipt of data, information, concepts and messages, and involves issues of how best to share, structure and extract meaning. Interaction refers to how people perceive and relate to each other, and involves issues of relationships, familiarity, credibility, trust and collaboration. Both strands need to be intertwined for success.

Despite the availability of technology, effective communication is as much about interaction as information. Technology may get information to people more quickly, but it is not a substitute for face-to-face communication.

Face-to-face contact – or 'talking' to use the full technical term – is still employees' preferred method of communication, and organizations need to do more to exploit its full value. Time is the most limited resource in most organizations, and better use can be made of precious face-to-face time which is too often used for the wrong purposes – to tell people things they could more easily read about, in meetings which are badly run and boring.

To get more out from this time people have to improve their interactions. More important than information technology is 'interaction technology' – becoming more capable of understanding how people can better work and deal with each other.

As mentioned earlier, effective face-to-face communication depends on conversation that allows information to be put in context. The moment of truth for communication is in conversation, which depends on how well people relate to each other – the quality of interaction. Managers have to be able to turn information into meaning and ensure understanding via conversation. Organizations need to help people create meaning and relevance at a local level out of the raw material of information. Since local relevance emerges from discussion with colleagues, organizations should add, to their information delivery, more opportunities for dialogue and conversation between people. People need to be given time to think through information, react to it and discuss it. The more they are force-fed with information, the less they make of it.

Face-to-face communication sessions often happen in teams, so teams need to be provided with tools and techniques to elicit the most value out of the time they spend together. Those who lead sessions should be trained in facilitation and interpersonal skills and in understanding how people relate and respond to each other. Briefing and presentation skills are not enough.

Turning information into knowledge depends on people's ability to process and apply it. The value of information is down to the individuals who bring their experience and knowledge to interpret it, and to reach a conclusion. Information is processed through the experience, insight and ideas which originate and reside between people's ears. This processing of information into knowledge and then into action, depends on the relationship between members of the team, as they pool their experience and expertise and spark ideas off each other.

Improving interaction requires greater attention to the human factors, to how well people work together in meetings and how well they manage interpersonal chemistry. Organizations need to invest time in coaching their people in how to deal with each other and educate them in the 'soft wiring' of how people think and react, and their own thought processes and reactions.

Middle managers can add real value by not acting as a mere conduit for messages, but by telling the whole business story and painting the backdrop of context. They can help their people understand the whole business picture and coach them in turning understanding into appropriate action. In order for them to do this they must be given a clear understanding of what the issues and implications are likely to be for their people.

Actions speak louder than words, and how managers behave is the most powerful communicator. Managers need to be trained in the skills of building relationships with their people, in presenting information clearly and in eliciting feedback to discover how they have been heard. Presentation skills are only the starting point.

Impact measurement

The goal of any communication programme is to have impact but this can only be established by measuring results against the original intention. Measurement is the only way to ensure that what is planned has happened and to show a return on investment.

Businesses are not doing enough to measure and track the progress and impact of their communication efforts, principally because they fail to specify the intended outcome of communication. Although many senior managers now have specific communication targets and are measured against them, their achievement is usually kept private. In measuring how communication is performing, there are two options – keep the measurement private, so that only the guilty manager knows how badly he has performed, or make it public by publishing scores.

Embarrassment is more effective than guilt in motivating managers to change. Good companies do regular surveys and measurement, include communication competencies in appraisals, track managers' performance via research and publish the results.

Communication standards make it clear what people have a right to expect in terms of communication, and to establish what is expected from them. By setting standards, the boundaries and objectives of communication no longer become open to interpretation and people know what will and will not be available. The organization needs to make clear, and commit to, these principles, demonstrating their importance and increasing their effectiveness. Performance against standards should be measured and reviewed regularly.

Making meaning: the business of understanding

The seven links in the communication chain described above are designed to reconnect an organization's people to its business agenda. However, this is based not just on repairing broken links but on redefining the role of internal communication.

Companies are now being forced into the business of understanding, needing to bring meaning, clarity and focus to their own information and to make the complex clear. Communication is about creating and sharing meaning, not simply about sending messages. It is not enough to tell employees that you have a strategy, and not enough for them to be able to repeat the corporate priorities or recite the mission statement.

Communication will continue to be viewed as a soft area until leaders are harder on themselves. Unless business leaders insist on early planning, well coordinated communication and clear and consistent messages with specific actions, communication will fail to deliver changed attitudes and behaviour.

A one-off roadshow by the chief executive may give employees a temporary awareness of the strategy, but their re-entry into the pressures of the next day's workplace may relegate the presentation to a fond, but irrelevant, memory. Organizations therefore need to move from this traditional view of communication – 'telling the troops' – towards engaging with their people and helping them understand what change means for them. Rather than simply adding new pieces to the jigsaw puzzle, management must explain the picture on the box so that staff can work out how the pieces fit together. Then employees have to convert that understanding into action.

To summarize, in terms of their internal communication, organizations must first do the right thing and connect it to achieving their business strategy and, second, do things right – have efficient and effective processes. These issues are explored further in the remainder of the book.

Part II
Talking Business

Creating differentiation

Organizations are having to pay more attention to their competitive propositions in an attempt to differentiate themselves. This is not easy. In a quickly changing world what was distinctive yesterday comes as standard today. One way of being distinctive is to have a powerful brand, even if what you actually provide is unremarkable. Another is to increase the value of what you provide, to change the way you deliver a service and how you serve your customers.

Whatever the route to differentiation, internal communication has a key role. The face that the business presents to the customer – accessibility, respect, friendliness, helpfulness – has to be reflected in how staff are treated, or the gap between the claim and reality will be clear to all. Unless the culture and the proposition to the customer are completely in step, it will neither be differentiating nor confer any competitive advantage. As well as meeting the promise made by marketing, employees need to understand how they can add value. This comes, in part, from their understanding of the typical problems facing the customer and their ability to meet these with the organization's capabilities.

The job that communication has to do will differ according to which route to differentiation an organization chooses to follow. Communication must be based upon the business's differentiating proposition or it will unknowingly work against it. Existing communication practices are based on the old, implicit, proposition and will work against the new one if not realigned.

Businesses have to maintain a balancing act between external and internal markets, as they attract and retain customers, and attract and retain employees. Differentiation is important in both. As the market shifts, and as customer expectations grow, the business has to stay ahead of the game by finding new ways to add value while protecting and building the equity of its brands. The ability of employees to meet customer expectations depends on their managers realizing that differentiation as an employer is also vital.

This chapter looks at aligning employees' values with those of the brand, and at the issues of employees' identification with a number of different claims on their allegiance. It also investigates the central role of internal communication as a process of converting employees' understanding of the proposition to the customer into action. This is followed by a case study illustrating how companies redefine the core value of what they provide and highlighting how internal communication helps employees redefine the value of what they do. Finally, the chapter discusses maintaining differentiation in the external market and the need to stay differentiated as an employer, as the organization moves through different stages in its life cycle.

What is differentiation?

Customers expect some basic things as a matter of course, and the supplier has to provide a foundation of these simply to be a credible option. These may include providing the basic service or product in a timely and professional manner, with prompt follow-up and servicing plus efficient back-up. These are things that the customer expects and only really notices if they are not there. They are not seen as remarkable, nor do they earn the supplier any Brownie points with the customer.

There are, though, those 'X' factors that customers may not at first think of, or expect, but which are more valuable to them and which

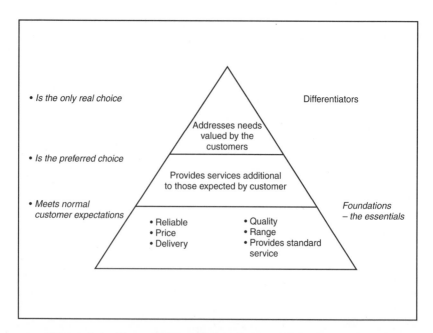

Figure 3.1   How differentiation has to be built on sound foundations

they appreciate. These include such things as advice, creative ideas and problem-solving. These do provide competitive differentiation and can justify higher pricing to reflect extra value.

Companies try to identify how to add greater value for their customers when they are in a competitive market and when they need to combat price sensitivity and customers' perceptions of them as undifferentiated suppliers of a commodity. Their quest is for an offer which the customer will value, which will set the supplier apart from the competition and which will create customer satisfaction and loyalty.

Customers expect the supplier they choose to meet good standards of product quality and speed and responsiveness of service. Only by providing them with unexpected additional value, such as advice, problem-solving and support, will a company create a differentiation. However, to have employees deliver that differentiation requires realigning internal communication. Playing the game by new rules moves the communication goalposts.

The following case study shows how shifting the competitive proposition redefines what information is relevant for staff and what information the company needs staff to capture and feed back.

Case study: Fraternal Finance

Fraternal Finance is a fictitious, though not untypical, financial services company whose internal communication strategy is out of line with its business strategy. It has decided that, in its marketplace, it will differentiate itself through closeness to the customer. It will be distinctive in its ability to understand intimately its customers' needs as they move through different stages of their lives. From childhood, to young married, to empty nester, they will provide them with appropriate financial solutions tailored to their changing needs, via staff in their branch network.

The new strategy requires branch staff to understand customers more deeply and also to have good in-depth knowledge of a wider range of products. This means they must receive and digest a greater amount of information and understand how to apply it.

Consequently, branch staff find themselves increasingly under pressure: more responsibilities and tasks are devolved to the branch network, resulting in increased workloads. A tighter regulatory environment means that they have to qualify as advisers and master competitors' product knowledge as more sophisticated customers increasingly shop around to get the best rates.

The pressure of time and workload drives staff to set their own priorities and focus only on the information that is of immediate use in completing their tasks on deadline. Staff feel there is simply no time to assimilate information for anything other than the immediate job.

Briefing sheets containing procedural changes and regulation changes – such as alerts to lost passbooks and stolen cheques – are circulated regularly, and in great numbers, to the branches. Everyone is supposed to read, assimilate, tick and then file the briefing sheets. To save time, however, the sheets are circulated and ticked off without anyone actually reading or understanding their contents. So, even for those tasks which are perceived as most important, there is a growing danger that staff are not up-to-date with crucial operational procedures.

Time pressure on staff means that they also have to be more selective in the information they use. Operational procedures are read first and, then, because there is commission to be earned, sales messages are studied next. Information about customers, though central to the strategy, is relegated to last place and is the first to be discarded if time is scarce. In other words, staff have developed coping strategies for selecting and prioritizing information from all the competing communication aimed at them. This is based on how they themselves believe they are supposed to be serving the customer – which may be at odds with the actual strategy.

The net result is that the business's espoused competitive positioning of closeness to the customer is undermined by its internal communication practices. Fraternal Finance has, in effect, three internal communication strategies which are simultaneously at work. Each is designed to support a different competitive strategy, and each works against the other. They are as follows:

1   the efficient distribution of information to allow compliance with operational procedures, and to ensure the best operational efficiency

2   the distribution of sales information to maximize the sales of distinctive and well designed products

3   the education about customers, the different stages of their life cycle and relevant needs, to enable staff to provide service to customers and colleagues.

Each is the legacy of a different strategy for competitive differentiation, which the organization has followed in succession. Each is championed by a different department, each of which has access to the branches, each with a finger in the communication pie.

The Fraternal Finance case study illustrates a number of issues that have to be addressed if its bid for differentiation is not to be undermined. Trying to educate staff about the new strategy will not be successful without addressing how they select and prioritize information, or without better coordinating the departments who communicate with the branches. For both producers and consumers of information, existing habits of communication are based on the past. While competitive strategy points to the future, communication habits, if unchanged, imprison the organization in its past.

Moments of truth

Lack of coordination in internal communication is a problem because it undermines the consistency on which a brand depends. There are certain critical points of contact between the customer and company. These include reception, telephone, meetings, PR, point of sale, advertising, mailings and so on. These points of contact are 'moments of truth' because, at each one, the company and its promises are tested and judged as to whether or not they are real.

Because organizations often do not clearly communicate their point of differentiation to their employees, it is not unusual to find different departments focusing on different differentiators. The sales department might act on the basis that differentiation comes from building close relationships with customers. The production department might believe that excellent products confer differentiation. The marketing department might believe in the distinctiveness of a trusted brand.

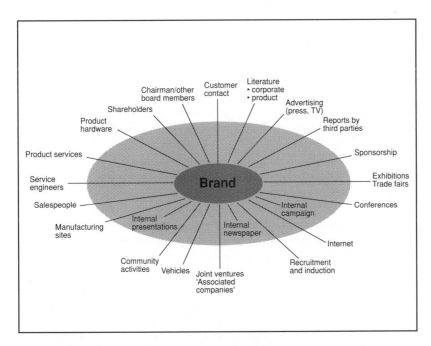

Figure 3.2 Moments of truth: points of contact with an organization's stakeholders

The greater the number of moments of truth, the greater the danger of inconsistency. Since a number of the moments can be owned and managed by different departments who may not share the same views and priorities, the danger grows. This means that there has to be tighter management of internal communicators. This is discussed further in Chapter 9, 'Repositioning the Role of the Internal Communication Function', and Chapter 8, 'The Management of Communication'.

Brand and behaviour

Brands are valuable to their owners because they can differentiate products and services from the competition: 'In a world of constant change, a strong corporate brand is one of the few sources of competitive differentiation' (RSA Inquiry). Companies are recognizing that their brands are an asset, which command premium prices.

In acquisitions in the consumer goods business, as much as 85 per cent of the acquisition price is attributable to goodwill – the difference between the acquired company's net asset value and the price paid. Despite the huge premium paid for goodwill, this is still seen as a more effective means of growing than trying to imitate the acquired company's brands. For example, Grand Metropolitan, which merged with Guinness to form Diageo, became the first large brand-based company to capitalize their brand assets and declare the value attached to its brands on its balance sheet.

Brands are seen as valuable, often expensive, assets and as passports to market growth. However, obtaining a return on these assets depends on aligning employee values with the brand's values. For brand owners business success depends on employees translating brand values into appropriate behaviour. That is not always straightforward. One of the ways in which customers build up a sense of a brand is by their daily interaction with the organization, especially its people. This means that customers' experience of employees can undermine the brand, when employees do not behave in line with the implicit promise, or when those employees in what were traditionally backroom jobs suddenly find themselves having front-line contact with customers.

Everyone has to be involved in delivering on the promise marketed to the customer. As Lew Platt, Chief Executive of Hewlett Packard put it in an interview with P. Doyle, 'marketing is too important to leave to the marketing department'. The scope of this challenge, and the risk of not achieving it, has grown. Nowadays, customers have more contacts with a wider range of employees, from front-line sales and service to backroom warehousing and distribution, and, as they deal with organizations on this broader front, businesses have to be able to translate the brand approach to a wider range of areas. For example it is easy to identify an appropriately branded way of recruiting people, but how would a credit control department behave in a way appropriate to its brand values?

For brand owners that manufacture products, the more frequent incursions of the customer into different parts of the organization puts them on their mettle. For service businesses, however, there's often no place to hide, since the customer is right there with the employee, looking over his or her shoulder as the service is delivered.

Two factors play a principal role in keeping employees aligned to new aims and objectives – the brand, which embodies the organization's shared culture and values, and internal communication.

As one of the strongest brands in the technology industry, Hewlett Packard takes seriously the link between the competitive advantage of a strong corporate brand and ensuring employees deliver on the brand promise. The organization has always had a reputation for product quality, especially in their business-to-business relationships. Now, as they move increasingly into consumer markets, selling peripherals and printers for home use, they are realizing the importance of the strength of their brand in consumer, as well as in business-to-business, marketing. They believe that creating customer loyalty comes from moments of truth, delivering brand values, through people.

Hewlett Packard sees one role of internal communication as getting every employee to understand what their brand value promise is, how they individually might affect it, which moment of truth they own, and how they are expected to deliver on the promise to the customer. Internal communication therefore has to:

- get all their people to understand their role in moments of truth
- provide employees with the information they need to fulfil their role
- educate them in the processes they will need to solve problems.

The company is, however, emphatic that simply articulating the brand promise, identifying the relevant moments of truth and expecting employees to deliver on them is not enough. Awareness of the brand promise, and their responsibility for living up to it, will be ineffective if employees do not have the means to deliver. There also have to be accountable owners of the moments of truth and quality processes to help ensure delivery and to remedy shortfalls.

Many companies, in contrast to Hewlett Packard, seem to believe that circulating a lavishly produced glossy booklet evoking the brand values will fulfil the need to communicate with employees, light the blue touch-paper of their enthusiasm and ignite their passion to deliver. It is no surprise, then, when such high-gloss communication turns out to be a damp squib.

Even for those companies who feel that they have clearly articulated their brand promise, and have their people firmly behind it, there are further complications.

Consumers want to have a relationship with suppliers beyond purchasing the basic product or service and are looking for more than brand image and product quality. Customers do not want to know only about today's product features, they want a deeper relationship and to be confident that suppliers can maintain commitments over time. Brand owners are building such relationships with their consumers, based on their corporate values. Virgin, Marks & Spencer and Tesco are all examples of strongly trusted organizations extending their influence into new areas, based on the strength of their brand. Their reputation is not just based on their products but extends to all their activities and values. Body Shop, for example, talks less about its products than about its commitments and ethics. At Body Shop the customer is not only buying traditional beauty care but is also engaging in a relationship based on a certain set of values. Similarly, Virgin sells its personality and characteristic approach more than its individual products.

The offer to the customer of trust, a deeper relationship and a link between brand values and the customer's values raises the stakes for companies. It increases the risk to the organization of its employees not delivering on a now more extensive promise. If, for example, you are selling yourself as a trusted adviser, you have to live up to a wider range of more demanding values throughout the organization. Furthermore, if there is a failure it is much more damaging, since, having put yourself on a pedestal, there is further to fall.

Brand versus barons

One of the problems of delivering consistently on differentiation is that employees in different parts of the organization have different views of what they are supposed to be doing. They identify with different sets of values and different priorities. This should raise two concerns for companies – turf and identification. Different organizational barons tend to compete for loyalty and their employees' time and attention. Managing levels of identification and avoiding identity clashes is key to consistency and differentiation.

There are a series of 'Russian dolls' of identification. While people do understand that they are part of a wider corporate entity, they also identify strongly with their own division. In fact, they identify with a number of different claims on their allegiance:

- the corporate brand
- the division brand
- the product or service brand

- the location where they work
- the team they belong to
- the customers they serve and have in common.

These differing claims need to be balanced, and the communication about each of the 'Russian dolls' must be orchestrated. The organization has to decide with whom or what it wants its employees to identify and what behaviour is needed to support its promise to the market. In short, it must decide where the 'centre of gravity' of its identification should be. Is it, for example, more strategically important for an employee to identify more with the product division than with the corporate brand? Having answered the question based on what's best for the business rather than on what suits corporate or baronial egos, it can then organize communication around that centre of gravity.

This requires strong coordination between a range of departments. Brand values are normally the province of the marketing department, corporate values are often developed by the corporate affairs or corporate communications department, and employee values and managerial behaviours are often developed by the human resources department. Each of these departments often takes a different approach, with a different emphasis, so that there is little match and an apparent confusion between the different values they promote.

Managers' personal style and skills often have the most powerful impact on communication, so there has to be a strong link between managerial values, corporate values, brand values and employee values to make sure they are all consistent.

Employees are more likely to deliver on the promise effectively, if they feel a sense of ownership and pride in what the company stands for. The corporate brand is critical to communicating this to employees. It also serves to signal to their friends and family that they stand for the same thing. Employees derive status from being associated with strong well known brands when they wear the employer's badge. Badged employees with aligned values make effective brand ambassadors.

Organizations which seem exciting in the external market also seem to attract and motivate employees. Body Shop, Virgin and Pret à Manger are all entrepreneurial start-ups which have grown by responding to the needs of customers. However, they are perceived as not solely focusing on profit but as having a wider vision of what can be achieved through doing business. In all these companies a strong external profile feeds back into the organization and gives a greater sense of worth to employees. In the future, then, creating a strong internal sense of mission is likely to require companies to adopt a high external profile, and a greater demonstration of a contribution to society.

Communication creates profit

There is a strong link between the quality of internal communication and greater profitability. Greater customer loyalty has been shown to produce greater profit but, in turn, depends on greater employee loyalty and satisfaction. According to Frederich Reicheld, author of *The Loyalty Effect*, employee and customer loyalty are very closely related. On average, US companies lose 50 per cent of their customers every five years and 50 per cent of their employees every four years, but the most successful US companies hold on to their employees and customers much longer.

Employee attitude research over the last 15 years shows that better communication creates more employee satisfaction and improves employee perception of their line manager. Higher satisfaction reduces staff turnover and higher retention of staff creates higher customer satisfaction and more customer retention. Finally, according to management consultancy Bain & Co. (C. Hopton), higher customer retention equals higher profitability (see Figure 3.3).

Using better communication to improve profit is easier to achieve if people have a strong identification with the product and with the values behind it. In response to external and internal pressures, organizations

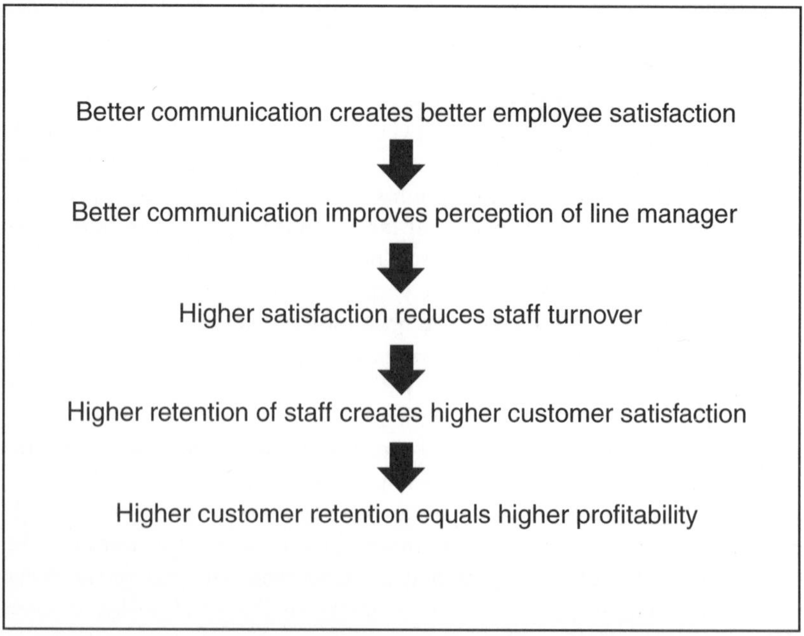

Better communication creates better employee satisfaction

⬇

Better communication improves perception of line manager

⬇

Higher satisfaction reduces staff turnover

⬇

Higher retention of staff creates higher customer satisfaction

⬇

Higher customer retention equals higher profitability

Figure 3.3   Better communication means higher profit
Source: C. Hopton, Bain & Co., 1994

are having to pay far more attention to creating shared values among their employees. Externally, customers are more interested in the values behind their suppliers; internally, shared values help create consistent employee behaviour.

The more organizations use their brands as an entry into new markets, the more they reach into different areas of their customers' lives asking for a much bigger 'share of life'. The greater the influence of a brand or organization on our lives through the extent of its operations, the greater the need for a new level of trust and the warier people will be about organizations' values and motivations. This is illustrated by the anta-gonism directed towards Microsoft and the suspicion of the dominance of its technology, and the examination of Rupert Murdoch's motives as BSkyB aimed to acquire the Manchester United football club.

Organizations' increasing focus on corporate values is not the harmless and irrelevant exercise of dreaming up value statements for display in the corporate lobby. Now, for both sides, it is about risk. The organiz-ation wants to protect its corporate reputation from the inappropriate behaviour of its own people; customers want to protect themselves from the power and influence of their suppliers. Internally, in times of change, the net of shared values keeps people together and acts as corporate glue. As organizations devolve authority to the front line, common approaches and consistent decisions cannot be achieved by providing rules and procedures. It is shared values and beliefs that help ensure common approaches.

Case study: Body Shop

In the past Body Shop has been synonymous with protest against animal testing and support for human rights and the community, and consumers consequently perceive it as a values-led company. Body Shop has 1267 retail outlets in 45 countries and trades in 23 languages. On average it opens a new shop every 2.5 days, and operates in several very diverse markets, each with its own culture and language.

Body Shop is emphatic that it is not a cosmetic retailer with values merely bolted on. It believes that if you buy its shampoo, you also buy the Body Shop values. Anita Roddick has described the ethos and values as 'not the brand, but the soul of the company. It's something you can see, and soul is something we feel.' The importance of these values to Body Shop is in their impact on customers and employees. However, in a moment of doubt and uncertainty, it became concerned about being too closely identified with values and campaigns and tried to detach its products from its values, only to find that its attempt to step away from 'soul' and closer to brand, undermined their success.

In terms of employees, Body Shop believes that you only get so much productivity out of reorganizations, systems and policies. It is by reaching the hearts and minds of employees and getting them involved that you gain surges of productivity and leaps of imagination. The company creates involvement through campaigns which staff and customers can support. They use 'Action Stations' to give staff the opportunity to collect signatures or write letters to MPs on such issues as stopping the trade in endangered species. They aim to use similar campaigns to influence the millions of people passing through their shops.

Every branch is encouraged to do community action in work time, with each department and shop making its own choice of project. Body Shop aims to provide its employees with the means to satisfy their desire to do some good, in the belief that work should change people's lives, not just provide a means to live. It also illustrates the strong link between a company's values and those of its employees.

To keep customers, companies have to continually improve the product and the service they supply. Service and customer satisfaction depend on the commitment and 'emotional labour' of employees. Companies with high-profile values attract and retain people who give high productivity, and high-quality work. Employees do not give that emotional labour to an organization that does not share their values and which seems to focus only on increasing shareholder value.

Case study: 'Store Wars'

For employees' enthusiasm and emotional labour to be channelled in the best way, employees have to fully understand how they are supposed to be serving the customer and to be able to convert that understanding into action (see Figure 3.4). The importance of converting awareness into action can be seen in the 'store wars' between the giant UK food retailers.

Food retailing is highly competitive and the way in which staff serve customers is seen as vital to the differentiation that competing food retailers are trying to establish. Over the past 15 to 20 years grocery retailers such as Sainsbury's and Tesco have invested in better stores, new 'convenience stores', employee training, consumer helplines and supply chain efficiency. This has yielded results, giving own-label brands a market share of just under 40 per cent, despite competition from branded products' advertising, image, packaging and line extensions.

With a £7.5 billion annual turnover, Safeway is currently number four in the supermarket league table. It has 75 000 employees spread over 471 stores in the UK. The Safeway brand promise is 'making shopping easier for today's family'. Delivering on that promise meant getting staff involved which, in turn, meant moving away from a command and control organization. Communication about what the company was trying to achieve not only helped employees understand the roles which

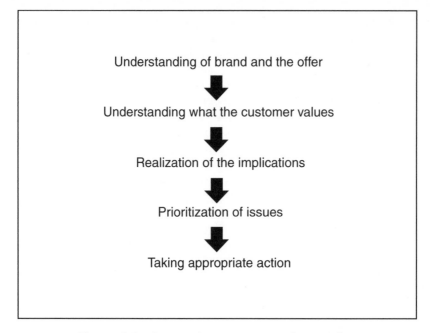

Figure 3.4   Converting awareness into action

they could play, it also challenged them to identify new ideas about how to deliver the Safeway brand promise. With over 90 per cent of staff contributing new ideas, customer services such as crèches, parent and child parking, baby changing facilities and Shop & Go were introduced.

The benefits claimed for this communication effort are impressive. Basket size increased by 12 per cent, while penetration of families was raised by 9 per cent. Even more importantly, brand share was increased from 8 to 9 per cent, and Safeway's share price increased by a third, from just under £3 to over £4.

Sainsbury's has also set out to change the way in which its staff work and manage. While store location and product range are key to attracting and keeping customers, the way in which people deal with customers is also seen as a differentiator. The company wants to alter the style of service its customers experience and it believes that the key to achieving this is to change the way in which it manages. There are 400 store managers aiming to involve their people more so that, in turn, staff will treat customers more personally.

Tesco aims to create greater loyalty among its customers, to increase their average number of purchases and to increase customer loyalty, all as keys to increased profit. They have recognized that the customer wants more time with staff in order to make shopping a more personal experience.

However, with 150 000 employees making contact with customers, the business has to treat its people as ambassadors or risk them becoming liabilities. To achieve its aim Tesco has been giving its staff a wider understanding of the brand, so that each employee can translate it into actions which are appropriate to them locally. The organization translates marketing speak into everyday language, avoiding the use of the word 'brand' and using instead the phrase 'every little helps'. The greater the level of understanding and translation to specifics, the greater is the likelihood of everyone taking action in the right direction.

Tesco is a good example of an organization taking action for customers by educating staff in brand values and helping them express them. However, this is not just an issue for front-line staff. Even if you can get employees to behave in line with the brand, value for the customer has to be delivered by the whole organization through supply chain leadership, product design, manufacturing, selling and servicing.

In Rolls-Royce, for example, the aim is to create the highest value by getting colleagues from different functional disciplines to work together as a team from the outset of a project. Specialists with a manufacturing background who know about the latest technologies, in conversation with designers, who have an intimate understanding of how the product works, and purchasing people who understand sourcing and supply management, share knowledge and open up new possibilities.

This kind of teamwork brings a significant benefit in terms of reducing cost, overengineering and time. It also calls for a shift in attitude, knowledge sharing, and cooperation. Trade-offs between volume and customization now have to be made by the whole team who have to work closely together. Because they have to forego concentrating exclusively on their individual specialized requirements and take decisions as a team, each member has to share an understanding of the customer and his or her priorities.

Moving from the core

The above are all examples of companies using communication to create greater differentiation, profitability and innovation. However, the real pressure on organizations is continually to improve the value they offer to their customers.

Understanding the customers' requirements includes understanding how their definition of value shifts over time. As services have become more important to what organizations offer their customers, so the role of the 'core' product they have historically provided has changed. Whereas in the past this 'core' – be it computer, telephone, bank account or copier – was what determined success, today the core is no longer enough to provide a competitive edge.

From the 1950s to the 1970s the core product or service was an organization's chief priority. However, as competition grew fiercer and goods became commodities much more quickly, there was a swift realization that more had to be built on the core product. Brand marketeers shifted to creating layers of added value, building emotional values into products and services.

During the 1980s and early 1990s marketing's way of trying to differentiate its offerings was by adding services to their products, such as financing, transportation and insurance (see Figure 3.5).

These add-on services, originally conceived as a promotional tool, became the principal differentiation. Customers could, in theory, obtain the 'core' items anywhere – although specifications and price would always be a major competitive factor – so, ironically, they came to place more value on the add-ons, transforming the balance of power between the 'core' and the additional parts of the offer. Customers were more interested in what they could achieve by applying products to their problems than the detail of the product itself.

Thus, the value added had less to do with the 'core' – be it a product or a service – and more to do with how it would be applied. This led to a shift of the traditional distinctions between services and manufacturing companies. Companies have had to become as good at providing new value-added services and solutions as they previously were at producing

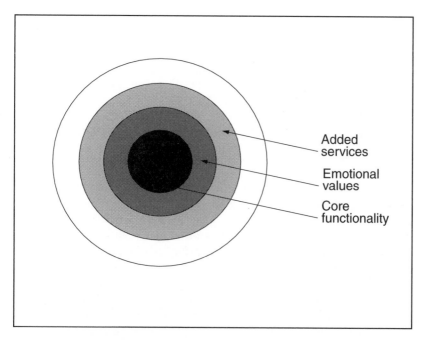

Figure 3.5   Adding value to the core product

their core product. Encouraging employees to make that shift is not easy, and demands a change in the approach to internal communication.

The implication for internal communication

As companies redefine the value they provide, they discover that what they used to give away as a peripheral to the core product – information, analysis, advice and insight – has become precisely what is now valued by the customer. The risk is that employees inside the organization fall between two stools, by focusing on providing the devalued core and giving away what is now valuable.

As a business redefines its value to the customer, this risk is considerable. Employees will still define themselves in terms of what used to lie at the core of their business, whether excellence in engineering or providing a good telephone service. However, the value of those traditional strengths, in which they take so much pride, may have evaporated. Redefining what's valuable to the customer, redefines what's needed from employees. This includes the kind of service they provide and the knowledge they need to gather and keep. Employees need to be re-educated about how to provide new value for the customer. Employees who take pride in providing excellent customer service are not necessarily providing great customer value. In one organization, for example, tens of millions of pounds were spent on a Total Quality Management programme speeding up the processes needed to create bank accounts for customers. While everyone worked their hardest to halve the time it took to process the necessary documents, their research showed that customers barely noticed the change and, where they did, did not value it.

Shifting the value proposition means emphasizing different values

Organizations are trying to use the strength of their brands to extend their activities into areas not traditionally theirs – examples are Virgin and Tesco which are entering the financial services market. This means that companies with good brands and good reputations, currently in very different markets, will find themselves competing with each other in new markets.

Such organizations, with trusted and innovative brands, must be certain that their employees' core competencies are closely matched to their brand values. As the brand is the passport to extending beyond the organization's traditional core, it needs protection. The customers' relationship is with the brand, so, at the very least, employees' behaviour must not damage that relationship. Where a company uses other partners or providers to deliver the new proposition, customers must perceive that the values and the people match.

Employees who cling to the past, or to corporate values which have become disconnected from a value proposition to customers, endanger this process. If a company redefines what it offers to customers, employees have to redefine the importance and value of what they do and how they behave.

What customers valued in the past is likely to be different to what they value in the future. For example, customer contact staff who get high job satisfaction from providing good service to appreciative customers may be surprised to discover that shifts in customers' expectations now mean that service is important but no longer valuable or exclusive. For these reasons, companies need to convey to their people that they have to find other ways to provide value if they are to have a successful future. Being proud of what no longer differentiates you can be a source of frustration and is often the cause of a perceived values clash between employees and their leadership.

Internal communication is essential to connecting employees' pride in the past with the company's potential for the future. Its role is to provide the necessary re-education and to bring the voice of the customer into the organization, in order to:

■ ensure consistency between the promise being made to customers and customers' experience
■ ensure that the promise being made to the customer market and to employer markets are consistent and reinforce each other
■ provide information to employees on their core products and services
■ provide information about customers, their different requirements and what they value, to enable employees to match customer needs to the company's capabilities.

Internal communications is needed to bring employees out of the past and into the present and is vital to preparing them for the future. Employees have to be educated about changing definitions of value to prepare them for fresh surprises ahead. Both companies and their employees need to understand how technology will change their relationship with customers and with each other.

During the 1960s and 1970s managers had one of two options – either produce products *en masse* for the generic end of the market or customize offerings for smaller selective niches. Then, as targeting became a more common approach during the 1980s, managers began to tailor their offerings to different segments of their mass markets. By the 1990s, thanks to technology, they could both have their cake and eat it. Mass customization meant that large numbers of customers could enjoy the benefits of mass-produced items with customized features to suit some of their individual needs.

In addition to mass customization, technology now also allows a shift towards 'one-to-one' marketing. Firms can track what their best customers buy, talk to them and tailor products especially for them. This ability is changing the relationship between customers and businesses, in that each customer is treated differently. With each transaction, the customer's needs and tastes are defined in increasing detail, and computers and databases allow every preference to be registered. British Airways greets frequent flyers with their favourite drink and newspaper, based on previous choices. The airline not only expects to gain more satisfied customers, it also hopes to reduce stocks and wastage on board. Amazon.com, an online bookseller, recommends books to customers based on past choices.

Most enterprises will not be able to treat all their customers so well; it is too expensive. Nevertheless the move from mass marketing to more targeted individual marketing via finer targeting and better data inevitably means that all customers are not treated the same. While the ultimate aim is to treat each customer as an individual, the flip side of the coin of individuality is selectivity. Companies are able to identify valuable customers and to concentrate on them, while holding back on, or even shedding, less profitable ones. This can lead to a clash of values with employees who have bought into the concept of providing customer service to their customers – all customers – and believe in fair treatment for all. In their eyes any selectivity should favour the more deserving, rather than more profitable customers for whom life is probably good enough already.

In a bid to attract more corporate patients, a healthcare organization introduced a 'club class' hospital bedroom for corporate patients. As part of this offer, they included a basket of fruit and a copy of the *Financial Times*. However, the nurses, whose vocation was to serve the sick, irrespective of their class or wealth, sabotaged what they perceived as the inequity of creating first- and second-class patients by redistributing the fruit baskets and newspapers among all patients, thereby defeating the purpose of the exercise.

One financial services organization found that the 80/20 rule applied: 20 per cent of accounts absorbed 80 per cent of resources, while the remaining 80 per cent of accounts had higher balances, more products, were less costly in terms of service and support and thus were more profitable. The business strategy devised was to shift towards offering more investment-related products, such as bonds. Customer research showed that their customers for these tended to be middle-class and fairly sophisticated and selective investors. This did not fit employees' traditional, and largely mythical, picture of the typical customer as a thrifty saver who had to count their pennies carefully. This outdated perception of the average customer, and the mismatch between those customers from whom the organization wanted to withdraw and those that employees wanted to serve, caused confusion.

The company had two communication tasks: first, it had to explain why it had to move away from the minority of customers who took up the majority of resources; and, second, it had to update its employees on the company's typical customer profile.

The possibilities of using technology for greater personalization means employees have to learn to respond to customers as individuals rather than as part of an undifferentiated mass. The more a business tries to respond to customers individually, the more its employees must be able to relate to customers differently, and understand the variations to processes needed to serve them. They have to understand that customers want different kinds of information, tailored to their needs, and delivered differently.

The issue, internally, is trying to explain to employees *why* there is this selectivity and difference among customers – especially where the staff hold a customer service ethic that involves treating customers equitably, if not identically. Improved customer information drives an organization towards selectivity, while also increasing the staff's empathy with the customer as an individual.

Research shows that service workers most value having the ability and the authority to solve problems and provide value to customers. They require high levels of information to be able to take action and prioritize demands. They also need to understand why things are happening, both for their own peace of mind, and to answer customers' questions. This means that the internal communication system needs to distribute a wider range of information, and to ensure that it is put in context.

First Direct is a prime example of an organization that established not only its own differentiation but a new approach to an industry. It was conceived as a result of Midland Bank asking itself how it could provide banking by telephone, avoid the need for a branch network, and gain market share by doing it differently enough to attract new customers. Although it pioneered telephone banking, the telephone has now become an accepted means of doing business, and not just in banking, as the growth of call centres testifies. Telephone customer service is still important but is not unique to First Direct any more. It is no longer quite so novel to, or valued by, its customers.

First Direct is a business that established a differentiating customer proposition and realizes it is not sufficient to do it once. Differentiation must be redefined as the market changes. The organization has 4200 employees and 1 million customers. It is the UK's fastest growing bank, with, it says, the most satisfied customers in the UK. It won the 1998

Unisys/Management Today overall customer service award, has one of the strongest brands and is respected as an innovator. Even so, it cannot afford to rest on its many laurels. The 1998 launch of Prudential's rival to First Direct, Egg, has added to the competition it faces from new sources such as Virgin, Sainsbury's and Tesco.

First Direct is well aware of three trends snapping at its heels. First, its differentiation is eroding, as customers become used to what was once unique and competitors enter the market with new offerings. Second, technology opens new possibilities not just for banking but for providing customers with useful and valuable information. Third, customers change and the problems they face in organizing their lives are no longer the ones that First Direct was created to address. Life moves on, and the business has to move too, making sure that it takes its people along with it.

With its moves into direct banking via personal computers (PC banking), its use of mobile technology and the introduction of its information problem-solving service, FD Octopus, First Direct is extending from its original core of telephone service-based banking to broader problem-solving. The company's basic strategy has not changed: it still aims to remove hassle from people's lives. At the outset, customer service was one way of reducing hassle; now it aims to remove more hassle from more people in more ways.

Its mission statement is 'tomorrow's bank today', and it aims to anticipate what customers' problems are likely to be in the future, rather than reacting only to those problems it was set up to tackle in the past. New technology makes it possible to move from telephone banking to banking via other channels such as PC banking, small messaging system, palm top computing, and digital television. PC banking and mobile phone banking means that you have greater control about where and when you want to do your banking. This shifts the traditional balance of the business, and redefines what activity will be involved and what takes priority. For employees it means doing new and different things that require new skills. Although the expression of their values might change, the values themselves will stay constant. First Direct believes that its core skills are enquiry, exploration of needs, active service and anticipation – and that these are still the skills which will be relevant in the future.

How shifting value affects internal communication

As a business redefines how it wants to serve its selected customers, its internal communication has to ensure that it educates employees in the following:

1 **Understanding the brand.** Employees need to understand the brand, the offer it makes to the customer and the values it represents. They should be able to translate that into specific behaviours in their own area and to have a clear sense of what would be appropriate and inappropriate to the brand.

2 **Understanding the real competition.** As a business builds on its core business and moves into what used to be peripheral areas in order to provide value to customers, it can find itself competing with new competitors. For First Direct, for example, the real competition is not high street banks, but brands such as Orange and Microsoft who could move into areas similar to theirs.

3 **Understanding customers and their changing needs.** While it is important for all employees to know their company's objectives, for a business focused on the customer, it is vital that they also know their customers' objectives and priorities. This is a significant issue in organizations which have decided to target new groups of customers. The traditional picture of the former customer can live on within a business long after the strategy has begun to focus on a quite different sector of the market.

4 **Redefining value and service.** How people define the nature and importance of service and value has to alter. Employees need to understand that good customer service is still a basic requirement, but that they have to take a further step to create value both for the customer and the company.

5 **Reappraising their role.** Employees have to redefine their own role and the importance of what they do. The way to add value in the future is to be relevant and valuable to what the customer wants to achieve. Since the customer defines value, organizations need people who can sense and respond to different kinds of customer in different kinds of way.

6 **Withstanding uncertainty.** Employees who have been successful in providing one product or service can feel wrong-footed and vulnerable when they suspect that it is no longer valued. There is a delicate balance to be struck between educating employees in the need to follow customers up the value chain and telling them that the great job they are proud of having done in the past is no longer valued.

7 **Staying connected to the organization.** As a business's definition of value changes what were previously fringe departments move to centre-stage. When car manufacturers began to make more money

from servicing a car than they did from selling it, for example, service departments became more important. Resentment between old-style departments and new-style departments can emerge as arguments over where money is best invested arise. Is money better invested in the increasingly outdated core, which nevertheless still brings in the most money, or should it be invested more in new areas which are going to be more relevant for the future? Departments or business units which feel they are being milked to fund the future begin to feel doubly neglected. They have lost their star status, and now investment is being diverted away from them to a newly favoured child.

Such a situation calls for internal communication to educate each department or business unit about the other in order to create a feeling of common interest and thereby minimize resentment. It also calls for education about what new areas are doing to avoid the 'unknown incompetent' syndrome. Research shows that where a department's activities are unfamiliar, colleagues in other departments rate its effectiveness poorly. In other words, if people do not know what their colleagues are doing, they think they are doing it badly.

Differentiating yourself as an employer

The importance of educating departments about each other highlights the fact that to get and keep customers, organizations have to attract and retain employees, as well as educate and engage them. The 1998 Fortune survey of the 'World's Most Admired Companies', identified companies' ability to do this as the single best predictor of excellence. Attracting and retaining those employees who best fit the organization's brand promise, means becoming an 'Employer of Choice' – the first stop for would-be employees. This means that the organization has to create a clear differentiation in the employment market, with as clear and consistent an offer to employees as it makes to its customers, and ensure that the promise to both markets is consistent.

Companies realize that it is not simply the recruitment costs of replacing employees that hurts the business. It is also the loss of the knowledge of customers' needs, often to the competition, which is painful. Becoming the employer of choice involves differentiating the employee's experience from that with competitors, reducing the time it takes to make them feel part of the organization and strengthening their feeling of belonging.

Because retention is such a key issue, organizations are trying to identify the key communication issues which will influence their employees' decision to stay. Some such factors, reported by employees, are that their experience has matched the employer's brand promise both to customers and to employees, and that they have had opportunities for learning and development. Also important is the chance to build relationships with colleagues, and a job that is not entirely task-focused. They also want to see that the relationship they have built up in their immediate team can also be established with others in the rest of the organization, so that they feel part of a greater whole.

Virgin is a good example of an organization whose brand helps make it an attractive employer. This makes it easy to hire people, with an employer brand premium that translates into paying a little less than the market rates. But while the wide spread of Virgin products may sometimes baffle brand consultants, Virgin's success underlines the importance of its core values – fun, innovation and an irreverence for authority. Virgin Cola, for example, decided that its differentiation would be as an alternative to their competitors. If Coke is the 'Real Thing', they wanted to be the unreal thing.

Virgin is very good at encouraging ideas and then letting them happen. There is a conscious avoidance of grades and hierarchies, and an expectation that people will come up with ideas and feel free to suggest them. It is they feel, cheaper to put an idea into action and see if it works, than go through a prolonged ideas testing phase. Virgin seems to take a Darwinian approach to ideas, if they thrive, fine, if they fail, little has been lost, and the culture of ideas has been strengthened.

Aligning employees with the brand values can reinforce differentiation, both to customers and to employees. The value of irreverence that Virgin fosters in its employees is clearly tied to their business success. Virgin clearly believes that success is a combination of competitiveness and confidence.

Virgin's differentiation, both in its consumer markets and employment markets, depends on its employees' close links with its brand values. It helps that some of those values have to do with irreverence, ingenuity and tongue-in-cheek humour. Parties seem to be the secret weapon. During the summer, 30 000 people – employees, partners, and families – all go to parties at Richard Branson's house over two weekends. Other Virgin companies take employees away for a weekend, be it a trip to Marbella or to Euro Disney, so that employees get to experience Virgin's planes and trains, see their company colleagues and feel part of the wider group.

Pret à Manger is another company that uses parties as a way to create a feeling of community, and, in this way, it has some similarities to Virgin and Body Shop. Pret à Manger describes itself as passionate about food and passionate about people. They are masters of the 90-second lunch, and with a current turnover of £75 million a year and 73 shops across the UK, their formula is obviously successful. The company feels that if you rely on employees' personalities, and give them the right environment to deliver service, they'll do it. Its approach is to provide a tight framework for processes and ways of working in its shops and, within that, allow their people to express their personalities. They define their employees as happy people who are being themselves, and who are being rewarded for being so.

Matching the promise of good food and fast service is easier when you recruit the kind of people you think are going to fit your values. In terms of selection, people are asked to go through an evaluation process for a day, for which they receive £25 whether or not they are offered a job. One of Pret à Manger's rules of thumb is that it only hires people with whom its existing employees would like to socialize, and a candidates' potential colleagues in shop teams have the final say in their selection. This underlines the importance of feeling part of a community at work. People want to work with people they like and can trust.

Like Virgin, parties feature heavily in the communication armoury of Pret à Manger. Those teams who win the star team monthly competition for best service, as perceived by the mystery shopper, go out together, with £25 per head as their budget. There is a weekly free bar on Friday evenings at a club in London, and parties for all employees are given twice a year.

The company has a number of things in common with Virgin, First Direct and Body Shop. Its values extend beyond the simple service it provides. In the same way that Body Shop married environmental concerns to soap, Pret à Manger does not stop at its passion for good sandwiches. It is environmentally green, using organic food. It is also involved with the charity 'Crisis', donating unsold sandwiches at the end of each day to feed the homeless. However, these values are not imposed on customers or employees in a cultural straitjacket. The individual expression of shared values, not corporate cloning, is what it seems to emphasize.

Interbrand Newell and Sorrel – the company that redesigned British Airways' corporate identity and developed their controversial multicultural tailfin design – maintains that the new strength of organizations will be in their diversity, not in uniformity. After facing a rash of copycat competitors, Body Shop feels that, although its current look can be mimicked and its products copied, competitors will not be able to recreate its core values or their cultural expression in local markets.

A shift towards recognizing diversity and serving a more varied range of customers, with a wider range of definitions of value, emphasizes the need to mirror that diversity internally among employees. A focus on diversity means that employees can no longer be seen as a mass market or as a pyramid of hierarchical grades. Organizations need to communicate with their employees in accordance with their values, life stage and job requirements.

Body Shop's decision to restructure and focus on retailing highlighted differences in values between its employees. After a nine-month review by their Chief Executive Patrick Gournay, aimed at making the company more profitable and competitive, Body Shop is revamping stores, cutting product lines by 25 per cent and ceasing to manufacture its own products. However, although the organization has moved to another stage in its cycle, it intends to retain its core values. Body Shop's diverse workforce includes left-of-centre graduates through to tabloid-reading production workers. How do those different groups of people buy into the organization's values?

In fact, retail shop staff buy into these values much more than production workers. Ironically, since senior management grew up with the development of Body Shop, they have a history of campaigning themselves. Discovering, as they get older, that some employees do not share their fervour brings them up against the problem of the company hitting maturity in its life cycle.

Pret à Manger is a good example of an organization which has been through the first burst of youthful growth and is now hitting what it describes as puberty. It grew rapidly with an idea that found its niche, and its culture was created by its founders – more likely by accident than design. With its recent creation of a chief executive and the introduction of functional directors at the centre, this culture is now changing.

As organizations mature, employees move from being enthusiastic early adopters to older and more settled, seeing the organization not as an exciting start-up but as a solid reliable bet. This process is mirrored in the life cycle of organizations. Most businesses go through a life cycle from enthusiastic adolescence to a more systemized adulthood. Unless internal communication is geared to the organization's stage in the life cycle, it will act as a barrier to progress.

At the outset, in the first flush of growth, people tend to share the same sense of direction and values. There's a pioneering spirit, and people are motivated by seeing progress made. People who join the company are attracted to its dynamism, excited by the product and reflect the attitudes and values of the founders. Colleagues have similar attitudes and enthusiasms, and communication takes place informally. At this stage, employees take a much keener interest in strategy and direction, since it keeps them alert to their own job prospects. Generally, when things are shaky and uncertain, people take a wider view, and stay alert for early warnings of approaching bad times.

As the business prospers, and the number of people in the organization grows, things change. There is more systemization of procedures and less reliance on informal communication. People are now on different sites and working on specialized functions, so there is less frequent contact between colleagues. Communication becomes more formal and impersonal. Meetings take place within the department, but departments have less contact with each other. Communication shifts away from relationships towards more task-focused information. As the company continues to grow, the leadership is seen to be less in touch with the customers or with employees. The first wave of employees who joined miss the contact they once had with the leaders, and see their lack of contact as the price of the company's moving on to a new stage.

Pioneers who have bought into the vision work hard to bring it to life but, as the company grows, new people join who do not share the original vision. These are like the homesteaders who follow behind the pioneers. For them the job is unremarkable, they do not have the same zeal, and they are attracted more by pay, benefits and job security. This means that, as a company grows, there is a hard core of enthusiasts who increasingly resent the less than 110 per cent commitment of their new colleagues. Leaders, distracted by growth and increasingly tied up trying to organize and systemize the business, become less visible. This is a greater issue for the pioneers, since their relationship and identification with leaders tends to be strong. Time becomes tight, and there is a high stretch factor as people turn their hands to more than just their own jobs.

At some point, as costs are re-examined, or as the value core shifts, the organization makes its first redundancies, causing a culture shock of betrayal. Despite good management intentions, lack of time tends to squeeze out communication The clarity of company goals and strategy decreases, as does the organization's perceived commitment to quality, performance appraisal and training and development. When an organization encounters turbulence and finds itself not flying straight and level, but blown off course, the first thing it often dumps to reduce the load is the parachute of communication.

There are other implications for communication as organizations move through their life cycle. Three things happen as organizations mature. First, employees become older and look to fulfil a broader range of their needs. Second, the organization gets older and moves to a different stage in its life cycle. Third, competitors start to offer the same kind of job and approach to employment, commoditizing what was once a unique employment offer.

As organizations age, they attract different kinds of people. Marketeers refer to the product life cycle and the adoption curve to identify the rate at which a new product or service becomes accepted. Be it the Walkman, CD players or the Internet, the pattern of successful adoption remains the same, rising from limited usage to widespread acceptance. This principle applies to employees' view of companies as potential employers.

In the first phase, early adopters are people who are willing to pioneer by joining a new start-up company. For them, the risk of the new, the time and cost of 'experimenting' and the lack of systems and procedures are not barriers. They may indeed be positive inducements. As the organization becomes more established and less of a risk, those who are more cautious, and who have waited to see the company prove itself, now join. In the final phase those who join the company are traditionalists, who have waited until the risks have fallen, and who see the job as more a necessity than an opportunity. They are not excited by the prospect of being pioneers, and place more value on the company's reliability and financial soundness.

Abraham Maslow's theory of the 'hierarchy of needs' suggests that people's needs drive their decision-making and their outlook. The pyramid hierarchy he identified consists of five stages, each building on the one before. At the foundation are physiological needs such as hunger and thirst. Then comes security and safety needs such as physical security, followed by social needs – to belong and be accepted. On the next level are esteem needs – both self-esteem and winning the respect of others. Finally, at the top of the pyramid, are self-actualization needs – to realize one's full potential.

Maslow's hierarchy of needs asserts that people are motivated by their immediate need and, once met, those needs cease to motivate, prompting a move up to the next stage of need. Normally people move up the hierarchy: moving down is more likely to be the result of circumstances rather than choice. However, when this happens, they do not move down stage by stage as they do on the way up. Instead they drop several stages at a time. A pioneering organization whose growth has galvanized employee enthusiasm can send people crashing with the first rumour of redundancies. Instead of dwelling on how career development can help achieve their personal aspirations, they start worrying about how they will pay the rent.

Early adopters and pioneers are mostly motivated by needs at the top of the pyramid – self-esteem and self-actualization. Those coming towards the end of the adoption curve are more interested in getting a job and satisfying their basic needs.

The importance of brand values is to those people at the end of the curve. These are the traditionalists, in a settled environment and a mature job proposition. It is at this point that employees can stop seeing work as a challenge or an opportunity, and see it as 'just a job'. Jobs, like products, can be commoditized. Here the employer brand is important as a differentiator to separate the job from competing employers.

The lesson to be learnt by looking at the life stage of a company, the kind of people who join it as it grows and employees' different motivations is that internal communication has a job to do in holding the organization together as it and its people change. To target that communication effectively organizations need to categorize their employees according to their values, life stage and job requirements. Early adopters want the excitement of new developments and pioneering strategies. Traditionalists want a more settled future with new products paying off well for the company. Meeting the needs of both means communicating the broad picture to them, so that they can look ahead to new developments and feel comfortable about likely future impact. Giving employees the big picture allows them to put their own small picture in context.

While insurance may not be a naturally exciting business to everyone, Axa Sun Life invests in projecting an exciting direction and future for the company. All staff attend a business context setting session which is followed up in their local team meeting. Body Shop uses days such as 'Company Day', when they close the business to explain to staff where the company is heading and to share its vision for the future. British Airways has a tradition of staging corporate events for all employees to give them a fresh picture of the business and the commercial context in which it operates.

Organizations also want to fight the slide into middle age and to revitalize their people. First Direct adopted a value of continually reviewing and improving to protect the differentiation they had established from competitors. This means that energy is put into fighting commoditization. For this organization the reinvention of its pioneering approach in a new form is a way to maintain enthusiasm and alertness.

Where employee values and the brand proposition are aligned there is a better chance that delivery on the marketing promise will be seamless. In the past few years organizations have rightly emphasized the need to balance the rights and responsibilities of the various stakeholders in the business, such as customers, suppliers, employees and shareholders. However, they have neglected employees' desire to feel a respected part of the organization and that their job can make a difference. The film *Barbarella* reminds us that 'a life without a cause, is a life without effect'.

Body Shop and Virgin are good examples of organizations which have recognized that what employees want from their working lives, and what organizations need to succeed can dovetail together (see Figure 3.6). Creating common ground involves using communication to combine four priorities among employees:

- **Cause:** a sense of wider purpose that gives employees greater opportunity for contribution and meaning
- **Customer:** an understanding of the customer proposition – a focus on, and a relationship with, the customer
- **Community**: a feeling of belonging to, and enjoying being part of, a community with interrelationships and mutual responsibilities
- **Company:** an understanding of the need to create financial success and to be responsible in the stewardship of assets.

Typically, an employee might identify with three out of these four priorities. One person might enjoy serving customers and appreciate the camaraderie of their colleagues but might not feel inclined to help gen-

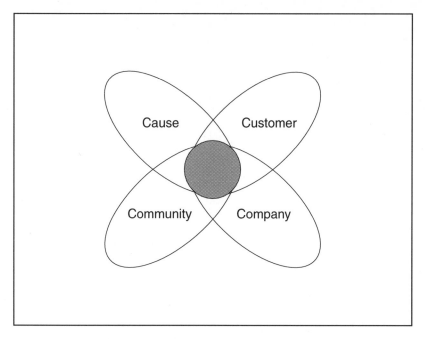

Figure 3.6   Creating common ground

erate profit or feel their job is significant. Another might feel that serving the customer and making money are essential, but dismiss the importance of relationships between colleagues. Some companies might manage to yoke together two or three out of these four. Success lies in combining them all.

Creating common ground is the key to successful organizations. Creating it requires internal communication to answer the employees' questions 'Who are we, and what's going on around us?', 'Who do we serve and how?', 'What do customers most value, and who's our competition?' and 'How do I help, and who can I trust?'. In a world of global brand building and shifting organization structures, in which employees are asked to 'think global and act local', the answer to those questions is not always straightforward. The next chapter looks at the impact of restructuring on identity and loyalty.

Restructuring and rewiring

Restructuring is one of the perennial issues that occupy chief executives, often for very good and very different reasons. This chapter looks at some of the communication implications of shifting to different organizational structures. In a world where employees are asked to 'think globally, act locally' this chapter adds the warning 'and communicate coherently'.

The chapter examines the different options for restructuring, from centralization to decentralization, and argues that not only are matrix organizations outgrowing their communication structures but that there is also a vital connection between structure and corporate and brand identity. After showing how better internal communication can help smooth the restructuring process and ease the pain of transition, it argues that the confusion and fragmentation of brands can be reduced, and provides a basis for competing corporate and business unit communicators to agree rules of engagement and mutual responsibilities. It goes on to highlight the role of communication in creating global attitudes, underlines the need to rewire lines of communication to fit a matrix structure and defines the changed role of internal communication in a global business. Finally, the chapter outlines how the management of communication has to change if companies are to realize the business benefits that their structure and brands are intended to deliver.

Restructuring is a favourite game of organizations which find themselves having to play by new rules of competition. Some organizations try to achieve the best balance between product and customer focus. Some try to gain all the advantages of size while avoiding central bureaucracy and allowing local operations the freedom to respond to their markets. Others are trying to respond to their customers' demands for global services, global consistency and for a single point of contact for global purchasing. Still others are trying to take advantage of their experience in problem-solving and their expertise in manufacturing by creating global functional networks to standardize what they do. The spread of global brands demands common worldwide approaches and consistency in marketing and manufacturing. Global clients want a consistent account management approach across all their markets.

The pressure to release shareholder value is driving organizations to reduce the range of different, costly and incompatible approaches to information technology, human resource policies, purchasing and marketing that have evolved across their business units.

Organizations are recognizing the desirability of operating on a global, rather than a multinational, basis. Their customers and specifiers can be given the reassurance of international quality standards. Global brands allow the company a greater return on its marketing spend. Costs can be reduced by efficiencies on a global scale. Heinz, for example, is shifting from being a traditional federation of virtually autonomous businesses in various countries, to becoming a global business, with local accountability, via the creation of eight global categories.

Unilever's culture is one of decentralized local companies and local trading. Business units have a high degree of autonomy, and historically they have acted as mini-businesses doing their own manufacturing and sourcing and marketing. Now Unilever is pursuing 'Unileverage', gaining the advantages of size and leverage as a global organization, while allowing its decentralized companies the freedom to respond to their local markets. This is being achieved by greater coordination across its business groups to gain the advantages of leverage in areas such as research and development, food science, advertising and marketing, innovation centres, and centres of manufacturing excellence.

These increasingly common efforts to gain advantage via restructuring or through a matrix of responsibilities differ from the traditional pendulum swing from decentralization to recentralization. This is more of a 'push and pull' approach, where some responsibilities are pushed out and decentralized, while others are pulled in towards the centre. This can mean decentralizing in operational areas to be more responsive to markets and recentralizing in 'back office' support services to regain the benefits of scale and synergies.

These push and pull approaches are all easier to achieve on paper than with people. A report by the Institute of Management said of restructuring that far from there being an end in sight to a relentless cycle of change, 62 per cent of managers who they surveyed said that their organizations had restructured during the preceding year. The frequency of restructuring is increasing with the average time between new structures now down to 18 months. A slight majority believes restructuring has increased profitability but more think it has harmed morale, loyalty and security and led to a loss of essential skills and experience.

In addition mega mergers are becoming more frequent and increasingly large. All of them are accompanied by job losses – usually 5–10 per cent of the combined workforce. The merger of Deutsche Bank and Bankers'

Trust is a good example, involving restructuring charges of $1 billion and $400 million spent on 'golden handcuffs' to retain key people in the new organization. Meanwhile, Exxon and Mobil expect to lose 12 000 people – 10 per cent of their joint workforce – and make annual cost savings of up to $5 billion.

Research has highlighted the failures to deal adequately with the people dimension of mergers. Worldwide studies reveal that most such arrangements, although apparently making sound commercial sense, generally fail to produce the promised benefits. Much the same occurs with restructuring. For example, US studies have shown that while nearly all of the country's top companies had implemented at least one major change programme over a 15-year period, less than one-third of these had led to an improvement in business results. Only half had led to any increase in the share price.

These mega mergers mean that, with the move to globalization, organizations risk alienating their people. However, even where restructuring is less dramatic, changing from a 'tribal' organization to a global one is difficult. Shifting structure, changing the relationship between the centre and business units, altering national perspectives to global ones and trying to create global outlooks from tribal loyalties all require more sophisticated management of internal communication.

A global company is one that markets a portfolio of global brands internationally. A multinational is a company which merely has operations in a portfolio of countries. Operating on a global scale involves difficult and often unpopular decisions on phasing out local brands, harmonizing standards across countries, and dealing with the self-interest and prejudices of local managers. This requires a fundamental change in organization, ways of working and cooperation.

Multinationals tend to have a history of the opportunistic establishment of operations in individual countries. In the past these overseas businesses tended to be run independently, since different local market conditions, distance and slow communications made control from head office impractical. Country managers used their initiative to develop their markets, creating their own brand names, developing their own products and quality standards and pricing to suit the local market. This created a wide variety of products, brands, pricing and manufacturing processes, with little standardization from market to market. Acquisitions and joint ventures in the local market exacerbated the problems by bringing in new brands with local strength and familiarity that overlapped and duplicated brands in neighbouring markets. The results were a lack of strong global brands, inefficient cost structures and inadequate investment stretched too thinly over too many new products. Decisions taken too far from the centre resulted in the costly reinvention of too many similar wheels.

Now the barriers to greater cooperation across markets are falling.

Deregulation and reductions in tariffs are reducing the idiosyncrasies of local markets. Telecommunication allows direct contact between the centre and local manager, and between colleagues in separate markets across the world. Levi Strauss Europe, for example, has moved to three regions within Europe in a bid to achieve greater standardization and consistency of products. While there are some variations between those regions, within each of them, the fashion tastes are broadly the same.

Similarly, car manufacturers are, for example, pressing for worldwide purchasing of oils and lubricants from a single point of contact, and for a consistent product wherever it is produced in the world. The drive for greater consistency of product has led to similar production practices and processes worldwide and a decrease in the autonomy of local management. Because the organization wants to manufacture in a few central locations, rather than having different factories in each country, local managing directors tend to lose their autonomy in production, development and distribution. Their sovereign power is diminished, and they have to focus on putting into operation approaches and frameworks which have been developed elsewhere.

Organizations are intent on taking better advantage of economies of scale and shared resources through better coordination. Cost efficiency is not all that's required. Also needed is a shift from an organization that is regional, functional and hierarchical to one which is far more flexible and organized around process teams and key activities. This involves moving away from local decisions taken only for local good to more decisions taken centrally for the good of the business as a whole. All this requires different attitudes and behaviours from employees.

Although an organization may operate worldwide, it often comprises a federation of subsidiaries which operate under different brand names and even joint ventures with competitors. All this results in a very national focus to individual businesses. Each market tends to be self-contained, with little cross-border product development, manufacturing and distribution. This discourages a global view and encourages lower horizons and the maintenance of national fiefdoms. It also means that employees identify with their local company name and local product brands, so that any attempt to change structure inevitably leads to issues of corporate identity, branding, employees' identification and loyalty.

Employees see themselves increasingly as members of different teams and tribes. In organizations, whether global or parochial, the challenge is to eliminate competition between different loyalties and, instead, to have them coexist and fit together like 'Russian dolls', one within the other.

Moving to matrix management

When organizations restructure they put themselves in danger. New organization charts may show the new formal structure, but the old informal structure of the past can linger to haunt management. The real organization comprises a network of informal allegiances and relationships in which influence is affected by credibility. Changing the structure does not change the informal network, and the formal and the informal run in parallel, with the informal commanding the grapevine and often enjoying higher credibility.

Moving to a matrix structure, for example, is challenging enough without having to contend with the guerrilla warfare of informal communication. If formal channels of communication are outdated and unreliable the management team will lose the battle. And whenever the structure changes, formal communication channels will become outdated.

This means that communication and lines of information have to be rewired to match the structure and achieve the benefits that the chief executive wants. Fatally, some organizations try to use nationally wired communication processes to make global change, with little success. This is because the communication infrastructure of a regional business trying to become global will be local, not global. In any revolution, the forces for change seize the radio station. Any chief executive who wants to communicate his plans for global progress to employees around the world has to realize that, in terms of communication channels, the local barons are firmly in possession of the radio station.

Restructuring means rewiring

Attention is only rarely paid to migrating the communication lines to a new structure. As employee survey after survey has shown, people prefer to hear from their immediate line manager and, in times of change, that is who they turn to. It does not matter, for example, that the reorganization says that they now report to a new manager of a new customer unit based in Houston. If, each day, they still go in to the Glasgow office, they will still continue to talk to their old manager who is close at hand and with whom they have an established relationship.

The term 'phantom limb' syndrome is used to describe how amputees continue to feel sensations from their amputated limb long after it has gone. Without a conscious effort to align the communication structure with the new organizational structure, organizations can encounter communication phantom limb syndrome. The old structure continues to make its presence felt long after the reorganization says that it should have gone, causing endless frustration to senior management.

Change in the role of the centre

Corporate rethinks have extended to reviewing the role of the centre and putting under the microscope the value of both corporate parenting and head office functions. Numbers of staff in head offices have fallen sharply in recent years as technology has made some former head office functions redundant and other functions have been decentralized to the operating companies or outsourced altogether. Some companies are outsourcing parts of finance; others are moving it into shared services. IT and human resources have been outsourced and decentralized with more reliance on SAP type systems to reduce the need for large numbers of information collators.

This is part of anticipating shareholders' insistence on greater value from all parts of the business. Reviewing the role of the centre goes beyond reducing numbers to identifying the most valuable role that the centre can fulfil. In the past, head offices either acted merely as banker to a portfolio of diversified businesses or, at the other extreme, involved themselves in operational detail. Both business models have now largely fallen out of fashion. A 1998 survey of 50 large companies such as Glaxo Wellcome and Cadbury Schweppes, by consultants Towers Perrin updated their similar survey in 1988. It showed that the majority of corporate centres now describe themselves as guiding, directing and giving strategic guidance to the operating units, and shifting to a more networked approach in order to realize the advantages of leverage and size.

Dual citizenship

Gaining the advantages of leverage and size in an organization which is evolving from working in separate national markets to applying common approaches across all markets puts a high demand on communication. One of the key demands is the need to create 'dual citizenship' among employees so that they identify with their own business locally, but feel part of a wider family and are willing to swap information, share success and adopt ideas from elsewhere. In this way employees can balance short-term parochial interests with the longer-term interests of the organization as a whole. The task of internal communications is to help enrol employees in the business strategy so that they reduce costs and improve efficiency. This means engaging managers so that they feel sufficiently part of the business as a whole to understand investment decisions being made elsewhere. Communication is also important for balancing a strong country focus with a greater focus on processes running across different countries, especially where there is an increasing use of cross-country teams working on specific issues.

As organizations globalize, global changes have a greater impact on individuals. For example, benchmarking and competition between manufacturing sites increase as manufacturing capacity is reviewed by companies on a global, not a country, basis. Employees who read about the colourful activities of colleagues on the other side of the world in the company newsletter can feel very differently about them when a product is switched from their factory to their colleagues', thereby effectively exporting their jobs.

Managing the transition from a divisional organization with a strong national focus, to a matrixed, networked organization requires careful management of lines of communication. The pay-off for good communication is a unified group of people who know where the business is going, and less speculation, misunderstanding and concern.

Internal communication and the corporate centre

The continuing debate about how the corporate centre can best add value highlights how internal communication has to be rewired and how the communication department's roles and responsibilities have to be revisited. Corporate centres target resources on business opportunities where they can outperform competitors. A corporate group may comprise a number of business units, each of which has its own chief executive responsible for developing its own business, within a clear strategic and financial framework. While it may provide services to the business units, the primary role of the centre is to ensure that the business units benefit from being part of the group through its role as a 'parent'. As a parent it will fulfil the traditional roles of financial management and control, and provide a short-term challenge to results as well as a strategic challenge to business units' plans. Increasingly, however, the role of the centre is to add value and release value across the group by facilitating the transfer of knowledge, expertise and best practice, standardizing processes and resourcing and developing senior managers. This new role means that the communication task must change. The parenting role of the centre will require internal communication to shift focus to create a sense of community, common interest and 'dual citizenship' among managers in order to encourage them to contribute, transfer and accept best practice.

Internal communication will have to be based on the best balance between the centre and the business units in a way that best fits their needs and style. To do that it has to strike a new balance between four elements:

- **Purpose and direction**: what level of understanding of corporate direction is needed at different levels within the business units.
- **Information**: who needs what information (for example, for strategy and direction, performance information), and how they can best receive it, how often, in what style and via which distribution process
- **Identification**: what is the right balance of identification between corporate, and business unit, and how corporate communication should best support that; to what extent people should feel part of the wider whole, and how communication should best act as a 'corporate glue'
- **Collaboration**: how communication should encourage the exchange of best practice, and foster sharing learning and networking.

While all this may be internal communication's job, what tools exist to carry it out? Five areas that help an organization restructure are:

1   management of communication responsibilities
2   managing the lines of information
3   redefining the role of the corporate communication function
4   redefining the role of the communicators' network
5   managing corporate and brand identity.

1   Management of communication responsibilities

A renegotiation of the relationships between the centre and the individual businesses should include redefining the communication responsibilities of the individual businesses. Managers tend to revert to past behaviour, and existing communication channels are often outdated and not designed to carry the business into the future. Clear expectations and targets for communication should be set, and managers tracked on their communication performance.

2   Managing the lines of information

Managers of corporate communication at corporate headquarters compete with operational managers in the divisions for employees' attention and loyalty. What share either should have, and the degree to which business units filter information from the centre, will depend on agreeing the proportions between communicators on both sides. Without agreeing explicit rules of engagement, the traditional tensions between the centre and the businesses will continue to damage communication.

3   Redefining the role of the corporate communication function

Becoming a unified business, and taking advantage of all possible synergies means taking key strategic decisions centrally and coordinating key activities across the group. Communication to support this must itself be centrally coordinated with the communication function, proving that it can take a more value-added role. The role of the corporate internal communication department should change to match the new role of the centre, and the following questions should be answered:

- What are the current expectations of corporate internal communication, and how well does it perform against them?
- What should the new role of internal communication be in supporting the new role of the centre?
- What are the new communication criteria and standards for success?
- How should communication best support other changes (for example, sharing knowledge and creating common values)?

4   Redefining the role of the communicators' network

Creating networks of professional communicators who collaborate closely translates into greater familiarity, improved relationships and trust, so that change happens more easily. Any alteration to structure changes the responsibilities of communicators. Communicators need to work together in a network to ensure that the organization enjoys 'joined up' communication.

Redefining the role of the corporate communication function and the communicators' network is discussed in Chapter 9.

5   Managing corporate and brand identity

Business units will have distinct targets and measures. Those targets will encourage units to focus on their market and customers. This may encourage self-interest and therefore some force for cohesion is needed to counter possible separatism. When an organization restructures it cuts across existing identities and loyalties and creates new ones. The corporate identity and employees' identification with it is a force for cohesion.

Rebalancing the 'Russian dolls' of identification, depends on managing the balance between corporate and local identity and agreeing how far into each business the corporate communication should reach. This means balancing the group-wide 'big picture' with local information and agreeing a share of corporate airtime in local communication.

Organizations need to ask themselves what is the role of the centre, what is the size, location and branding of the business units, and how important is having a common culture across the group? If some employees need to feel part of the wider business, how far down the organization should identification with the corporate name extend? In a decentralized business does the employee on the shopfloor really need to know who the ultimate owner is and is there any value, beyond corporate vanity, for them to have this knowledge? The following section provides a basis for agreeing this balance.

Communication adds value or destroys it

Normally, the change in an organization's structure is an attempt to find a solution to a problem. For the organization to achieve the solution that gives it the best value, communication has to match its brands and corporate reputation, and fit with the way it has chosen to structure and run the business. If the way in which communication is structured does not match and fit, it will destroy value rather than create it. Communication that does not fit, does not help; it hinders.

To ensure communication adds value senior managers have to:

1   calculate where the 'centre of gravity' for employees' identification and loyalty should be, which brand employees need to represent, and the structure of the business – how centralized, centrally co-ordinated or decentralized it is. These are questions around two things:
    – *Brand structure*: the relationship between corporate identity and brand
    – *Business structure*: the organizational framework for running the business
2   understand how the business has balanced business structure and brand structure to create best value
3   identify how the structure/brand balance might change
4   match communication 'wiring' to structure and brand
5   identify how communication can add value by greater:
    – consistency
    – coordination
    – accountability
6   identify how communication should be managed to add most value.

The following subsections expand on the first four of these. The description of how to achieve the remaining two is continued in Chapter 8.

Calculating the centre of gravity

Traditionally, how communication is managed has depended on an organization's degree of centralization or decentralization. In more centralized organizations the corporate centre had a claim on the employees' brainspace; in more decentralized organizations, the local barons ran their own communication show.

When organizations want to turn their employees into brand ambassadors and ensure that they deliver on the brand promise, the question should be asked 'for which brand?' – corporate, business unit or product? To resolve the counterclaims of the corporate centre, business unit or matrix line of management on employees' loyalty and attention, the question to ask is 'Where does the business strategy require the focus of employee loyalty to be?'. Employees who are expected to deliver on a brand promise should have their attention and identification aligned with the brand proposition.

In a business like Marks and Spencer, consistency and reliability are the core of what customers are offered at whatever shop they happen to use. It is therefore important that employees at any one of the network of stores identifies with the values of the brand proposition. Similarly, the essence of McDonalds' offer is consistent standards, wherever you go. There is therefore an obvious advantage in employees feeling part of the whole of McDonalds, its approach and values, and not trying to reinvent any of its wheels.

However, a customer looking for a pub may be more interested in one with quaint individuality, rather than looking for one of a uniform chain. Should the bar staff feel part of the King's Head, or part of the pubs division of a diversified leisure group? While pub managers may feel happier as part of a larger group, seeing its range of career opportunities, do the part-time bar staff need to feel the same corporate connection?

When an organization's strategy is to present a local brand to the consumer, communication should be focused on encouraging employees to identify strongly with their local unit. Employees of Rank Hovis McDougall may feel proud of producing Mr Kipling cakes. They may, however, feel there's no advantage to being part of the same family of businesses as Smith and Wesson guns, even though they are owned by the same group, Tompkins. At the corporate centre of a federation, like Tompkins or BTR, there will be little desire to communicate directly with the plants or offices of its businesses. That will be the province of local management, and there will be little benefit for employees in knowing that they are, ultimately, part of a larger whole.

Having decided where the employee's identification should be to give best value to the business, managers have to abide by the discipline which that decision entails. This discipline depends on both business structure and brand structure. For example, what freedom does a decentralized, autonomous country manager have when he is marketing a global brand? Can he do what he likes or must he follow guidelines from the centre?

What is the corporate identity and branding of the organization?

Any shift from the traditional roles of business unit and corporate centre to more of a global network will highlight the issue of corporate naming, and with whom employees identify. Brands and logos are the tribal flags and totems around which employees form their loyalty and identity. When organizations become more global, people become more tribal. Alvin Toffler, the futurist author, discovered that when people feel they are amalgamated into larger geographical blocks, such as Europe, they seek comfort and identity in smaller regions. This may explain why, while the UK gravitates towards Europe, inhabitants of Cornwall want to secede from the UK. Similarly, as organizational life becomes more complex, global and multidisciplinary, employees look for a simple local tribe to join.

In every organization identity and structure go hand-in-hand. If businesses within a group share a brand which is seen as a valuable asset, they will be held accountable for protecting and building that asset. Their accountability to the centre and to each other will be higher than in businesses in a group which has no shared brands. Their room for independent manoeuvre will be smaller. Where businesses promise a consistent service worldwide to global clients, epitomized by a brand they share across all the countries in which they operate, their interdependence and accountability will be all the higher. Organizations have to reconcile how they want to manage their brands with how they want to run their business.

Organizations fall into three groups: monoliths, portfolios and federations.

The monolith has a strong single business identity which is shared by its divisions: examples are 3M, BP, Virgin and ICI. The fundamental strength of the monolithic identity is that, because each product and service launched by the organization has the same name, style and character as all the others, then relations with staff, suppliers and the outside world are clear, consistent and easier to control and manage. Employees in each of its divisions will have a strong loyalty to the name and will be constantly seeing it in advertising and on the High Street.

The portfolio is an organization with individually branded businesses, owned by a group which is itself branded, such as Kingfisher, Storehouse, Rover and Whitbread. The companies forming a group are perceived, either by visual or written endorsement, to be part of that group, such as

Nestlé. Consumer goods companies traditionally have portfolio identities while banks traditionally have monolithic identities.

The federation comprises a collection of businesses, each with its own identity, owned by organizations such as Hanson, Tompkins or BTR. The owners' identity may be visible only to the City, and is irrelevant to the consumer.

Such federations have grown largely by acquiring competitors, suppliers and customers who have their own individual name, culture, and reputation. They are concerned to retain the goodwill associated with the brands and companies which they have acquired but, at the same time, they want to overlay their own management style, financial practices and rewards on to their subsidiaries. They have certain audiences, such as the financial world, opinion formers, and corporate customers, who they want to impress with their total size and strength. Communication to these audiences aims to emphasize uniformity and consistency as opposed to diversity.

Of these three types of organization, portfolios have the most difficult job. Some portfolio organizations have acquired competitive ranges of products in different countries with varying reputations. They therefore have problems of competition and confusion among suppliers, customers and often their own employees.

Companies seeking to create an identity covering a wide range of activities with subsidiaries that often compete face a complicated task. At the corporate level and for corporate audiences, they want to project a single but multifaceted organization that has a shared sense of purpose. However, at a local level they also want to allow the identities of the companies and brands that they have acquired to flourish in order to retain goodwill, both in the marketplace and among employees. Different portfolio organizations take different approaches to this balancing act.

There are two types of portfolio organization – the high-profile portfolio such as Rover Group and the low-profile, such as Whitbread. The high-profile portfolio owner's name will be known to its customers and to its employees, whereas the low-profile portfolio owner operates through a series of brands or companies which are apparently unrelated, both to one another and to the corporation. Especially in pharmaceuticals, food, drink and other fast moving consumer goods such organizations separate their identities as a corporation from those of the brands which they make and sell. Low-profile portfolios include such organizations as GrandMet, Unilever and Procter & Gamble. In such setups, so far as the final customer is concerned, the corporation does not exist. What the customer perceives is only the brand. This allows the brand to have a life cycle of its own, distinct from that of the company. It also allows brands from the same company to compete with each other. That perceived competition might be reduced in the eyes of the consumer if they were known to all belong to the same owner.

Business structure

A company has to identify the right 'centre of gravity' for its employees by matching the brand they need to understand and deliver with the structure and way of managing the business. The way of communicating should differ according to how centralized, centrally coordinated, or decentralized it is.

Communication in a centralized organization   A centralized organization is characterized by close, central control of decisions. Typically, a small number of people at the centre have the authority to take decisions which affect the whole organization. In a centralized organization with a monolithic brand, for example, communication is run on the 'Roman empire' model. Strategy and planning happen at the centre, and prepackaged messages are distributed with minimal local change.

There may only be a few organizations which are actually completely centralized, but there are certainly a number of organizations who run their communication as if they were.

Communication in a decentralized organization   Decentralization allows greater closeness to the customer and faster responsiveness to the market. Senior managers in business units are allowed to get on with the job, within clearly established frameworks.

In a decentralized organization communication should create greater closeness to the customer and faster responsiveness to the market. Employees should feel that they are working for the local business unit, so that greater identification and loyalty encourage greater motivation and productivity. Employees should be focused on local issues and priorities, with low exposure to the wider corporate picture.

Senior managers in business units can be allowed to get on with the local communication job, reporting regularly to the centre on progress against agreed responsibilities. Managers at the centre should maintain a hands-off approach and concentrate on identifying opportunities which can be rolled out across the divisions.

Communication at the business unit level should aim specifically to foster strong identification with the unit. The centre will communicate only occasionally to all employees and have only the top management tier as its regular constituency.

Communication in a centrally coordinated organization   Typically, in a centrally coordinated structure, technical functions, such as IT support, are centralized at headquarters, while daily operating decisions remain decentralized. Centralized purchasing takes advantage of group negotiating muscle and common human resources policies are often adopted across the business.

When organizations become more centrally coordinated, communication should prompt managers to look beyond the needs of their local units and to feel a part of a greater whole. Employees can still identify primarily with their local units, but occasional communication from the centre can create an additional sense of being part of a wider whole.

In other business functions formal planning and review procedures are established, and each business has to compete for corporate funds. New coordination systems aim for a more effective allocation of the company's limited resources. Similarly, in internal communication, common planning frameworks are needed to ensure the best use of employees' time. Communication needs to be coordinated more strongly by the centre, and common standards, planning frameworks, and measurement should be adopted across the business units.

Balancing business structure and brand structure to create best value

Internal communication should match the organizations' structure and fit the brand. Matching the management of corporate identity and brand against how the business is managed yields a chart which helps identify the best fit. Figure 4.1 shows how different organizations combine their

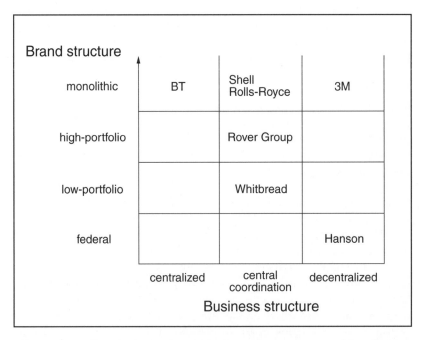

Figure 4.1 The balance between brand structure and business structure in different companies

approaches to management and brand. Rolls-Royce, for example, combines strong stewardship of its brand with a desire to allow business units to get on with their job, while retaining the advantages of any synergy. It has a monolithic brand, and manages its business units by central coordination.

Chapter 8 looks at how internal communication should best be managed for each of these types of organizations with some rules of engagement for internal communicators, both at the centre and in business units.

Identifying how the structure/brand balance might change

Organizations rarely stand still. They move from one box to another, on a migratory path from decentralized federation to monolithic global network and back. They can move between boxes like knights on a chessboard. So what do they need to change in their communication structure to help them arrive at and sustain their desired state? What do they need to keep in place to plan ahead for the next move?

HSBC, originally the Hong Kong and Shanghai Banking Corporation, used to be a federation of banks and financial services companies, located and managed within the communities they served. Managers were asked to focus on the local rather than the global, and operated with minimal involvement from head office. However, the global nature of its competition and the need to produce greater value for customers and shareholders alike has meant a move towards central coordination and the adoption of a single global identity.

To present itself more coherently to customers, employees, shareholders and the financial community, HSBC clearly believes that it needs to adopt one single unified brand and to be much more disciplined and focused in the way it presents itself and communicates. This has involved, for example, changing the long established and well respected names of Marine Midland in the USA and Midland Bank in the UK to a single name, used worldwide – HSBC.

This unified brand is intended to help the customer understand what the organization as a whole can offer, making cross-selling easier. Cross-selling also requires that employees know and understand what different parts of the organization are, feel that they are part of the same organization and owe each other some allegiance and cooperation. HSBC's name change shows a clear link between how it presents itself, with whom it wants employees to identify, its business rationale and what behaviours it wants from employees as a result.

Another organization to move around the chessboard of structure and identity is Hanson. Once a traditional federation, Hanson owned a range of businesses and added value in ways which meant more to the City than to the customer. For example, it could immediately reduce acquired companies' cost of capital, since it had a strong credit rating and could get money more cheaply. It could also extend to acquired companies the low rate of tax that it had achieved and also add value through its management techniques. These strategies worked well for low-technology businesses or with several factories making the same things, since it was then possible to rationalize the number of factories, and squeeze more from the assets.

Hanson is now shifting from a diverse conglomerate to a focused building materials producer as the group looks for acquisitions. It has 'Hansonized' its three operating companies. Cornerstone, the largest business, became Hanson Building Materials America, ARC is now Hanson Quarry Products Europe and what was Hanson Brick is Hanson Brick Europe. This entails rebalancing employees' identification with the Hanson name and style.

Matching communication 'wiring' to structure and brand

Case study: Rover

Rover has been through the full range of these issues. As a group it has moved from decentralization to central coordination and has had to redress the balance between its individual brands and its corporate name.

In 1991 Rover was organized into business units. This made managing directors accountable for their businesses, and they were given their own manufacturing and engineering units. The business units represented a mixture of brands, locations and support services, comprising Rover Cars, producing small and medium cars at Longbridge, and large cars at Cowley, Land Rover at Solihull and Body Pressings, Swindon.

These business units had grown up independently on four sites, with sufficiently different ways of operating to require being pulled together more consistently. The aim behind this was to reduce complexity in the engineering process, with more customer-focused, branded, front-of-house operations serving the customer, and more coordinated back-of-house operations providing common standards, methodologies, parts and platforms.

Rover combined a move to greater central coordination with a shift in its corporate identity. It had to balance its group identity under the Rover Group name, with the growing integration with its owner, the BMW Group. Creating a Rover Group identity was part of the move towards greater central coordination, with a single engineering group and common processes and standards.

The profile of the BMW Group within Rover then rose dramatically with the creation of a centralized engineering group and the Hams Hall engine plant providing engines for vehicles across the group, under the BMW name.

These issues of identification and badging are always challenging but were all the more so because, while Rover is a portfolio of different marques, BMW is a monolithic brand, which is marketed in a very focused way. Employees within BMW, identify with BMW as a whole, more than they do with the products.

Despite its troubles, Rover had been very successful in creating a corporate reputation and an employer brand, with 86 per cent of staff reporting that they were proud to say they worked for Rover. In the past, associates – as employees were called – might not have been ready to admit to working for British Leyland, the forerunner to Rover. Rover's success transformed that attitude. Nevertheless, the associates have strong local loyalties, even to brands and companies that no longer exist except in their folk memory. Traditionally, the associates identified first with the manufacturing plant's location, like Longbridge, and then with Rover. Getting associates to provide customers with quality cars, service and back-up, meant the employer brand, the corporate brand, and the product brand needed to be strongly connected, balancing local tribal identification with a sense of common purpose. This meant that there were a number of 'Russian dolls' of identification, that had to be fitted one inside the other:

- location/plant
- function – engineering, manufacturing
- brand
- Rover Group
- BMW Group.

The replacement of the Rover Group name by the BMW name made getting the balance of identification among employees all the more difficult, especially when BMW was seen to be reversing to distance itself from Rover.

Rover Group's experience teaches a number of lessons about the management of communication. Whatever the recriminations about BMW's communication, Rover's own internal communication had achieved a great deal, in difficult circumstances.

In Rover's first wave of improvement, communication was used to create a clear focus on the team and on improving individual performance by making people feel part of a smaller unit. This meant using the team leader to communicate and giving small teams responsibility for quality and improvement. This was successful in creating a strong team culture, but it also created strong local identification. Leaving communication at that level would have created a cellular organization, in which people concentrated on their narrow local interests rather than on the bigger picture. Encouraging a wider group identification and accountability for product quality, meant communicating an understanding of the group business context. Rover did this initially by bringing different groups of employees together from outside their locations, more closely coordinating communication between business units and sharing information. It created a common team meeting process that combined group information with local information and followed up with management conferences, and then conferences for all associates.

This shift from a local cellular organization to a more networked organization illustrates some of the ways in which communication can be rewired to create value, once the organization is clear what identification it needs to create among its employees. If the business strategy calls for a decentralized organization with local brands, business units can target their internal communication on creating their own cultures. If, on the other hand, the strategy demands a centrally coordinated organization, internal communication should be focused on creating a common group culture with common ways of doing things which facilitate cross-functional networking.

The first approach gives more discretion to the business units, and a much lower profile to the centre. Although there will still be a communication framework, the content and style will be determined to a much greater extent by the businesses. The second approach requires a higher level of centrally coordinated internal communication, as well as greater visibility of the corporate name among employees. From a communication perspective this means a greater reach from the centre into the business units, and more communication resources at the centre to deliver this.

Case study: SmithKline Beecham

A similar communication rebalancing act was performed by SmithKline Beecham, first as part of a merger process, then after a major acquisition, and finally as part of creating a European consumer healthcare business.

SmithKline Beecham has become world-class in terms of both global scale and rates of growth, and has become the foremost consumer healthcare company in Europe. SB Consumer Healthcare aims to concentrate on its key brands that can be built up in every market.

Many retailers will only stock the number one and two brands in addition to their own label in a given category. This has led the best marketers of consumer goods to rationalize their product portfolio and focus on core brands. For example, Unilever has announced that it will discontinue or sell off 25 per cent of the brands that it markets in order to concentrate on core brands. In this way, the companies aim to eliminate costs, increase investment in product quality and put increased advertising behind core brands.

To achieve this, SB Consumer Healthcare is applying global processes in individual markets. For example, although the company's oral products might have different names in different local markets, they are likely to have a striped toothpaste, or a mouthwash – global product concepts – sold under locally well known brand names. This gives an opportunity for global product formulations, global new product development and global creative concepts and advertising approaches.

The organization's strategy is focused on greater operational efficiency and the most efficient and effective exploitation of its portfolio of brands. The aim is to drive greater innovation and creativity across the business, to reduce costs and to reduce duplication by sharing services. One of the main drives behind this approach was to instil process improvement as a routine way of doing business, and to drive the business forward using reliable processes rather than one-off initiatives.

SB Consumer Healthcare focuses clearly on standardizing processes for two reasons. First, once a process is standardized and documented it is easier to improve it. Second, standardizing processes frees up innovative creativity in new areas, rather than using it to reinvent products that already exist elsewhere in the business.

One example of this is the 'Marketing Leadership Programme', which aims to standardize and share best marketing practice across European markets. Best practice procedures are provided for market research, advertising, media buying, brand planning and development. This is part of the philosophy of freeing up the local organization to concentrate on those unique local things it needs to do well, and to apply standardized processes in a way appropriate to their own individual markets.

Good internal communication is vital to strengthening a pan-European approach, and to creating stronger local ownership of global processes. SB sees internal communication as helping managers from each country understand and support a European approach to the business. It has consciously focused communication on the 200 members of the European leadership group with the aim of creating understanding and ensuring a continuous flow of information. Such continuous communication needs to be strongly coordinated to make sure that mixed messages are avoided. In addition, communication forums and functional networks have been established, so that professionals who do not share the same reporting lines can come together to discuss relevant technical and professional issues. Electronic discussion databases allow them to continue debates and pool views, approaches and experience, despite geographical separation.

All this helps deliver a better knowledge of the European business, a better understanding of the future commercial environment, greater local

ownership of standard SB processes and better cross-functional networking.

SmithKline Beecham is typical of organizations which are structuring
themselves to have the best of both worlds – market-facing units which
are organized to focus on customers, and product units which are organized by product or capability. The goal is to combine a sensitivity to
customer needs with industry knowledge and expertise, while gaining
economies and efficiencies of scale.

Case study: ICI

ICI is typical of an organization trying to achieve the best balance of
coordination and autonomy, and achieving synergies of belonging in
the same corporate family. It, too, created communication forums and
networks as a key to realizing business benefits.

Following the demerger of Zeneca, ICI redefined the role of the group
centre. Instead of being a holding company with a portfolio of autonomous business units, it wanted to operate as a federation of
autonomous businesses within a collegiate network. This network would
be linked together by the corporate glue of a common brand, shared
values and with a strong corporate parenting advantage.

The business units tended to be sizeable, all carried the ICI prefix and
ranged from turnovers of £600–700 million through to £1.5 billion.

To create greater focus, the organization clarified responsibilities and
structure, balancing a matrix of geography, function and product line,
to create product line businesses, organized globally.

To provide additional communication glue, it created networks termed
'Driven Networks', which were led by a chief executive of one of the
major global businesses. These networks comprised representatives of
all the businesses, drawn from the top 200 people across the company.
The aim was to foster excellence in such areas as manufacturing, marketing, purchasing and information technology.

ICI's move to a matrix organization, and to networks, rather than
a hierarchy, required a more flexible approach to management and
communication. The emphasis in such networks is on solving problems
quickly by bringing together cross-functional teams which are formed
to tackle a particular problem and may be disbanded once the problem
has been resolved.

Networking is what makes networks work

The shift to a matrix organization often leads to an explosion in communication activity. Newsletters, roadshows and websites proliferate, as

does the number of Christmas parties people attend as members of different teams. This is no accident. It highlights the complexity of a matrix in which an individual is simultaneously a member of several teams organized for different purposes, and has to balance different aims and priorities. It also illustrates the importance of a shared sense of community and relationship. The importance of social events, or of seminars and meetings outside the immediate day-to-day job, is that they provide the goodwill, common interest and interrelationships that hold the organization together.

Operating in a matrix poses some real challenges for internal communication. Organizations are rapidly becoming networks with matrices that are very complex. Decision-making is often by consensus, and implementation is via influencing colleagues and subordinates rather than by diktat. Professional and functional responsibilities have to be balanced with line responsibilities. Each employee can have two or more managers, each with different priorities and performance measurements. All managers are free to communicate, and all lines of the matrix may have their own professional communicators competing for employees' time and attention.

The matrix approach drives consensus-seeking but can slow down decision-making – a real concern during times of change. The complexities of the matrix can obscure where accountability lies and hinder changes. Because of this, good communications and a shared understanding of direction and priorities are essential.

Matrix management depends on shared responsibilities and leadership, and it is often ruefully noted in matrix organizations that 'shared leadership equals no leadership'. When responsibilities are shared there is a greater cost in terms of discussion, coordination, and in time and effort. Working across different teams is at the heart of the approach, but incurs costs in terms of responsiveness and speed and, if poorly handled, can reduce efficiency.

Relationships and goodwill are key to resolving 'shared leadership problems', and good communication is as fundamental to making a matrix work as electricity is to a lightbulb.

Professional service firms were among the first to encounter these problems and are in the vanguard in terms of their knowledge about working in collegiate multidisciplinary teams. The professional service firm, says the management guru Tom Peters (*Financial Times*), is 'the best model for tomorrow's organization in any industry'. These firms – consultants, auditors, civil engineers, IT professionals, lawyers and so forth – are typically informal and flexible in their structure and good at teamwork and knowledge-sharing.

Now, while organizations look to these firms for lessons on how to manage in the future, these professional firms are trying to master the lessons of global networking, project coordination and matrix management that some large corporations have already had to master. There are lessons for both kinds of organization in how to rewire lines of communication for the future.

The lesson that professional services firms learned first was the importance of communication and teamwork. They have had to carry off the neat trick of continually creating new teams to work on assignments, while ensuring that those newly created 'tribes' also felt part of wider national, regional and global organizations. Operating in a matrix structure, they have understood the importance of communication to balancing complex lines of identity – client, industry, firm, specialization, and geography. They also recognized that their accumulated experience is a precious asset whose value can best be realized by their people sharing knowledge with each other, and how important good communication is in getting them to do so. They also realized that there are some inherent tensions in the structure of a matrix that need careful communication. Objectives that should be complementary can become competitive.

One form of the matrix which will serve to illustrate some of the issues is the resource management model, variations of which are used by consulting firms, engineering firms, accountants and, increasingly, by in-house IT departments. The principle behind this model is pools of people organized in specializations managed by resource managers. Customer-facing groups with knowledge of industry issues work with clients to identify their problems and then assemble an appropriate mix of specialists from these pools to man a project. Once the project is over, the specialists return to the pools to await the next call.

However, matters do not always work out so neatly. The traditional line manager function of making sure that an employee is both doing the task and being developed is split. A project manager may be responsible for keeping the individual occupied on productive work, while a resource manager focuses on ensuring that the individual is developing the necessary skills and their career development is being managed. This can liberate the project manager to focus purely on the task while leaving the softer issues of employee development and well-being to the resource manager, who is more distant from the day-to-day realities of project work and therefore has less knowledge of the people he or she is developing.

While project managers are assessed on profit, resource managers are assessed on efficient use of capacity. Project managers want specific skills available for a specific job; resource managers want to limit the risk of being left with idle people once the immediate need for their skills passes.

Industry and market knowledge is important to winning and keeping clients so customer-facing groups want to retain people who have built up industry experience on a project, rather than release them back to their pool. Project leaders also want to keep good workers for their next project, and will also try to avoid returning them to the pool. Having hung on to such people, project leaders need to keep them busy, productive and paid for to justify their existence. This leads to customer-facing groups and service groups competing for work, with customer-facing groups using their own people rather than specialists from the service groups. The idea of the client getting the best team for the job is sacrificed to meeting utilization targets. Goodwill erodes and there is a shift to greater self-interest.

To stop such an erosion, a wider view of the whole is necessary. However, the nature of project work militates against that vital sense of the whole. Staff are at different locations, often feeling isolated and uncertain about future work. They work in teams that are physically separate, serving a range of different clients, providing pieces of a jigsaw whose whole picture they cannot see. Large projects can become a loose federation of mini-businesses, in which individual employees are constantly monitoring their own job security, and where self-interest can never be far from their minds.

Regular communication is the antidote to many of these problems, but communication is the first thing to be discarded when time is tight. The strong focus on cost, time, and resource budgets often means that there is little time or budget to spend on communicating. As a consequence, it can be viewed as an overhead to be minimized or to be hidden away on client project work. People focus on day-to-day pressures, and lose sight of any bigger picture. At junior levels, they keep their heads down, intent more upon their professional development than on the organization's direction. This makes retaining good people all the more difficult.

Individuals are likely to have a reasonable degree of clarity on their day-to-day objectives, and on what they personally are supposed to be doing. They may also have a fairly clear view on what their immediate team is doing. Beyond that everything is much less clear. If your nose is close to the grindstone, your horizons tend to be low. This leads individuals to identify with their immediate teams and to have low familiarity with other areas with a resulting lack of understanding of their priorities and problems. A final outcome may be a cellular organization, with low cooperation between the cells.

The most important lesson that professional service firms' experience teaches us is that a matrix organization must consciously create strong identification, goodwill and relationship by investing in regular communication between its people. Furthermore, creating a sense of community and relationship is vital.

Where organizational structures become both complex and ambiguous, it is people's relationships that make the system work. This means people who get along with each other help each other out. They do not stand on their dignity or insist on keeping only to their own precisely worded job description. The quality of relationships, goodwill and cooperativeness form a safety net for the inevitable imperfections of the structure. Where good relationships do not exist, or are allowed to erode, that safety net disappears and creeping schizophrenia can set in.

The complexities of a matrix create ambiguities, and the nature of project work is communication-unfriendly. Professional service firms have a sobering range of business issues which they have to address if they are to be successful. They are not alone. Such issues also arise in a knowledge-based business. Since businesses will become more knowledge-based as they aim to provide value by applying their knowledge and experience, many other organizations will face these issues as they shift to similar structures and ways of operating.

Companies which provide their customers with value by applying their knowledge in multidisciplinary project teams will have to attract and retain the best people. To be successful, a project-based organization needs to resolve a number of issues:

- People need to be able to identify at least with the programme within which their project lives.
- They have to have a clear understanding of how the other projects work, and how the individual projects fit together to form a bigger picture of the programme.
- They have to have a clear understanding of the rest of the organization and the wider agenda for change.

This kind of organization requires a continual, significant investment of time in communication to hold it together. People tend to identify most strongly with their project team and, while bonding team members together on the job is important, there also has to be an ability to 'unbond' people at the end of an assignment. When projects end and the team breaks up, do people feel that they're returning home or to strangers? People have to perceive the resource pool as a warm place to return to, or they won't want to unbond. Worse, like the end of a holiday romance, they may feel the pain of separation so much that it may prompt them to look for another job, since returning to the pool would be like joining strangers anyway.

Project workers have to feel connected with the wider organization and the leadership. Giving them an understanding of the business context gives them a greater sense of control and reassurance. However, where leaders are largely invisible, and there is no opportunity for contact, trust is undermined. Employees fill the vacuum by building a picture of the leaders' motivation and agenda from isolated incidents.

Where leaders are largely invisible, employees tend to be unclear about their roles and responsibilities – what exactly do they do up there on the management floor? Employee attitude surveys and communication reviews consistently reveal that greater contact between individuals creates greater familiarity, greater familiarity creates greater trust and greater trust creates greater cooperation. The reverse is also true. Lack of contact and familiarity leads to distrust, and lack of familiarity leads to lack of respect. Where one team does not know or understand what another team does, they rate them poor at doing it – the 'unknown incompetent' syndrome, mentioned earlier.

Organizations which apply multidisciplinary teams to customers' problems will aim to encourage collaboration between different service areas, and to share and apply knowledge gained in different parts of the organization. To achieve the benefits of cooperation, they will have to increase their employees' willingness to collaborate, reduce the likelihood of interpersonal friction and reduce the cost of coordination. For such organizations internal communication is both a corporate glue and a corporate lubricant.

They will also have to avoid overengineering, and added cost, by better project management. This, in turn, will entail educating their employees to understand the best business balance of customer satisfaction and commercial management and the trade-offs involved between them.

Internal communication is needed to make an organization's people able and willing to do all this. It has to give employees the information they need to do the job, while motivating them to want to do the job well both for the customer and for their company. It has to help decrease self-interest and increase mutual interest.

Strengthening the team ethos, and improving the bonding of project teams, with a shared sense of direction, and common understanding and values, requires using communication to link three agendas:

1   The company's agenda: the strategy and direction of the business
2   The customers' agenda: what they need and how they want the company to give it to them
3   The employee's agenda: a clear career path and what experience and skills he or she wants to gain.

This is a clear remit for communication. But to fulfil it, professional communicators need to understand how the shifting sands of organizational structure can swallow their well meant messages and bury their traditional communication channels.

Shifting the corporate communication remit

Communication is the glue that allows structures to thrive. Changes in structure from decentralization to central coordination demands shifts in identification, information and relationships. The bad news is that it also increases the number of communicators active in the network, and the need to manage and coordinate them.

The traditional remit of the corporate communication centre is ownership of the corporate communication channels – the corporate video, the corporate newspaper – and drafting, crafting and distributing senior management thinking and messages. However, restructuring is likely to change its remit. A change in structure leads to the need to shift the balance of employees' identification with the corporate identity, brand and product.

Case study: 3M

3M is a good example of an organization which has faced the issues of restructuring, the creation of a matrix organization, the rebalancing of levels of identification and the need to use communication to create different relationships across its business units.

3M is a federation of 35 businesses, producing a range of different products from sandpaper to hip replacements, organized by product and market focus, each with its own marketing function. As part of a radical reshaping of the company's European organization, it has created a series of European business centres (EBCs). These are clusterings of businesses around nine European locations.

Since the headquarters of EBCs are in different European countries, the extent to which employees identify with their EBC rather than the country in which they work varies. The healthcare EBC, for example, which includes the dental, the pharmaceutical and the medical businesses, is headquartered in the UK – although the French members of the EBC may have greater affinity with 3M France.

Internal communication is directed towards creating a greater sense of identification with the European business centre, using existing face-to-face communication structures in the businesses. Each EBC managing director produces a briefing on the European business centre and its results, which are used by communication team leaders to brief employees.

Having divided people into units, 3M is keen to encourage salespeople to look for other opportunities to cross-sell. They are therefore using communication to create familiarity and goodwill between different business units. Salespeople from different business units, who would not normally meet, are brought together for breakfast meetings to get to know each other and to share leads. They are also provided with audiotapes and sales communication packs to educate them about each others' products.

3M defines the role of internal communications as 'creating employee understanding in support of the business strategy to generate profitable growth'. It sees itself very much as a global organization, and has put a great deal of effort into integrating its communications, so that there are shared messages and shared tools across the different regions worldwide. Whereas ten years ago the UK would have had its own, and very different, internal communications strategy, now there is a more integrated worldwide strategy in order to avoid duplication and competition between messages.

The 3M case study illustrates the internal communication issues that are likely to be encountered by other organizations. Organizations will have to rewire lines of information to sustain new structures, reposition loyalties so that employees within individual companies also feel part of the wider family, and create a global network of communicators so that communicators in different business units work together effectively.

The communication function will have to imitate the business as a whole by shifting from its traditional core of channel ownership and message provision to a more value-added role. This will help create greater business value through networking knowledge, fostering links between different parts of the business, encouraging a sense of global identification and creating a greater understanding of the new roles and behaviours that will be needed. These issues are taken up again in Chapter 8, 'The Management of Communication', and Chapter 9, 'Repositioning the Role of the Internal Communication Function'.

Networking knowledge

Chapters 3 and 4 looked at the how internal communication can help achieve differentiation and help restructuring deliver value. Differentiation for some businesses has involved a move away from their traditional core products to add-on areas – adding value by problem-solving. Consequently, the heart of their businesses is now not simply in products or their production technology, but in their experience, knowledge and expertise. This in turn means that their focus has to be on information and knowledge as a key to providing customer value. Knowledge needs to be identified and captured, and best practice in one area transferred to others in the organization.

Chapter 4 focused on the drive behind restructuring to achieve synergies between different parts of the organization. To achieve these synergies, it will be important to capture and share information, and to network knowledge for global consistency and global customer satisfaction. In organization's pursuit of a clear differentiation, making the connection between the capture and transfer of knowledge and its application will be vital to success. This chapter looks at how internal communication can be used to make that connection and create better networking of knowledge.

In an information business, knowledge and skills are the real assets, and they reside within individuals. Organizations aiming for greater competitive differentiation and customer retention may have to rewrite the statement that 'our people are our greatest asset' to 'what's in their heads is our greatest asset'. In either case, organizations will still want to 'sweat the assets'.

Organizations realize that their knowledge about what they do and about their customers is a crucial tool for strategic advantage. Capturing and sharing that knowledge has become a key means of creating value for both the customer and the supplier. Since the key productive resource of the new era is neither labour, land nor capital but knowledge, it is no surprise that knowledge management is an idea whose time has come. In the USA the proportion of knowledge workers – those working with information rather than materials – will have risen from 17 per cent to

59 per cent over the course of the twentieth century, while those handling materials will have halved to 41 per cent. It is expected that seven out of eight employees will soon be knowledge workers, and predictions for 2001 are that 20 per cent of jobs will be unfilled because of the lack of employees with the right knowledge.

Sir Francis Bacon argued the usefulness of 'filthy lucre' when he said, 'Money is like manure – it does no good unless it be spread around'. This chapter argues the same of knowledge – that it has to be shared and applied to achieve a benefit. Spreading it around and applying it is primarily an issue of relationship and interaction, not just the management of information. For this reason, this chapter argues that instead of knowledge management we should be talking about knowledge networking.

The chapter discusses first what is knowledge management and why it is important. Then it looks at the role of internal communication in knowledge management and argues the importance of correctly linking two strands of internal communication – information and interaction.

What is knowledge management?

Knowledge management is the deliberate leveraging of employees' collective knowledge to increase the organization's ability to create value. It requires turning personal knowledge into corporate knowledge so that it can be shared throughout an organization. Doing this effectively enables an organization both to increase profitability and create new knowledge.

Companies adopt two broad approaches to knowledge management:

1 capturing and sharing existing knowledge better – making implicit knowledge more explicit and putting in place mechanisms to move it more rapidly to where it is needed
2 innovation – making the transition from ideas to commercialization more effective.

Why knowledge management is important

When downsizing many companies discarded the people who had the knowledge they needed. Knowledge management is now being seen as a first stage that stops or reverses that loss, and provides processes for the capture and re-use of valuable knowledge.

Many innovative companies have long appreciated the value of knowledge in enhancing their products and customer service. There are three main reasons why the level of interest has grown dramatically during the last few years.

1   Total Quality Management (TQM), Business Process Re-engineering (BPR) and similar initiatives have helped organizations become more efficient at what they do. Now companies want to make the best of their talent and differentiate themselves in the marketplace.

2   Applied knowledge can enhance the value (and hence the price) of products and services. Examples are the hotel chain that knows your personal preferences and so can give you a more personalized service, or the food retailer who knows your regular order of staple items and can deliver them regularly without you having to reorder.

3   By retaining knowledge during downsizing or restructuring, organizations can avoid costly mistakes or 'reinventing the wheel'. Companies save millions a year by taking the knowledge from their best performers, sharing best practices and applying them in similar situations elsewhere. This has resulted in improved customer service, faster problem-solving and more rapid adaptation to market changes.

Companies that have successfully applied knowledge management techniques report bottom-line business benefits. One of the best known examples is 3M. Innovation is encouraged by the '15 per cent rule' (which allows employees to spend that amount of time on their own projects), and the governing principle that 25 per cent of company turnover must come from products introduced in the last four years. 3M scientists in hundreds of divisions produce a stream of new products, sometimes based on completely new knowledge, but more often by recombining existing knowledge in different and creative ways.

Hoffman La Roche has reduced the cost and time in achieving regulatory approvals for new drugs, through their 'Right First Time Programme'. Dow Chemical has generated over $125 million in revenues by the active management of their patent portfolio and from licensing. Texas Instruments has saved the equivalent of investing in a new plant by sharing best practice between their semiconductor fabrication plants. Hewlett Packard now brings new products to market much faster by more effectively sharing existing expertise within the company with their development teams.

By using knowledge to make processes more efficient, companies can achieve their end result more quickly, and get products to market faster. Even marginal improvements can have significant effects. In the pharmaceutical industry, for example, each week of delay in launching a new drug means many thousands of pounds in lost revenue.

Every organization is in business to offer a service and/or product. Every day, employees make key decisions throughout the chain of processes that create value. By focusing on these decisions, and the information needed to make them, the quality of both product and process can be improved and errors can be avoided. This reduces costs of labour and raw materials and so raises productivity. This, in turn, increases profitability since the organization can charge the same price and pocket the difference brought by increased savings, charge more if it has added to the value of the product, charge less and undercut the competition, or share the savings with its customers.

So, knowledge management is important because:

- capturing and sharing knowledge is important for creating value within the organization
- delivering on the promise to the customer involves the whole organization delivering consistently on that promise which, in turn, requires the harnessing of knowledge and expertise across the organization to avoid reinventing wheels
- organizations want to leverage their expertise for greater innovation, process improvement and product development.

However, realizing these benefits requires taking knowledge-sharing seriously and systematically. Successful knowledge management is not achieved by organizing knowledge transfer programmes and trying to share absolutely everything with everyone. Rather, an increase in shareholder value is achieved by concentrating on strategic knowledge and tying knowledge management to the organization's mission and strategy or to a specific business issue, with a clear link between knowledge and the bottom-line business benefit.

Internal communication is critical in to achieving that bottom-line benefit because:

- more employees are becoming knowledge workers
- the business strategy dictates what knowledge is useful. Internal communication which is not aligned with the new strategy hinders its successful implementation
- changing how you serve your customers changes the information you need to capture, store and share
- information that is not relevant and cannot easily be turned into value becomes a deadweight
- employees need to know the wider context in order to transform information into knowledge.

More employees are becoming knowledge workers

As commoditization of their core product or service forces organizations to find new ways of providing value for customers, value is more likely to be found in providing additional advice and information. This means that employees are more likely to become knowledge workers.

Five or six years ago, Unisys was essentially a mainframe computer manufacturer. As such, employees were viewed as being contributors to the process of making a product. Today, about 60 per cent of its business is in services. Its product increasingly is its people – their knowledge, capabilities and skills. Now they are not just an input to the product, they *are* the product.

Knowledge-based organizations have a high proportion of knowledge workers and their expertise is composed of knowledge and skill in specific fields. In addition to using their knowledge to interpret incoming information, they also create it. Knowledge workers are typically more productive and better paid and are more mobile than typical workers.

Changing customer strategy changes information needed

Moving employees' focus from producing the best products to under-standing and solving customers' problems redefines what information is relevant and valuable. Where customers are more interested in getting their problems solved, employees need to concentrate on better problem-solving rather than on improving product features in isolation. For example, in a company that has traditionally followed a strategy of product leadership and which is proud of its products, employees' defi-nition of providing customer value can be adding in more product features. As a result, information about products, not customers, is what gets communicated.

To be able to transform the information they receive into valuable knowledge, employees need to be aware of the larger context, understand the whole of their customer's situation and be able to link the two. Educating employees in the broader business context, enables them to understand and bring clarity and meaning to corporate information.

For some organizations better management and knowledge-sharing is central to their strategic ambitions. This is particularly true for the 'Big 5' accountancy and consulting firms, although the general principles hold for most organizations. The 'Big 5' firms are all keen to build their distinctive brands and to win business from rivals. Their problem is that they do not sell baked beans but a diverse set of sophisticated services. David Maister, the guru of the professional service firm sector, believes that there is an inherent barrier to creating the kind of brand premium such companies are seeking. He maintains that people pay a premium for Campbell's soup because it delivers what it promises more than 99 times out of 100. If that reliability drops to 70 per cent, the brand value simply evaporates. He maintains that professional service firms have a long way to go to get brand premium because they do not have the internal controls to deliver every time.

Instilling global partnerships with the kind of disciplines that underpin a brand is the challenge now facing the managers of the new 'Big 5'. Three obstacles lie in the way. National partnerships value their collegiate independence, which promotes individuality over 'corporate' discipline. The constraints of regulation and culture make it difficult to get national partnerships to work smoothly under one set of values. And, finally, the diversity of the 'one-stop shop' model offering businesses everything they want under one roof makes specific branding difficult, if not impossible.

Overcoming these obstacles demands greater management of the knowledge within the firm and getting employees to focus externally on the client and the issues facing them in their industries.

It is the knowledge of the industry issues, as seen by clients, which demonstrates familiarity with clients' situations and helps win their business. Creating value demands that people have an external focus, and know what product or service will most help the client. This requires a clear understanding of the end objectives and issues facing the client.

There are two types of knowledge that are relevant for a professional in one of these firms:

- knowledge and understanding of client issues and needs
- knowledge of company capabilities and processes.

The challenge is how to connect these two to create value for the client.

The Big 5 are not the only companies which have clearly linked their knowledge management with their customer proposition. Hewlett Packard, for example, is changing its internal communication and knowledge management to align with its competitive positioning and its desired relationship with customers. 'If Hewlett Packard knew what it knows we'd be three times more productive', Lew Platt, HP's chief executive has observed.

Hewlett Packard's heritage is strongly based on its product leadership and innovation. With a strong brand, it operates increasingly in consumer markets as well as with strategic accounts among multinational businesses. It therefore has to balance a number of different strategies across its sales organizations.

Redefining core knowledge

Open systems are driving the commoditization of both Hewlett Packard's and its competitors' traditional products, and customers are adept at 'cherry-picking' from their offerings – getting technical expertise from one vendor, then buying the hardware from another. Its sales strategy is to become its customers' 'trusted adviser', moving upstream from commodity supplier to partner. This is what Xerox did when it repositioned itself from a photocopier seller to the Document Company.

The aim is to get customers to appreciate the value of dealing with the Hewlett Packard organization as a whole and to begin charging for those services that they used to give for free. Customers will have an opportunity to configure for themselves the best mix of core and peripheral services, such as technical support.

When the product was the core, relevant information was information about the product. Now that the product is simply part of a wider offer, more information is required about the other components of the solution available. The organization therefore has to be much better at formulating and communicating messages to customers, to third-party partners and to the sales force.

Becoming a problem-solver, and tailoring specific solutions to individual customers' wider needs, requires a much broader familiarity with the customer's situation, their industry's issues and their strategic ambitions. This kind of information allows salespeople to talk to a potential customer on the same wavelength.

They then need a deeper understanding of the capabilities and resources of their own organization so they can select the best option for the customer. This means they have to juggle a much wider range of information from a greater number of sources.

Senior management may already be experienced in providing the most appropriate solutions to problems in large, complex customers. However, the sales force as a whole also needs to have that information and understand how to apply it in their own accounts. The role of internal communication is to provide the channels to disseminate that experience from top to bottom, and to accelerate the pace at which the organization's capabilities are matched to customer needs and experience.

Aligning salesforce communication with strategy

Moving from a product to a market focus redefines what information is relevant to the job. Changing strategy without revisiting the kind of information being captured and shared is a recipe for failure. If it is not realigned with the new strategy, the distribution of outdated information will continue to reinforce old approaches.

Over the last few years some organizations have tried to position themselves not as suppliers of components, but as providers of total systems. They have also restructured from product divisions to customer-facing business units, in an effort to become less internally product focused and more outward-looking and customer-led. Such an approach can lead to two problems:

■ Salespeople are not always convinced, and are happier remaining product pushers in the interests of a short-term pay-off, and a less complicated life.

■ Salespeople still have to hit their monthly targets, and it is easier to do that by dealing with customers who are already in shopping mode and are interested in product features rather than in the organization's capabilities as a whole.

During the transition a degree of schizophrenia sets in, with different individuals showing varying degrees of product/market orientations. Organizations with a strong heritage of product leadership, where product divisions have been the profit centres, will have a culture of technical fascination with product features. This will be reflected in their communication which will be product-focused, and poor internal communication could therefore derail their strategy.

What information salespeople will access, how they prioritize it and their definition of its value will depend on their perception of their own role. Product pushers, for example, may want primarily product information. Salespeople who see their role more as consultants, on the other hand, will want more information on industry trends and issues to help them identify relevant opportunities and needs among their customers. A typical mismatch is when salespeople are given densely written technical information when what they need is information on customer issues which they can use to jumpstart a conversation with a senior-level contact who is relatively uninterested in detailed technical issues.

Turning information into value

There are useful lessons which organizations have learned from managing salespeople that can be extended to other employees who are becoming knowledge workers. Salespeople are pioneers in the application of knowledge, because they apply their information to customers' situations. They have to be able to demonstrate to their customers, in a compelling way, the link between their company's capabilities and the customer's own needs.

Salespeople make the connection between customer and capability and turn information into value. They have learned lessons in dealing with customers that the rest of their organization could usefully learn. Their job has traditionally been translating information about products into customer relevance. They intend their communication to result in action, and they focus on the 'localization of the message' – they know that their job is to communicate information framed from the customer's point of view.

However much companies may debate what information employees should receive, there is rarely any argument that their salespeople should be provided with the information which they need to do their job. However, providing them with that information comes with a clear expectation of an outcome. Salespeople are expected to do something as a result of communication – sell. The expectation is that they will build relationships with their customers, understand their concerns, and use their knowledge to take the best action. All these expectations are just as relevant for internal customers.

Localizing the message

In the past, the salesperson acted as the link between the product divisions and customers, identifying what was relevant for customers and sifting and translating information to ensure that it was relevant. Marketing focused on sending overall general messages out to the market; salespeople focused on translating general information into specific messages for specific customers to a specific timescale. The job of the salesperson was to be the final link in the chain of making general information relevant and specific to the local market.

Salespeople's role is to add value to the information they receive by making the connection between product features and their benefit to the customer. This value-adding role is something organizations have automatically expected of salespeople, because they recognize that someone has to act as negotiator and mediator to make sure that the organization's agenda and the customer's agenda connect.

The lesson for internal communication is that this value-adding role now has to be filled not just by salespeople but by all managers within an organization. Making the connection between the company's business agenda and the employee's agenda requires managers to translate general information into specific individual relevance. They have to be the final link in the chain of communication to their people.

Providing valuable information

If salespeople are to fulfil a more demanding role, those providing information to them need to provide it in a more relevant form. If organizations want a deeper relationship with customers, communication needs to be focused on customer and business problems. Nowadays customers are less interested in the hardware and more interested in the application and the solution. Internal communication has to make the vital connection between a 'product out' approach and a 'customer in' approach, providing practical tools for sales and customer service people.

Internal communication should provide customer service and salespeople with general information about business trends and issues as a whole, and product information organized from the customer viewpoint. It should also provide profiles of the organization's capabilities, to help salespeople identify solutions to needs, speeding the perception of them as advisers rather than as product pushers.

Hewlett Packard makes life easier for the salesperson by structuring the supply of information to what is required at each stage of the sales cycle. It runs seminars for salespeople on business issues relevant to their target customers' industries, as well using its intranet to provide information on technical issues and position papers on its approaches to industry developments. It provides its people with information about the most pressing business issues in the markets they serve, industry issues in both its own industry and those of its principal accounts, and issues facing major customers. This provides the background necessary at the outset of a relationship with a target account. Salespeople can also use the intranet to get information on their own company, its track record, number of locations and its business partnerships.

In structuring a proposal for a customer, salespeople can access information about similar problems dealt with elsewhere by the organization, reference sites, issues and problems, potential pitfalls and so on.

Information and interaction in knowledge networking

Knowledge management combines the two strands of information and interaction – information that is circulated through the organization; and interaction – how people relate to the organization and to each other. In terms of the information strand of knowledge management, there are some clear lessons which apply in all areas of internal communication. If organizations are to improve their knowledge management, they will also have to get much better at information management. They have to provide clearer information which managers can easily link to local situations. Organizations have to be much more disciplined about the prioritization of information and the management of employee brain-space, and provide information in a more user-friendly way.

Managing information overload

The problem of information overload is twofold; information is relevant. Part of the problem that employees face is first, the sheer volume of information and second, 'meaning underload' – unclear relevance. In order to convert data into information, a human mind has to process data and find it meaningful. Even the most skilled human being has a limited capacity to absorb information. As businesses rely more on extracting value from knowledge, that limited capacity will become more and more precious. This means that they have to get better at organizing and communicating information, or be consumed by it.

A recent survey (Pitney Bowes, 1998) revealed that 1 billion (1 000 000 000) pages of paper are generated every day in the USA, with the majority (60 per cent) being used as input to computer systems. Furthermore, 40 per cent of respondents found it hard simply knowing where to look for information. This problem is increasing as the amount of information available increases: 50 per cent of respondents in organizations over 5000 people said that they rarely had information available on time, and almost one-third felt they had too many sources of information.

Prioritizing information
Managing knowledge requires getting all of the right information in front of the right person at the right time. This is another reason why organizations have to be much more disciplined about the prioritization of information and the management of brainspace.

As communication within organizations becomes more frequent and more chaotic, especially with the increasing use of voicemail, e-mail and the Internet, reducing information overload should become a priority for the communication professional. Instead of being information 'producers' a more important role will be that of information 'reducers'. In many organizations people are drowning in information but starved of knowledge. People need help in determining what they need to know, where to find it and how to use it. Communicators must develop more effective ways to sort the useful from the useless, removing 'communication' junk before it alienates employees like junk mail.

Writing it right

Often, knowledge-sharing is undermined at the most basic level. Poor writing skills can derail the process by making information difficult to understand, by increasing the time it takes to understand what is being said.

Most managers believe that they have good writing skills, yet often those skills are developed by writing long, formal reports. In a fast-moving business that is not what is needed. Toyota, for example, relies heavily on written communication in its product development process. However, it does not suffer from the mountain of paperwork we associate with bureaucracy. In most cases, engineers write short, crisp reports on one side of A4 paper. The reports all follow the same format so that everyone knows where to find the definition of the problem, the responsible engineer and department, the results of the analysis and the recommendations. The standard format also helps engineers make sure that they have covered the important angles. The result is a clear statement of a problem and solutions that is accessible not only to people within a particular project but also to those working on other projects.

Writing these reports is a difficult but useful skill, so the company gives its engineers formal training in how to précis what they want to communicate. Toyota has also created a culture in which reading these reports is seem as a valuable exercise and essential to doing the job well, with some senior executives refusing to read any report that is longer than two pages.

Sharing knowledge through stories

One of the problems with gathering information is that it tends to become sanitized and one-dimensional. The stories, anecdotes and colour that make information live are precisely what people tend to extract. In some technical and specialized areas where knowledge is not easily captured or codified, people learn from each other through stories, not from manuals. War stories and catastrophes become the basis for future sales pitches or new products. Recalling war stories spontaneously in conversation, rather than in the bullet points of product information, is the way to engage colleagues and get them to identify vividly with the issues being raised.

In one corporate communications company, the case studies which described the company's best solutions to typical client problems had sanitized the messy truth of experience. New employees who read the manual of case studies were wistful that they could never seem to apply such neat solutions to their own more awkward clients. When a senior manager started telling the war stories behind the case studies employees' learning soared.

This topic is continued in Chapter 8 'The Management of Communication'.

Turning information into value

Knowledge management centres around creating, distributing and applying intelligence to achieve business goals. Turning information into value is a process. In today's information age, the only way to add value is by turning information into knowledge and then into wisdom.

Knowledge is different from information and data. Data can be thought of as musical notes. Information is the musical score – data arranged in a systematic way in order to yield order and meaning. Knowledge can be thought of as the know-how and talent that enables a jazz musician to improvise upon a musical score.

Knowledge can be described as knowing what to do in situations and skill in knowing how to do it. It includes the assumptions, beliefs and values that often result from an individual's or an organization's experience. Effective knowledge management is therefore crucially dependent on making explicit what is implicit so that it can be shared.

Data does not become information until we have successfully linked meaning to it. There is a process of transformation. If we fail to build common meaning and understanding, data remains just a bunch of unconnected events. At the root of information is 'to inform' – to bring form to, create form from. Information is a creation from the basic compound of data: by looking at relationships and patterns that occur in data, we assign meaning to what we see and create information. Identifying how to use that information to do something creates knowledge. Adding experience to that knowledge creates learning and wisdom.

Sharing and using knowledge involves four unnatural acts: people have to be willing to share best thinking, use other people's ideas, collaborate with other experts and evolve their own thinking. If knowledge is a valuable resource, a natural tendency is to hoard it. To enter our knowledge into a system and to seek out knowledge from others is not only threatening, but also hard work, so we have to be highly motivated to do it.

People need to have a shared definition of what is valuable to the customer, since that is fundamental to a shared understanding of what knowledge is valuable, and how it can be applied to create more value. A company's knowledge management strategy should therefore reflect its competitive strategy: how it creates value for its customers, how that value makes money for the business, and how the company's people work to deliver value to both customer and company. For their part, employees must understand why customers buy the company's products or services rather than those of its competitors, the value that customers expect from the company and how they can use the company's knowledge to provide the kind of value that customers expect.

Companies focus on how they will compete, what they will offer and how they will go about providing it, predominantly in one of the three following categories:

1   **Operational efficiency.** This means providing customers with reliable products or services at competitive prices and delivered with minimum difficulty or inconvenience. DHL and FedEx are good examples of this kind of company.

2   **Closeness to the customer.** This means segmenting and targeting markets precisely and then tailoring offerings to match them. Knowledge of the customer and flexibility in their operations allows the company to fulfil particular requests or to tailor individual products. A merchant bank or an IT consultancy would be a good example.

3   **Product leadership.** Sony, Apple and Microsoft are good examples of companies which compete by offering leading edge products and which aim to produce a continuous stream of innovative products and services.

Depending on which of these competitive routes a company chooses, different kinds of knowledge are needed – explicit or tacit knowledge. Explicit knowledge is knowledge that can be captured and codified, such as simple software code and market data. This kind of knowledge is extracted from the person who developed it and packaged in a way that others can use, whether in documents or in an electronic repository. Tacit knowledge, on the other hand, is difficult to capture and express in writing and is acquired through personal experience. It includes scientific expertise, operational know-how, insights about an industry and business judgements. It is transferred from person to person, either by continual contact over a period of time, as between an apprentice and a master craftsman, or by tuition, coaching and conversation.

Where the company's employees use explicit knowledge to do their work, the company can rely on gathering and sharing that knowledge and packaging it in documents, guidelines, databases and electronic repositories. When people use tacit knowledge to solve problems, companies have to encourage its transfer from person to person.

Whatever route a company chooses, it has to balance capturing and codifying explicit knowledge and getting people to share tacit knowledge – basically balancing information with interaction – then it has to ensure that its internal communication is geared to supporting that balance. However, for all organizations, whatever their competitive strategy, internal communication has to foster four elements among employees:

1   a feeling of being part of a community with common cause
2   a willingness to contribute or to have one's knowledge extracted and
    bottled
3   a willingness to consult and use other people's knowledge
4   the skills for conversation, brainstorming and discussion.

Achieving the best mix of these four elements depends on companies
making the connection between their internal communication, knowledge management and their competitive strategy.

Internal communication for operational efficiency

Companies pursuing operational efficiency minimize overhead costs,
eliminate intermediate steps in the service or production process, reduce
costs and standardize business processes across departments' boundaries.
They continually refine the process from order entry through to product
or service delivery, and use information systems to measure the timing
of component parts of the process. Such organizations aim to reduce the
range, variety and complexity of their products, processes and services
by adopting fewer, standardized approaches. For them, success relies
on employees keeping consistently to specified approaches. For such
companies empowered and creative employees are an extreme hazard,
since any innovative approaches could involve the expensive reinvention
of wheels, risking inconsistency.

Creating standardized products or relying on standardized processes
involves well understood tasks and explicit knowledge which can be
readily captured and codified. Once an approach is invented it will be re-
used many times. That opens up the possibility of achieving economies
of scale in knowledge re-use and so growing the business. It also enables
a reduction of cost by reducing duplication, complexity and avoids
having to retain a large number of employees who would be necessary
if different systems and approaches were used.

For businesses competing on operational efficiency, knowledge management should be based on re-use, with an approach that enables many
people to search for, and retrieve, codified knowledge without having to
contact the person who originally developed it. This requires a significant
investment in high-quality, reliable and fast information systems that
codify, store, disseminate and re-use knowledge.

In addition, internal communication has to provide a context so that
the messages that employees receive fit the competitive strategy and the
knowledge management approach. For example, senior managers tend
to be divided in their views about employees' empowerment, either
passionately for or warily against. Following philosophical debate in the
board room, internal communication can encourage empowerment with
senior managers encouraging innovation, seeking suggestions and
encouraging initiative. While this is praiseworthy in its care for realizing

people's potential, it may not be appropriate to the company's competitive strategy. In a tightly regulated industry, such as the rail, water or nuclear industries, empowering employees to devise new approaches could be catastrophic. In these industries people should not feel encouraged or tempted to develop a novel solution to a problem even when a perfectly good solution already exists in the electronic repository. Unnecessary innovations are expensive and departures from standard procedures may be risky.

Therefore, internal communication has to be geared to creating an understanding of competitive strategy, and to fostering the right kind of knowledge management to support that strategy. What can be counterproductive is creating forums and workshops as the prime means of knowledge-sharing. This not only involves expensive travel and meeting time, but may encourage the reinvention of standardized processes which have already been painstakingly agreed upon.

Companies that pursue operational efficiency will want their people to acquire about 80 per cent of their shared knowledge from documents and databases. However, there will still be a need for selective contact between colleagues for knowledge networking via face-to-face meetings or by telephone. Such communication is needed to make sure that information is not blindly applied to situations for which they are unsuited. To make the connection between databases and personal knowledge-sharing, companies should encourage the use of e-mail and electronic discussion forums.

For companies competing through operational efficiency there will be a number of jobs internal communication will have to do. Standardizing processes can mean reducing the number and complexity of processes used. However, while standardization is a fine thing for the individual whose method becomes the standard, others may dismiss it as 'not invented here'. Such people should be encouraged to contribute to databases, consult and accept best practice from elsewhere.

The job internal communication has to do here is to encourage a sense of community and common interest. It should focus on creating greater understanding of roles and priorities across functional and structural boundaries, and building stronger personal relationships between colleagues in different departments. Team meetings should be used to discuss ways of eliminating snags in the process, and to give updates on measures of efficiency, progress on costs and the implementation of the team's ideas. They should be run by the team leader, assisted by a facilitator from elsewhere within the business, to give a broader view. Representatives of departments that share a process should attend each others' meetings to create greater familiarity and understanding of each other's pressures and objectives. They should also alert each others' teams to upcoming changes, to problems that have arisen from their areas, and feed back remedial actions.

Internal communication for closeness to the customer

A company that competes through closeness to the customer charges premium prices for highly customized solutions to unique problems that meet particular customers' individual needs. Because those needs will vary dramatically, there will be no database of standardized approaches, nor any codified explicit knowledge. This is because providing creative advice on high-level strategic problems demands the appropriate application of experience. Knowledge transfer is done person-to-person, via conversation, brainstorming and coaching. Personal relationships are more important than databases.

These types of organization develop electronic document systems, but invest only moderately in IT. This is because the purpose of the systems is not to provide exhaustively codified knowledge but to provide the names of people in the company who can act as points of contact and provide further advice. Their systems are not the last word in knowledge-sharing but the first port of call for networking. Employees can review summaries on a subject area to get a general idea and to find out who has done work on a topic. Then they speak to those people directly.

The key competitive differentiator for such companies will be how close they can get to customers and how well they manage their relationship with them. Providing valuable advice and innovative ideas depends on the adviser's ability to become familiar with the client's problems and the ability to network knowledge and expertise within his or her own organization.

These organizations need to match internal knowledge to increasingly diverse client needs, concentrate resources in the best location and keep expensive headcount down. This makes networking knowledge and expertise their prime challenge. Increases in efficiency among knowledge workers will therefore come from internal communication making strong connections between people with expertise, wherever they may be located in the business.

The job internal communication has to do here is to develop networks and forums so that tacit knowledge can be shared via conversations. Internal information, in directories or on-screen, should show who can provide expert advice, and in which area, to speed up problem-solving. Selection, induction and training programmes should stress the creative decision-making skills needed to respond to individual customer needs.

For this strategy, flexibility and responsiveness is key, and communication systems have to be tailored to meet the different needs of different departments, rather than using a 'one size fits all' approach.

Communication is targeted on feeding customer views and attitudes into the organization. Team meetings concentrate on customer feedback, complaints and commendations. Customers are brought in regularly to provide feedback directly. Upward feedback sessions are run, at which front-line staff update senior management on customer reactions, needs and requests. Communication focuses on stories of ingenious ways in which employees have solved problems and how they put themselves out to help customers.

Internal communication for product leadership

Companies that pursue product leadership aim to produce a continuous stream of state-of-the-art products and services. That involves creating applicable and relevant new ideas and speed in getting them into the market. As the organization's employees need both information and insight to innovate, the knowledge management system should provide access to repositories of information on market and technological trends. It should also provide opportunities for people to share directly with each other information whose potential and implications might be lost in document form.

Innovation demands creativity, which in turn means recognizing and embracing ideas that originate outside the company. Internal communication should focus on inputting ideas from elsewhere and monitoring competitors' activities. Team meetings should include feedback on customer experiences and problems, competitors' advances and brainstorming exercises on improving products and processes. In companies competing as product leaders, internal seminars on technical developments are complemented by overviews of social trends and the circulation of reports by subject experts. Outsiders – whether customers or suppliers – are regularly brought in, and forums are held to identify areas for improvement, together with advisory panels and customer user forums.

To increase the speed of getting innovative ideas into the market, internal departments spend time familiarizing themselves with each other's roles and identifying ways of accelerating the development process. The marketing and research and development departments hold joint team meetings, and communication is organized along project team lines with the project leader coordinating lines of communication.

However, as with all internal communication, the rule is, if you alter your strategy, shift the focus of your communication. For example, if a company changes its business strategy from product leadership to operational efficiency, or from operational efficiency to customer closeness, the range of information that has to be captured and exchanged will also need to change. So, too, will the mix of information and interaction and the balance of using databases and relationships. However, what remains vital to the strategies of customer closeness and product leadership is person-to-person contact for greater knowledge-sharing. The next section looks at stimulating greater networking to encourage this.

Stimulating knowledge networking

Knowledge usually exists in pockets within a company's informal networks. A company's communication infrastructure is not usually designed to encourage sharing between these pockets. In fact, the more valuable the material, the less likely is the infrastructure to allow access to it. In old stable organizations people knew where to go to get things done and how to make connections via personal networks. Who you knew was more important than what you knew. However, dramatic downsizing and continuous restructuring have depleted many of these networks. Employees find it increasingly difficult to identify who knows what they need. This hinders a firm's competitiveness when speed is at a premium. The communicator's job is to identify these pockets of expertise and connect them one to the other. For example videos, publications, management presentations, intranet sites and resource guides can direct people to the places where they can learn.

Although technology attracts the most attention in knowledge management, it is not the most important factor. While databases can highlight who has relevant knowledge and experience, conversation is the best way to find out what is distinctive and relevant. That is why managers prefer to get information from people rather than computers; people add value to raw information by interpreting it and adding context.

People with the knowledge need to be willing to share it, even when they are busy and they gain nothing by it. Such a degree of altruism and cooperation is a function of relationship, and of a sense of belonging to a community and wanting to help fellow members. When it comes to knowledge, people need to care before they share.

Organizations need to use their internal communication to create a sense of community and mutual interest to encourage sharing. Employees will be members of a range of different teams and networks – best practice forums, industry teams, functional networks and customer teams. The competing claims of these on employees' time and attention should be carefully reconciled to allow sharing and collaboration. This will require companies to be more conscious about creating different levels of identification and tribal loyalties to these teams in order to foster networking.

Consultants Booz Allen, for example, have a knowledge management system which provides a 24-hour-a-day electronic database and data map of what the firm knows and who knows it. The programme operates at three different levels: as an educational tool to foster basic consultancy skills among new joiners; as a repository of functional, knowledge and standardized methodologies for journeymen consultants; and as a means of developing leading edge strategic thinking among the partners at the top.

Their experience is that knowledge management does not happen automatically. The chief resources required for this kind of knowledge work are time and space for conversations between colleagues, a minimum of IT to cross the time zones and, crucially, the community of interest to provide the spark that makes things happen.

Networking knowledge through trust

Organizations need to be able to rewire their lines of information and relationships because networking lines are different from hierarchical lines. Knowledge is networked and transferred through trust, and networks are built on relationships. Trust networks are built from face-to-face meetings which provide the atmosphere for people to share freely and the common interest to want to share at all. These connections, or networks, of trust are the veins of a natural resource of knowledge. Encouraging face-to-face contact creates greater familiarity, and where people build relationships greater trust follows.

To network knowledge, communication centres on establishing networks as a means of creating cooperation and sharing knowledge. Conferences of key managers are held frequently to focus on major problems. Business forums are held to keep people up-to-date on industry issues, customer plans and activities in other divisions. Senior managers tour the units to listen to employees in informal sessions, and upward feedback is seen as vital to progress.

People who need to cooperate with each other are brought together both for social occasions and to discuss business issues. The aim is to create contact and familiarity, and so increase trust and relationship. Managers from areas across the business are brought together at off-site sessions and are trained in behavioural skills for better teamwork and resolving conflicts.

Communication is organized across the network as well as within units. Forums are held in which colleagues from different divisions present and discuss solutions to common problems. Breakfasts and lunches are hosted to allow people within departments that rarely meet formally to get together, in the expectation that contact will create greater familiarity, leading to a higher rating of each other's effectiveness and greater cooperation.

Managing networking and interactions

Trust is what drives networking, and this depends upon people's ability to have conversations with each other. This requires companies to pay more attention to coaching their people in improving their interaction with others, in order to create the relationships, that create networking.

Technology provides many options and channels for distributing information, but few companies are concerned with how people actually use information once they get it. Most of the information that people really care about is not on computers. Evidence from research conducted since the mid-1960s shows that most managers do not rely on computer-based information to make decisions. The results of these studies are remarkably consistent: managers get a third of their information from documents, most of which come from outside the organization and are not on the organization's computer system; the remaining two-thirds come from face-to-face or telephone conversations. In short, managers prefer to get information from other people. People add value to raw information by interpreting it and adding context in talking to each other. In other words, people turn data into information into knowledge, via conversation.

Case study: BP

British Petroleum's introduction of virtual teamworking using videoconferencing speeded up their solution of critical operation problems. BP, now BP Amoco, recognizes that data has to be processed into information and turning information into valuable knowledge depends on people's ability to apply it. It also depends on how people relate to each other and the opportunities they have for conversation.

Take the example of exploding a seismic charge to check the oil bearing potential of a geological formation. The value of the resulting data depends on the individuals who bring their experience and knowledge to interpret it and reach a conclusion. The information is processed through their experience, insight and ideas.

Focusing on this importance of mental processing, and the importance of the interrelationships between team members to spark ideas off each other, BP values their intranet as a resource for spreading human capability.

BP's fostering of this human approach includes their knowledge management team – a cross-business team which champions an integrated approach to knowledge management and innovative pilot projects. An example is the Virtual Teamwork Programme, a group-wide business change programme. This has a long-term objective to enable radical business improvement through the creation of virtual work teams of employees, customers and business partners.

The aim for its intranet, therefore, is not to create an encyclopaedic cookbook of solutions, but rather to keep track of people who know the recipe. In other words, it keeps people connected, and nurtures:

- the technology to give people access to each other
- the culture that will get, and keep, people talking.

One of the facilities offered on their intranet, for example, is tracking down colleagues whom you are likely to meet, or from whom you might need help. This is done by means of the 'Yellow Pages', which tells you who knows what and where to find them. Each individual has their own page, with a photograph, relevant experience, why you might want to contact them, what they can offer, and their contact details.

BP believes that part of its business success depends on how quickly its people can learn and spread expertise around the organization. Their focus, then, is on connecting people with people, and so people with knowledge. The BP case study demonstrates that knowledge is about people and their interrelationships and shows how BP sees part of its knowledge management job as strengthening those relationships.

People are reluctant to give up what they know in the spirit of the 'greater good', knowing that it will give away their intellectual advantage to their colleagues. It is therefore important to be realistic in what knowledge management asks them to give. For example, one of the high street banks does not seek to take people's ideas but rather create a network so that it knows who to direct people to for the answers. By contrast, Andersen Consulting's staff are more willing to contribute, since this increases their chances of advancing their careers.

A company whose culture is open and people-friendly will achieve far greater success in networking knowledge than one which throws money at the problem. It may install the appropriate technology and skills but if people do not contribute, or do not make time to store information appropriately, the investment will be wasted. Ironically, a company with less sophisticated technology but a more open attitude towards cooperating is more likely to manage knowledge successfully.

Building a blue tit culture

A successful knowledge management programme requires the creation of a collaborative, sharing mindset across the organization.

Companies' sociability has a great affect on how they learn, shown through the contrasting experiences of blue tits and robins with milk bottles. In the early twentieth century bottles had no tops, and both types of songbird learnt to use their beaks to siphon off the milk. When the dairy industry placed aluminium seals on the bottles, the blue tits – but not the robins – learnt to pierce the tops.

The explanation – according to Allan Wilson, a prize-winning US biologist – is that the blue tits are more sociable than the robins. Although an occasional robin has cottoned on to the technique, there is no method for transferring this knowledge through the species as a whole because robins are territorial birds. While tits group together from an early age, male robins will not let other males anywhere near their patch.

Similarly, in any sizable organization there are bound to be a few innovators. But it is no good just having them around; that alone will not lead to the development of good, marketable ideas. Arie de Geus (1997), formerly of Shell's planning group, believes 'you will not have institutional learning until you have developed the ability to flock'.

Trust drives networking, and this depends on a willingness to share and cooperate and people's ability to converse with each other.

In terms of their relationships and interactions, people need first to have a shared definition of what is valuable to their customer, since that is fundamental to a shared understanding of what knowledge is valuable and how it can be applied to create more value. Second, organizations need to create a sense of community and mutual interest to encourage sharing and foster greater networking.

Talking it through

Employees' ability to internalize and act on information comes only when they have an opportunity to reflect on, challenge, question and clarify it. Because dialogue is critical to creating and sharing knowledge, there need to be meeting places where ideas can get tested against the thinking of others. One major car manufacturer assembled a group of managers, familiarized them thoroughly with the strategy and then put them in front of employees to discuss it in detail without the aid of any elaborate communication tools. Managers then simply asked employees: 'What do you not understand? What needs to be clarified? What do you want to change?' They also talked about what was important to them and what kept them awake at night. As a result of these dialogues, employees provided valuable strategy input, exposed critical areas of resistance and gained a higher understanding of the direction.

Making it safe

Learning takes place when things go wrong or do not go as expected. If an organization has a culture in which mistakes are not tolerated, people will not share what went wrong and so opportunities for learning will be lost. Changing requires companies to pay more attention to coaching their people to improve their interaction with others and to get better at holding productive conversations. To make the most of electronic communication, employees must first learn to communicate face-to-face.

Charles Handy underlines the importance of trust as a key ingredient in collaboration and virtual organizations:

For trust to work large organizations need fairly constant smaller groups. . . . Paradoxically, the more virtual the organization, the more its people need to meet in person. . . . (Handy, 1995)

Membership of a network can replace a sense of belonging to a place with a sense of belonging to a community.

Face-to-face communication

A sense of community can be created using face-to-face communication to create more contact and a greater understanding of each other's constraints and priorities. The value employees derive from formal communication sessions often takes the form of an opportunity to network informally, and the really valuable communication happens informally by osmosis.

However, where communication is left to informal networking alone and there is insufficient investment in formal communication processes, there is a greater risk. Informal networks rely largely on length of service. People who have been around a long time know where to go and who to talk to when they need something. New staff do not have the time to build their own networks and are left at a disadvantage, which, in times of fast growth, is a vulnerability.

In order to create better collaboration and understanding amongst members of different divisions, there needs to be opportunities to talk informally with members of other departments, to be able to put faces to names, and to have a point of contact for referrals, tips and introductions. Information that is presented to each other has to be presented in simple, clear and memorable form that is, above all, brief.

Getting the most from face-to-face communication demands that managers gain a better understanding of group dynamics, how groups work and how individuals react and are motivated to interact within them.

Greater collaboration, whether at a distance or in the same room, requires less focus on information technology and more on 'interaction technology', such as understanding the ways in which group members influence each other, understanding the feelings of inclusion and exclusion among individuals within the group, building trust and maintaining motivation.

This topic is continued in Chapter 10 'Information Into Interaction.'

Putting knowledge to work

Knowledge networking is another aspect of how better internal communication can create value for organizations. Effective internal communication allows employees to work together to turn information into well informed decisions. This calls for a better management of internal communication and the ability to connect, share and structure information. Also needed are the interrelationships and interaction that enable people to work together to turn that information, first into understanding, then into decisions that add value.

Internal communicators can help network knowledge by taking the following seven steps:

1   Create an understanding of the organization's mission and the strategic issues it faces.
2   Communicate its competitive strategy and its differentiation.
3   Circulate information on client needs, and educate about industry issues.
4   Put the disciplines in place to manage information more effectively.
5   Provide information about key processes to improve operational efficiency.
6   Strike the best balance of information and interaction to support the organization's chosen competitive strategy.
7   Create familiarity with, and goodwill towards, colleagues in other parts of the organization to foster networking.

Effective internal communication is a key ingredient in helping organizations turn their knowledge to business advantage. The more effective management of internal communication and the repositioning of the communication department will help achieve this. These are discussed further in Part IV.

Part III
Changing Communication

Making change happen

Chief executives are generally preoccupied with becoming more competitive and more innovative, improving processes and reducing cost. All of these are likely to require some kind of change in their employees' attitudes and behaviours. Chapter 4 looked at the change involved in globalization and restructuring, and the implications for organizations and their employees. This chapter continues the theme of change, focusing on how to bring employees along, rather than leaving them behind.

Managing change has become an important issue among senior management, yet studies consistently show that most change initiatives fail to deliver their planned benefits. At the heart of this failure is poor communication, despite the recognition that well managed communication is central to managing change.

When change shoots communication to the top of the management agenda, it exposes the weakness of existing communication practices. Like being forced suddenly to run a marathon when you have not routinely kept fit, you realize, too late, that day-to-day fitness is vital. If you want to be able to use communication to achieve change successfully, you have to get your internal communication up to daily fitness. Effective communication minimizes the pain, prevents problems and helps the organization arrive at its desired goal more quickly.

This chapter describes the case for change, why change can fail, and how communication can be used to bring about change more effectively. It focuses on identifying specific approaches to communication for different types of change, addresses the problem of selecting the right communication media, provides a case study of how one company used communication to support change and concludes with some advice on how to communicate change more effectively.

The case for change

Change is a given in today's business environment, and the ability to make change happen is now a core competence. Organizations face a stark choice; manage change or become its victim.

Change is difficult to carry out. Hammer and Champy, in their book on re-engineering, found that between 50 and 70 per cent of organizations failed to achieve the results they wanted by changing processes and procedures. A survey by Larkin and Larkin (1994) in the USA showed that 66 per cent of companies which underwent change did not achieve the cost savings they sought. Although, for example, a large mineral extraction corporation achieved 50 per cent of their training goals and 50 per cent of their participation goals, they only achieved 5 per cent of their results targets. Similarly, one of the largest US financial institutions implemented a Total Quality programme. After two years they had experienced no bottom-line performance improvements. The American Electronics Association (1991) reported that 73 per cent of US firms have improvement schemes but 63 per cent of them fail to improve quality defects by even 10 per cent.

Managing change well minimizes the risk of failure. Change itself usually involves a large investment in people and resources, and it takes time to bear fruit. Minimizing the time it takes to make change happen is at the top of the management agenda, because allocating business resources to implementing changes diverts them from their real job. If momentum flags, people become demotivated and sceptical and eventually the process runs out of steam.

Why does change fail?

Most of the factors which undermine change relate to people:

1   **Lack of motivation.** John P. Kotter (1995) found, from his research, that over 50 per cent of companies failed in the first phase of change because they did not establish a great enough sense of urgency. Other researchers have found that only 9 per cent of companies implementing a change programme had any success in actually converting people to the new values involved.

2   **Not understanding the full picture.** Failing to understand the context for change is a barrier. If people do not understand the 'why', they are less able and willing to implement the 'what' of change. For example. the implementation of a new computer system for a subsidiary of a large manufacturing organization failed because neither

the system developers nor senior management understood the wider context. They did not realize that the project would involve so extensive a redesign of their business processes or their management structure.

3 **Loss of stability.** While chief executives reassure their people that the only constant is change, people want to be in control of their environment and to preserve stability. People try to regain their equilibrium if it is disturbed. Welcoming change is directly commensurate with the degree of power people have to control their environment.

4 **Failure to answer 'What's in it for me?' and 'What do we want employees to do?'** Employees' resistance to change can stem from their lack of understanding. Poor communication is often cited as the single most substantial barrier to achieving necessary change within organizations. This is because it is too focused on announcing the 'what' of change rather than the 'why', and then fails to spell out the implications and the 'what now?'.

Unfortunately for those trying to make change, the force of an organization's existing culture is designed to maintain the status quo and builds in inertia to protect it. Culture is the means by which we bring stability to the threat of change, by rationalizing our way out of it or by going into denial of it. The mental starting position for most people is 'We do not need to change – we're already doing a good job. But if we do, it's them, not me that needs to change'. We are brilliantly equipped to rationalize our way out of changing.

Communicating company vision is fine, but people want to know how they will be affected, and why they should change. Employees are likely to be bemused by the failure of managers to specify what precisely they are now supposed to do.

In order to address these failings, organizations have invested in change management processes and teams, to help coordinate and make change happen. Change management has three main roles: the delivery of benefits; helping to arrive at the desired destination more quickly and with minimal pain; and accommodating the needs of the business and of the workforce. Good internal communication is central to each of these roles.

How much change is manageable?

Rather than try to manage separate waves of change, organizations need to become flexible and continuously responsive. This involves becoming more knowledgeable about how their people respond to change, and how they can foster the responsiveness their employees need to compete. Organizations need to shift from managing incidents of change towards developing the capacity to respond fluidly to events as they arise. This is rapidly becoming a critical factor – the ability to change continuously in a continuously changing world.

Traditionally, leaders will drive change, alerting the organization to the need to change in the face of changed competitive conditions. They will spotlight an external crisis, or the 'burning platform' for change – something that threatens survival and demands urgent action. In the longer term the aim is to push the responsibility for driving change further down the organization by creating greater understanding of business issues and allowing employees to identify where change is needed and to drive it on their own initiative. Change can then be driven from the bottom of the organization, and top management need not constantly rearticulate direction to employees.

However, before they can reach that happy state, organizations have to deal with the issue of employee 'change-lag' – a situation where employees, threatened with the dire consequences of not changing, cannot take any more. Suffering from corporate 'combat fatigue' they bunker down in their foxholes and take each day as it comes. Without good communication, employees are liable to become sluggish and resistant, with the consequence that each successive change introduced will become more problematic. Involving people early translates into a greater understanding of change and smoother implementation. For this reason, a number of organizations have moved the communication function into their change management department.

What is the room for manoeuvre?

People are not keen on change which destabilizes them and reduces their ability to control their environment. Thus, communication about change has to highlight for people the freedom they still have and be clear about the non-negotiable framework within which their area of autonomy and discretion lies. This strategy serves both parties well – it allays the nervousness of senior management who fear that allowing employee debate will undo all their good work. It also fulfils the desire of employees to identify their remaining areas of discretion.

Psychologists describe people's perception of the degree of power they have over how things are managed and affected as their 'locus of control'. There are two kinds of locus – internal and external. Those who have an internal locus of control fundamentally believe that they call the shots and that they are omnipotent in their world. Typically, newborn babies feel that they are the centre of the universe, see no distinction between themselves and the outside world, and do not see themselves as victims of bigger forces. After babyhood, we all swing from an internal to an external locus – from a sense of omnipotence to a greater sense of helplessness in the face of outside forces we cannot control.

When change happens, people ask themselves what they can affect and what they are likely to be affected by. They tend to see themselves as more powerless than before and to worry about those things they feel they cannot affect.

Apparent resistance to change can be a consequence of not clearly outlining the space for control that employees will have in the future. People are more stressed by uncertainty than by bad news. With bad news, they can identify their 'decision space' and get on with regaining as much control as possible and making what decisions they still can. Where this space is not clear, people create ways of increasing their comfort and denying the control of others over their lives.

Communicating change therefore has to tackle the danger of a clash between the management agenda and the individual's agenda. Senior management typically want to limit employees' locus of control – they want to publish their plans and have the workforce comply. They fear involving people in discussion in case employees come up with the wrong answer and that, like children, they will have to be brought back to the correct answer after a diversionary bout of discussion.

Employees on the other hand, try to maintain their locus of control and, if possible, extend it. Practically, this means that it is not enough to simply make people aware of the plan, or describe their part in it and what they are expected to contribute. It is far better to focus on, and reinforce, those areas that they still can control and decisions that remain within their remit. This encourages employees to look beyond their area of control, to areas which they can influence.

In times of change, when people are nervous about what they can control, leaving that 'decision space' unclear can cause employees to become overcautious and create resistance while they try and fathom their room for manoeuvre.

Communicating for change

Managers who want to communicate change typically ask, 'How do I convince employees of the need for change?', 'How do I motivate people to change?' and 'How will I know when staff have bought into change?'

In times of change, companies have to communicate far more just to stand still. The amount of change has increased employee suspicion and reduced management credibility. MORI's norm for the credibility of management is 66 per cent under normal, stable conditions. For organizations going through change, it drops to 49 per cent. Similarly, the norm for understanding the organization's objectives is 48 per cent normally, but in periods of change it drops to 34 per cent. This is exacerbated by the communicators' desire to push change at people, as if it were a desirable product, with self-evident benefits. Organizations typically set themselves to 'sell' any change to their people and become frustrated when their people decline to buy what they are selling. Managers make their case, strongly advocate their position at the outset, and then try to push for a close. This itself tends to create resistance as pushing hard provokes a strong reaction, and apparent dismissal of others' views provokes opposition.

Too many managers see discussion as a sign of weakness, or fear that discussion will unravel what's already been achieved. Yet, by trying to limit discussion, managers signal that communication is a one-way process. To persuade means both listening to others and reflecting their perspectives along with our own.

Senior managers tend to focus on what they believe employees need in order to fulfil their task, rather than what they need to understand and to feel part of the organization. This mismatch hurts most when those at the bottom of the organization receive only narrow communication on the specifics of implementing change. The lower down the organization you are the less you are aware of the wider context, the less rationale you understand, and the less sense the specifics make. This kind of approach makes it difficult to know when staff have bought into change, because it focuses on trying to convince them of management's case rather than allowing them to raise their concerns. For example, is the lack of questions at the end of a manager's presentation to staff a sign of acceptance or rejection?

The difficulty communicators encounter in assessing the impact of their communication is that they often have no clear idea of the impact that they are trying to create. Communication can focus on the distribution of mission statements and visions which are too abstract to guide employees to what, specifically, they are supposed to do. If there are no clearly identified outcomes that communication is intended to produce it will be impossible to measure whether they have been achieved.

At the outset of change a company's leaders can usually identify specific examples of what they need. The people in the finance department, for example, should be answering the telephone more quickly when the customer service representatives try to contact them about a customer's billing query. However, in communication, these specifics are lost, because they are turned into the more abstract 'need for greater interdepartmental customer focused responsiveness.' This translation of concrete examples into abstract exhortation makes it harder to achieve the desired result. It also makes it difficult to measure whether the communication is being effective. Ideally, what should be measured is whether, in this instance, the telephones in the finance department are being answered more promptly. Instead, what the communicators end up measuring is whether people attended the change roadshow and whether they can recall the key messages.

Hoping for culture change while carpet-bombing employees with management-speak is a recipe for disappointment. The first challenge is to be clear about the outcomes you are trying to produce. Once you have established these it is easier to detect whether you have achieved them.

A framework for communicating change

In answer to the questions about how best to motivate employees to change, this section offers some principles for communicating change. These apply specifically to the issues of culture change and structure change – two of the four types of change discussed later in this chapter.

1   Create a sense of urgency

Senior managers are often grateful for a 'burning platform' – a crisis that provokes an undeniable pressure for change. In the absence of a crisis, organizations are often tempted to set fire to their own platform by creating a crisis that gives them a mandate to drive change through. This is a tactic that can backfire if employees see little sign of the threatened crisis materializing. It damages management's credibility and portrays them as doom-mongering Cassandras.

In the absence of a crisis, and where employees are mistakenly feeling 'fat and happy', it is best to try the re-education route, taking employees to the top of the strategic mountain and showing them the oncoming threat to continued survival. Urgency is best created by taking employees through the same learning process senior management have undergone. A shared sense of urgency comes from a shared understanding of the business threats, on the principle that 'if you can keep your head while all about are losing theirs, you do not know what's going on.'

Later in this chapter Rover Group provides a good example of both approaches.

2   Communicate the context and the full picture

In their study of more than 200 big business managers, John P. Kotter and James L. Heskett (1992) show that there is a positive relationship between the strength of a business's culture and its performance. They also conclude that a business's performance depends more on how well its culture is *adapted* to the business environment than on how strong it is. That means having employees who understand the business environment and knowing clearly how they need to respond to it.

A recent significant trend has been towards creating greater business literacy among employees, educating them about the wider context of their industry, consumer trends, changes in competition and the likely implications for them and their job.

Pepsi, for example, places great emphasis on building business literacy. After its research revealed that employees were not sufficiently aligned with the organization's goals they developed a programme for employees, centred around communicating an understanding of the business and its direction. This had the aim of closing the gap between individuals' and business goals. Similarly, Rover Group runs business conferences for its managers and associates (employees). The Royal Mail runs business education sessions on the changing mix of personal and business mail and the increase in competition. First Direct runs annual conferences on business direction, strategy changes in technology and updates all its employees on these twice a year. Intel runs business update meetings for all employees each quarter.

The BBC is facing a wide range of changes such as the debate about maintaining its public funding, the move to digital television and the introduction of 24-hour news-gathering. It has developed a series of briefings for managers called FutureWorks which explain changes in viewer types and preferences and puts the BBC's strategy in the context of wider social, technological and regulatory change. In addition, BBC News ran sessions called 'The Big Picture' to give people the 'why' as well as the 'what' about their market, providing the wider context in terms of its audiences, competition and distribution channels.

Rolls-Royce staged 'One Small Step' one-day workshops for their employees. The intention behind these was to expose employees to the need for change as well as to give them the context and the rationale for change, and a unified picture of change initiatives. In addition to sharing the thinking, the emphasis was on how each individual could take one small step to make change in his or her own area.

3   Communicate the 'why' as well as the 'what'

Objections at the implementation stage to the 'what' are often loosely disguised symptoms of an underlying lack of buy-in to the 'why'. Unless you draw the bigger picture, and prepare the way with the 'why', it is difficult to get change properly understood, let alone implemented. For people to accept and cooperate, they have to share the thinking. Announcing senior managers' conclusions gives them no chance to assimilate the thinking or understand the context. Without the context, information does not make sense or have the intended impact.

Those in the organization who have worked on change projects often already possess the rationales, detail, messages and benefits. That information simply has to be channelled into internal communication.

Nevertheless, crafting clear and well presented messages has much less impact than management style and visibility, and the leadership's willingness to be challenged and tested on their case for change.

The Body Shop keeps employees in touch with the big picture and uses local communicators to marry local detail to the wider context by means of two different processes. First, sessions are held to ensure that people understand what the business is trying to achieve, so that they can help deliver it. Second, line managers run a monthly cascade meeting which includes corporate information. In addition they make use of a network of departmental communication coordinators to give information to, and get feedback from, employees on their understanding of issues.

First Direct takes a similar approach to educating their people about what is going on in the marketplace, changes in technology and what their customers need and value. Each year each employee participates in a series of sessions given by the managing director. These engage employees in debate about changes and their implications for the business. These are then followed by half-yearly updates by heads of businesses, who relate some of the broader business changes to their own individual areas. First Direct also has a series of cross-functional and cross-sectional communication groups which are used both to gather views and to disseminate information. They are also used to give people a better understanding of what is going on in other parts of the business.

4   Maximize the sense of continuity and stability

To create a sense of urgency change is often sold as a 'revolution' but such an approach risks being perceived as a too extreme and sudden a departure from traditional values. Employees who see change as violating their sense of values will resist it and cling to existing work patterns for stability. On the other hand, employees who perceive change as evolutionary, not revolutionary, see a greater continuity with the past, which reassures them.

During the 1980s banks went through a financial services revolution which called for managers to shift from focusing on whether or not to grant loans to customers and begin selling them products and services. The resistance of some managers to this was based on their perception that this was a complete break from their previous jobs. Only when communication began to emphasize that selling was a natural extension of the good service they had traditionally provided did resistance decrease.

5   Do not wait

When faced with a situation in which you are uncertain of the outcome it is very tempting to decide to say nothing until you are certain. Failure to communicate is based on the assumption that communication is under the control of management and can be turned on and off like a tap. This is a mistake. The grapevine will communicate if management does not. Therefore, be proactive and manage communication rather than having to respond to the latest rumour. There will always be something that can be communicated, even in the most uncertain situation.

6   Communicate probabilities and scenarios

As part of its restructuring, Cable and Wireless decided to sell off its pager business, Mercury Paging. Its management team decided to communicate with staff from the outset of what was a long process. They took the view that, while you cannot predict the future, you can talk about what might happen. They did not know who might acquire them, so they talked to employees about the sorts of different businesses which *might* buy them. People would have speculated anyway. By being proactive, the management team were better able to manage uncertainty, to respond to outlandish rumours and maintain morale.

Run low-key open forums or management briefings to discuss what might happen and the different scenarios you envisage. By conducting them in a low-key way, you will be better able to communicate that you are speculating, rather than announcing, what is going to happen.

7   Give the timescale

As you will almost always know the timescale to which you are operating, you can tell people when you will be able to communicate specifics. Communicating a timescale allows you to say something while you are still analysing and debating the way forward. However, it must be a timetable that you can keep to. You will seriously damage your credibility if you fail to keep to your own deadlines.

Communicating a timetable brings two benefits. It allows managers to separate specific implementation questions from big picture strategy questions and respond to them separately. It also lets employees know precisely when they can ask specific types of question and receive answers.

8 Make face-to-face the main communication channel

Research shows that people prefer to receive information about change from their immediate manager, face-to-face. This is because people want to get news from a trusted source, in such a way as to allow them to ask questions and assess the truth of what they are being told. By communicating in this way you will be better able to assess what people's concerns are, correct misperceptions, gather feedback to inform further communication and minimize the chances of sensitive details leaking.

Communicating face-to-face also enables you to communicate nuances and the fact that some things are still uncertain.

9 Explain the implications for the individual

It is possible to make sure that people remember the business's objectives and have recall of key messages but for employees to *care* they have to see the link between their personal agendas and those of the organization.

Often, employees' first questions are about how the change will affect them personally. This means that communication has to spell out the 'what's in it for me?' for employees and specify what they are expected to do. In addition to understanding the role they will play in the future, employees also need to understand how they can succeed and how they will be measured.

Sometimes, especially when communication begins early to prepare people for change, these details are not yet thought through. While it is unlikely that employees' questions can all be answered at the outset, the process and timetable for deciding should be explained, so that the organization can limit people's uncertainty.

10 Use involvement to get commitment

Commitment comes from a sense of ownership, and ownership comes from participation. People need to be actively involved in discussing how the change can be implemented in their area. The less they are involved, the less committed they'll be.

People dislike being presented with a *fait accompli*. Even where they may have agreed with the conclusion, being excluded from the debate can be perceived as a slap in the face that fails to acknowledge them as thinking people who are important to the company's future.

11   Train managers in new skills

Managers often believe that the secret of communicating change lies in presenting great arguments. This is because managers have usually been raised to develop communication skills based on an old model of successful behaviour. They are good at presenting information, rebutting challenges and winning the argument. In situations where they are challenged, they can be masterly at authoritatively putting down questioners.

However, in communicating change, other abilities are more important. Managers need to be trained in new skills. Success depends more on the manager's credibility and his or her ability to listen, connect on the right emotional level with an audience and communicate through vivid language that make arguments come alive.

12   Invest enough time

Communication is affected by the quality of relationships, and relationships take time to build. Creating a change in a relationship takes time, and both sides need to see investing time as valuable.

Communication is a process, not an event. It is unlikely that a shared conclusion will be reached on the first attempt. Communicating change involves listening to people, allowing them to test your position, allowing them to share the thinking and process information, and then trying again.

Senior management must 'walk the talk' if they expect those they manage to do the same. This is true in terms of their following new procedures, letting go of the status quo and not holding personal agendas too tightly. In any organization going through a transition from one definition of successful behaviour to another, there is bound to be apparent hypocrisy. If this is not recognized there are always going to be instances of an apparent mismatch between managers' behaviour and their words.

A framework for developing change communication

If the above are some of the principles that underlie communicating change, what are some of the practicalities? This section offers a framework for developing appropriate change communication. It outlines four types of change so that communicators can select the most appropriate communication approach. The section identifies what is most important to each type of change, and then advises on the selection of the most appropriate communication media.

As a first step to communicating change it is important to define what the change is. Change may be significant but limited to one part of the business such as the reorganization of a function, or of a factory. It may be limited to a change in procedures or the redesign of a process. The introduction of IT or the restructuring of IT legacy systems may bring root and branch change intended to have a more long-term impact on people's behaviour.

The following are four types of change, each of which requires a different communication approach:

1 **Culture change**.
   'Culture change' can mean a wholesale shift in attitudes and behaviour, and a move to a completely different way of operating. However, the use of the term is itself often confusing because those yearning for it often cannot define in what ways they want to see things changed. If culture can be defined as 'the way we do things around here', culture change is changing the way we do things. This begs the questions, which things need to be changed, in what ways and why? Asking these questions is vital to turning 'culture change' from rhetoric to specific and observable outcomes.

2 **Structural change**.
   These are changes which affect the organizational structure of a business – for example, restructuring, divesting non-core businesses, making an acquisition or merging with another organization.

3 **Initiative**.
   A change initiative has more long-term impact and is intended to have a greater effect on people's behaviour. Introducing anything with a three-letter acronym – business process re-engineering (BPR), value-based management (VBM), enterprise resource planning (ERP) – usually qualifies as a specific programme of change, intertwining strands of change within an overall umbrella theme.

4 **Campaign**.
   Often what is characterized as a change can be defined as a campaign. This is communication with a finite life and a clear end goal, which aims to raise awareness and influence perception. This may translate for some groups of people into action or changed behaviour. Com-

municating about Year 2000 millennium bugs or the changeover to a common IT operating environment would fall into this category.

The Handbook of Internal Communication (Scholes, 1997) defines the aim of campaigns as:

> ... to gain commitment from the targeted audience to a specific business objective. Typical examples might be a customer care or service quality programme, a cost reduction exercise, or an attempt to persuade people to join a voluntary scheme such as an Employee Share Ownership Programme.

These distinctions are not clear-cut and depend on the remit and perception of the person championing the change.

A campaign to raise awareness in the run-up to a workforce ballot can be one aspect of a wider cultural change, as part of a productivity improvement initiative, prompted by a restructuring. The raising of awareness about the Year 2000 bug and millennium compliance may be part of a wider change in how the organization uses its IT.

It is important to distinguish between these different types of change to avoid overcommunicating and undercommunicating. Overcommunicating is done by those managers who are tasked with getting employees to save electricity by turning off unnecessary lights, but who launch a series of energy management roadshows in the last quarter of the financial year when employees are most busy, because they see an opportunity to extend their remit and create a more eco-conscious culture change.

Undercommunicating can be more of a problem. This is the failing of the manager who, faced with communicating a fundamental restructuring of the organization, uses only a complex PowerPoint presentation and an attractively laminated mission statement.

Do not confuse one kind of change with another. Initiatives which are communicated as if they were campaigns, for example, create awareness but do not create long-term shifts in attitude and behaviour.

What is important to each type of change?

Communication principles relating to culture change and structural change are set out earlier in this chapter (see pp. 131–36), while campaign communication is dealt with in a case study later (see pp. 146–49). Initiative communication is discussed in Chapter 7.

One of the key issues in communicating change is the degree of change involved and its impact on the employee's sense of power and self-determination. How much it disturbs employees' equilibrium and how easy will it be for them to restore it? The deeper the change, the greater the disturbance, then the longer the learning journey you have to take employees through.

There are two strands intertwined in communication – information and interaction. Interaction involves how managers relate to, interact with, employees, and their personal style and credibility. The degree of change experienced by employees determines which of the two strands will be more important to them and how the two should best be balanced.

Some changes demand more information; others depend more on interaction. Changes to car parking arrangements might generate some temporary heat, but they would be less worrying than the announcement of a takeover. The communication need in car parking changes would largely be for information. However, the announcement of an acquisition would provoke a very high requirement for both information and inter-action because people would need a great deal of information and their reassurance would depend on the credibility of the managers delivering it, as well as the climate of trust within the organization.

In a campaign, for example, information issues will be more important than those of relationship. Clarity of presentation, the use of plain language, with clearly labelled points will be what's needed. Reliable distribution, timely alerts to change, and the relevance of information to individuals will also be key factors in raising audience awareness.

Where structural change shakes the bedrock of employees' current assumptions, and creates uncertainty and insecurity, relationship issues come straight to the fore. In addition to clear and reliable information, employees will look for quality of interaction. They will judge managers on their perceived openness and on how well they acknowledge existing concerns or whether they try to ignore them. They will be affected by how managers listen to them, and whether they have the opportunity to voice concerns. They will also want the time made available to feed back their concerns, to raise challenges and to feel that they have some input into the final outcome. The size of the groups in which they gather should be small enough to encourage interaction and help staff feel comfortable and safe to speak up. This is because the degree of inter-action between people in face-to-face sessions affects their relationship, their feeling of being respected, and their willingness to respect others and their views.

This is why people's interpersonal skills are critical to creating a responsive organization. The main hindrance to becoming agile and flexible is too narrow a repertoire of skills held not just by managers but by any employees who have to work together to pool ideas and create solutions. The importance of interaction is examined further in Chapter 10.

Selecting the best balance of information and interaction depends on the degree of change involved and the nature of the change – whether culture, structural, initiative or campaign.

Typically, the formation of a communication strategy begins by asking what are the target audiences, what are the key messages and what are the best media and communication channels for delivering them. This traditional approach is based on a view that communication is the distribution of information to readily identifiable audiences.

This is a good strategy for a campaign, because campaigns require a high need for information and a low need for relationship. However, this approach does not work well for the three other types of change.

To become committed to a course of action, individuals typically undertake a journey. They consider whether the broad concept of doing something suits them before moving on to examining its feasibility. Only when they are satisfied it could fit in with the rest of their lives and is generally acceptable do they become interested in how the 'nuts and bolts' details will work out. This is a journey from awareness to commitment. The full journey means becoming aware of the change, understanding its implications, supporting it, becoming involved in deciding how it might be implemented and finally being fully committed to making it work.

Different groups of employees need to go on journeys of a different length. Some may need, for the moment, only to be aware; others to be wholly committed.

Equally, there are groups of employees which the organization needs to move to different stages of the journey, and at a faster rate. In organizations trying to use communication for change, the focus has to be on the outcome – what the organization needs from employees in terms of attitudes and behaviours. Investing time and resources in communicating to employees should be based on their importance to achieving the strategy rather than on their status in the hierarchy. For the best investment of scarce time and resources, the organization will need to differentiate between employees and to prioritize from whom it needs what objective over what time period. The first step to this is identifying what is required *from* different groups of employees, not just what is needed *by* employees. This process is discussed in greater detail in Chapter 7.

Having identified what is needed from employees in terms of awareness, understanding, support, involvement and commitment, the next question is how to begin to achieve it.

Which medium?

Few of us have a clear sense of which channel is most appropriate for a given communication. However, communicators should be aware that wrong choices create information overload and confusion, and waste time.

Anyone who wants to communicate can use first-class mail, express mail, voicemail, e-mail, fax, electronic bulletin board, videoconferencing, intranet, newsletter, poster, business television or the telephone – not to mention a face-to-face meeting. The proliferation of technology has increased the options for communication but has created a new problem: how to choose from all the alternatives. One way of choosing is to understand the principle of 'richness' in information and media – that is, the capacity of different media to carry information and emotions. Whether a medium is 'rich' or 'lean' depends on how much it allows of the following:

- interactivity
- multiple cues
- language variety
- social and emotional cues.

Interactivity

Does the medium allow quick response, conversation and involvement? Examples of media which are richly interactive are those that allow conversation in real time such as face-to-face meetings and telephones. Media such as e-mail or voicemail are leaner on interactivity because they do not allow people to interact at the same time, but take place with a time delay.

Multiple cues

Does the medium provide a variety of signals which help convey both literal meanings and underlying subtleties of message? Face-to-face communication is richer since it provides all the non-verbal cues which aid further understanding. Written text is leaner because there is so little beyond the literal message to go on.

Language variety

To what extent does the medium allow a mix of types of language – for example, verbal, visual, musical and numerical? Different people respond to different types of language. The presentation of numbers on a spreadsheet aids precision but is not as engaging as the presentation of the same information in pictures and words which give a wider variety of cues and help spell out interpretation.

A spreadsheet or numeric database is lean on language variety, while videoconferencing is richer.

Social and emotional cues

To what extent does the medium allow personal feelings and emotions to infuse the communication? A high proportion of what is communicated is non-verbal, and we take our cues from each other's tone and gestures. Communication is not just the information transmitted, it is also the impact we have on each other. Emotion, emphasis and pace all have an effect. A rich medium such as face-to-face allows all of these to add to the communication. A channel such as e-mail is lean in these and would not, for example, be a good choice for communicating the chief executive's inspirational vision.

Telephones are a surprisingly rich medium, despite the lack of visual cues. Perhaps that is why Alexander Graham Bell initially thought that the primary use of the telephone would be for broadcasting opera.

Deciding on the richness of the medium

There is a trade-off to be made between the desire to be clear and the need to use communication media efficiently. Choosing too lean a medium means the risk of too little information, which might result in different interpretations, misunderstanding and ambiguity. Choosing a richer medium than the issue warrants risks information overkill that results in 'noise', distracting from the key message.

Richer media are important for creating shared understanding where the risk of misunderstanding is high and there is a real need for minimizing ambiguity. If this need is low, leaner media are both more effective and efficient. This means, in practice, that you do not need face-to-face seminars to alert people to changes in the day's menu in the staff restaurant and that you should not try to enrol your employees in a major organizational change by pinning the announcement on the noticeboard. The first option would result in communication inefficiency; the second in communication ineffectiveness.

A general rule is: the less the chance of misunderstanding or misinterpretation, the leaner the media you can use.

Working together

Everyday we process information to assess the world around us and to coordinate the tasks that we are doing. These tasks usually involve an element of uncertainty either because information is missing or because it can be interpreted in different ways. To communicate successfully then, we try to do two things:

- reduce uncertainty by gathering more information
- develop shared understanding with colleagues with whom we are working.

This means that we have to find the best way of using communication media as efficiently as possible so that we transfer the information we need without tipping into information overload. We also want to be as effective as possible in creating a shared understanding, without short-changing each other and creating misunderstanding, or conveying only part of the whole meaning.

Achieving the right balance depends on recognizing the considerable potential for misunderstanding and the importance of guaranteeing clarity. Where is the danger of misunderstanding greatest? At the outset of change. Where is the need for clarity greatest? During change. This is because there is no pre-existing shared context and because, in the early stages, general approaches and ideas are still being sketched out, and specifics are hard to come by.

The stages of change

There are three main stages in the change process:

- **Stage 1.** Those planning change go through a process of funnelling their thinking from 'blue sky' possibilities where any option can be considered, to developing a specific option which promises the greatest value.
- **Stage 2.** The specifics of a preferred approach are worked through and investigated.
- **Stage 3.** A detailed implementation plan is developed with mile-stones, key responsibilities and performance indicators.

The first-stage 'funnelling' process progresses from abstract general approaches to specific feasible proposals and, finally, to concrete action plans. All those involved in the funnelling are familiar with the issues, have an input to the changes proposed and have had the time to work out the implications not only for the organization but for themselves. In terms of their 'locus of control' they feel that they have some handle on the change.

In the first phase of this process there are few specifics to share and, because conversation is general and the terms are abstract, the change planning team realizes that they must create shared understanding with others outside the team. They know that this is particularly important with the organization's leaders, in order to reduce uncertainty and prevent later misunderstandings. Since senior managers have the power to veto or derail change, they are courted and prepared for any develop-ments long before they emerge. For this purpose, rich media, such as face-to-face meetings, are used and are recognized as important: no project leader would simply e-mail his conclusions to the chief executive and hope for the green light. Later, once a shared context has been established, less rich media, such as written progress reports, are used for efficient project communication and effective collaboration.

However, the sound logic behind this process of communication and enrolment is often abandoned when the time comes to communicate with the rest of the organization.

The communication process with the rest of the organization should involve taking people through a line of logic – a thinking process. People whose attitudes or understanding you want to change have to go through the process; they cannot just be given its end-product. The aim of internal communication should be to share the thinking, not to announce the conclusions.

The communication task at this point is twofold: take people through a thinking process from 'blue sky' proposals to concrete plans; and use communication media of the right degree of richness to do so. However, there are some obstacles at this point. First, managers may have mastered the issues involved and may want to cut out the debate and focus on implementing the solution. However, employees will resist the manager's attempt to push them to the specifics; they will not cooperate until they have assessed how much the change will disturb their equilibrium and how difficult it will be to restore it. Second, those managers who are driving change have been using lean media such as e-mails, graphs and project reports to manage the change project. Having all that material ready to hand makes it tempting simply to package it up and use it to communicate to everybody. Third, although the change team has done a good job in enrolling powerful and influential senior managers in the change, they neglect to consider the power and influence of employees in making change happen.

When a change planning team who are familiar with all the issues themselves, talks to others who do not yet share that understanding, and where the planning team does not share the thinking and uses lean media to communicate in the interests of efficiency, there will be a collision of agendas. The greater the degree of change, the more likelihood of misunderstanding and the greater the need for shared understanding. This means sharing the thinking using rich media at the outset.

If you do not take employees through the thinking, communicating to them can feel like trying to herd cats. Discussion of nuts and bolts issues can suddenly veer into debates about rationales and hidden agendas. Carefully prepared and pithy presentations can suddenly erupt into argument. This is not necessarily because employees are resistant, it is more likely that presenters are making the wrong assumptions about where employees are in the learning process, and are using an inappropriate channel to communicate.

Employees must be allowed to match their own agendas to that of the organization. If they do not have the time and information to do that, they will be forced to find some other way of increasing their decision space.

Specifics are often rejected by staff because the foundation of shared understanding of the general approaches has not been laid. Pushing too quickly for compliance can actually end up costing more time than taking things more slowly at the outset. Change communicators then find themselves having to run more time-intensive sessions to flush out the real issues and try to repair the damage. Once suspicion has set in you have to use richer media, such as face-to-face meetings and seminars to explain even simple operational details which normally could have been communicated via the noticeboard.

Trying to move change along too swiftly only succeeds in putting you further back. However, if you take people with you from the top of the funnel, sharing the thinking, you can then use leaner media to clarify operational detail.

Taking your employees through the thinking can seem expensive in terms of time and resources, but those who want to take their people with them cannot afford to push them down the road of change without a good look at the map. As in trying to beat road traffic jams between you and your destination, sometimes the longest way round is the quickest way there.

Avoiding the information overload and initiative indigestion that seem to clog the path of change, requires four things:

1   the right identification of the type of change involved
2   the right selection of communication approach
3   the appropriate selection of rich and lean media
4   the correct application of both to the stage of change.

Earlier in this chapter four types of change were outlined – culture change, structural change, campaign and initiative. The following case study is an example of a campaign, which was part of a wider structural change and culture change.

Case study: Rover Group

The importance of matching media and message is underlined in Rover Group's communication during the turbulent autumn of 1998. Its future apparently lay in the balance and government ministers were pressed for funds to support BMW's substantial investment in the Group.

Rover is no stranger to change, and has seen its industry and economic goalposts shift repeatedly. Rover is a company which has learned the importance of internal communication and the need to manage it as well as possible. Its transformation from its earlier incarnation as British

Leyland had been due to raising the understanding of its people to take on board a radical culture change. The organization needed the commitment and contribution of the entire workforce and its recognition of the pivotal role of internal communications was central to making that change happen.

The company had been faced with an environment in which both upward and downward communication had traditionally been done through the union shop steward. They had to re-establish the communications channels and infrastructure in the company to ensure that their people understood their job, the job of their team or department, the company's goals and strategies, and Rover's position in the wider international business community.

In 1994 Rover had won the first ever UK quality award. Their then chief executive, John Towers, received the communicator of the year award from the British Association of Communicators in Business, and their internal communication team won the communication team award.

BMW then paid £800 million for the company which British Aerospace had bought five years earlier for £150 million.

While Rover has been working to improve quality and productivity, the competition globally had been doing it better and faster. The competitive threat came not just from the UK but from the Far East, Eastern Europe and the USA.

This required Rover to introduce a number of change initiatives, including flexible working practices which were used by its competitors.

BMW invested £400 million in its Oxford plant to produce the Rover 75, the first vehicle to have been entirely developed under BMW's ownership. It was designed to evoke and update the premium brand values that the Rover marque represented in the 1950s and 1960s, and thousands of jobs depended on its success.

Rover Group and senior trade union representatives reached an agreement on shift arrangements and working practices for the Rover 75. At the Rover Oxford plant this culminated in a draft agreement which was put to the workforce by ballot. In the run-up to this, there was a need for clear communication of the issues and the options, so that associates could decide which way to vote. This task was divided between senior managers and union representatives. Senior managers communicated first with all the managers and the union then communicated with its members.

Managers prepared themselves for the task by first understanding the issues themselves. In small groups, they worked through the complex and detailed proposals in order to understand what the agreement meant for their staff and for the business as a whole. The aim was to prepare them to brief their staff and feel comfortable dealing with questions and concerns. More importantly, they were given the time to ask questions and challenge assumptions behind the proposals.

Managers participated in a half-day workshop by way of preparation. The presentation of the proposals was followed by a break-out session in which managers identified their questions and issues.

Senior managers often find it hardest to communicate when they themselves have unresolved issues. In most organizations it is difficult to raise such issues without being perceived as negative or self-interested. At the time of the communication process, one of the unclear issues was what the new role of managers would be under the new system. This meant that managers were trying to answer their staff's specific questions without knowing the answer to one of their own fundamental questions.

However, by acknowledging the issues, it was easier to get managers involved, since it demonstrated a willingness to grapple with tough issues – be they managers' or employees'. Managers were then able to work together to resolve employees' questions and propose new roles and responsibilities for their own future.

What was good about the managers' approach to communicating the changes, and what helped them to succeed were the following under-pinning principles:

1 **Communication is face-to-face.**
   The only way to communicate changes which affect how people do their jobs is face-to-face. Videos, publications and large meetings can be valuable, but should not be used alone.

2 **Facts, not exhortation.**
   How will this affect me? Employees need hard facts about change first and, in the absence of facts, will resist exhortation, hectoring and threats. Briefing packs and information literature should present the facts of the change, without management 'spin'.

3 **Create advocates by adding context.**
   Managers and supervisors must feel that they can support the proposals, in addition to delivering the facts. People are influenced by those they trust and whose opinion they value. Managers and front-line supervisors need to be aware of the context, arguments and counterarguments for the changes so that they are prepared for face-to-face conversations with their people and can act as advocates for change.

4 **Prepare the briefers/session leaders.**
   In change, communication is often contaminated by the concerns of senior management rather than those at more junior levels. Senior managers find it most difficult to counter those objections with which they secretly agree.

Enrolment of the management is essential – they are not necessarily already convinced. The context and facts should be first discussed between the senior managers associated with the change and their immediate subordinates. Only then will managers feel comfortable and able to lead discussions at the front line.

5   **Use feedback to retune the messages.**
At each stage of communication questions and recommendations need to be captured to give a better understanding of how facts are being interpreted and to amend the content for the next round of communication.

6   **Provide more information than communicators need.**
People who are running sessions must be given more background information than they need for a presentation. This gives them the confidence to lead the discussion rather than sticking rigidly to the line of the presentation. It also gives them credibility, in that they can be seen to be adding value to the information they are presenting, rather than simply reading from a script.

7   **Make questions and answers as straight as possible.**
Most question-and-answer documents are written to rebut queries and questions from the audience. They follow the format of question-and-answer sessions designed for handling the media and aimed at controlling the discussion. This has the effect of closing down any conversation. The aim here should be to open up conversation, and to encourage people to feel safe about speaking up about what some of their, or their friends, issues are. Questions and answers should therefore couch questions in the audience's language. Answers should be as straight as possible, with the promise of further detail where it is not yet available.

8   **Explain the benefits to employees, not those to the company.**
Because the internal team first has to sell its proposals to senior management, the implications of change are usually spelled out as benefits to the company rather than to the employee. However, using the same slides for employees can be fatal.
The benefits should be reworked to reflect employees' concerns, not management's. This means being able to see information from the recipients' viewpoint.

The success of Rover's approach was a result of the partnership between management and union in their communication roles. Once managers had prepared, and briefed the management population, the union presented to its members.

Previously, at Rover Oxford, the union would have gathered 2500 people in a mass meeting on the lorry park, and then addressed them through a megaphone. This time, the union appreciated that it was a complex issue and that the traditional approaches were not going to work. Instead, they brought their members together in groups of 150 people at a time, for a presentation, using the more up-to-date technology of a PC projector. Management cooperated by stopping production for four to five hours so that the union could walk their people through the rationale, issues and their recommendations.

The investment of time in the preparation and communication of a complex set of issues by both management and union teams paid off in producing a clearer understanding about what was needed for the future. It also helped that, for all the hours of discussion and the numbers of slide presentations, the issues were summed up in a series of simple key messages – it was the best deal on offer, any alternatives would be worse, and the union were happy to back it.

As a result, 85 per cent of associates turned out to vote, 70 per cent of whom voted 'yes' to the proposals.

Following the success at Rover Oxford, the Transport and General Union supported rolling out the deal to the whole group, claiming that the agreement would become best practice for the rest of the UK manufacturing industry. As part of the joint management–union campaign to sell the deal, Rover hired the National Exhibition Centre in Birmingham to stage presentations outlining the agreement to its production staff. The favourable vote by Rover production workers of nearly 18000 to 7000 followed six weeks of hard talking between unions and management. The size of the vote in favour of the deal was in marked contrast to the wafer-thin majority which had first allowed the introduction of some flexible working in 1992.

Communicating campaigns effectively

The Rover case illustrates some of the issues of campaign communication – aiming to raise awareness and influence perception, with a clear end goal.

1 **Give managers something to say – or they'll make it up.**
   When it comes to dealing with uncertainty, middle managers are in the front line. They will be asked by their staff what they know, and may find themselves in a situation where they know no more than their people, but are believed to be privy to the latest thinking. Middle managers may wish to create the impression that they *do* know more than their staff, or they may wish to protect their relationship with their people by joining in with the speculation.

The solution is to give them something to communicate in order to fill the vacuum.

2 **Set up a feedback loop.**
Do not rely on feedback just from management briefings. Set up hotlines, e-mail addresses or electronic forums to allow staff to raise questions and give feedback. Doing so will help you keep your finger on the pulse and allow you to respond quickly to the changing currents of communication. Make sure the feedback loop is connected to senior management, since they are the only ones who will be able to address many of the issues raised.

3 **Assume there will be leaks.**
It is wise to assume that anything which is written down will leak at some stage – hence the emphasis on face-to-face communication. Plan in advance how you will respond to leaks; make sure your internal and external communication plans are linked.

4 **Ensure that the words and music match.**
Management credibility is determined by the extent to which managers do what they say they are going to do. Do not plan one thing and then try to communicate something else. People will either catch you out as you go along, or figure out afterwards that you lied to them. Either way, you will destroy your credibility and have to manage a workforce which resents you.

5 **Use plain language, not management-speak.**
Plans are usually sketched out in management-speak, with the benefits of proposed actions framed as advantages to the company. The same information is then used to sell the change to employees. Without the same strategic insights as board members, and access to the same market and company data, employees often find the plans difficult to follow.

6 **Acknowledge employees' concerns.**
It is important for people to understand why change is needed, so you should communicate about such things as market and industry pressures and rising customer expectations.

However, it is equally important to acknowledge employees' needs and requirements – such as job security, job interest and pride in their employer. This does not mean that you must guarantee job security, but does mean that you should explain the options that you considered and why redundancies, for example, are the only feasible way forward.

7 **Communicate change even-handedly.**

People are not stupid and will ask you difficult questions. If you are being 'economical with the truth' they will quickly sense it. Therefore you have to be straight and credible about what changes are involved; overweighting one side of the balance will be seen as either incompetence or deviousness.

Make sure there is a summary that spells out both the good and bad implications of change – people usually forget the positive aspects and focus instead on the negative aspects and drawbacks, and only stumble on the advantages some time later.

8 **Explain the options.**

Expand on the rationale and need for the change, and the likely scenarios if the organization does not change. Do not use this as an excuse for scare stories that will damage your credibility. Discuss the likelihood of new and different competitors entering the market, and project the consequences of not responding to competitive pressures. Finally, discuss other options that have been considered by the organization and why they have been rejected.

9 **Crash test your change presentation.**

A good way to test senior management cohesiveness and understanding is to get them to field test a presentation. Getting them to role-play being a union official or a cynical employee helps flush out misunderstandings, misinterpretations and lack of agreement among the management teams.

10 **Put it in writing.**

Managers have different philosophies and value systems, as well as differing hopes and expectations of the change. Creating a brief summary document as a handout for employees is a good strategy for flushing out these implicit disagreements and ensuring that there is a robust, coherent story that all can agree. The process of drafting it and getting it approved will take much longer than you think, especially since you should assume that anything written will leak.

Communicating initiatives and projects

Change has provided the pressure to force organizations to look at how they communicate and to try and improve it. Today's world has very different rules for communication and, to succeed, organizations will have to learn them.

The following chapter continues the theme of communicating change but focuses on using communication to achieve the intended benefits of projects and initiatives.

Communicating projects, campaigns and initiatives

This chapter looks at the specifics of communicating initiatives, campaigns and projects, with some rules, hints and tips for doing it better.

It presents key steps for using communication to produce better results:

1   dealing with the pitfalls of project communication
2   coordinating project team members, and linking them with other communicators
3   linking different communicators together to form an internal marketing approach to project communication
4   developing a communication plan.

Some of the issues in initiative communication are highlighted by the following case.

A business decides that, in order to secure its future, it has to reorganize its internal processes to get more for less. Part of this reorganization includes unifying IT into a single business-wide system. This factor turns the process into a major change programme in which the way people work together, and the processes which they operate, will all alter.

So important is this change to securing the organization's future that it is carefully planned and programmed. Recognizing the importance of good communication both to its success and to the eventual achievement of the promised business benefits, a dedicated communication team is assigned to it.

Initially its job looks relatively easy. There is already high expectancy and a strong desire for information coming from within the organization. Senior managers are keen to show their commitment and start the implementation. They appeal for information, videos, brochures and roadshows with which they can begin to motivate and inspire their own people.

The communication team includes members who are very familiar with their organization's culture. They are personally enthusiastic about the project and believe that the right kind of communication is vital.

They have seen so many previous initiatives run aground because of a lack of clarity, internal competitiveness and sudden surprises about detail that they view this as their opportunity to strike a blow for clarity. Personally they feel that it is important that people like them are involved, since their colleagues on the project tend to be far more technically focused and, although excited by the technical developments, are uninterested in, and naive about, the likely human reactions of their colleagues and the rest of the workforce.

The team develops a painstakingly scheduled and carefully produced communication plan, including which audiences should receive which messages, via which communication media and with a calendar of events. They then begin assembling some communication products – a video for communication to the workforce, scheduled roadshows by the team and its leaders to begin education, a newsletter to keep everyone updated on developments, and slide packs for use both by team members and by senior managers. An intranet site is also developed, where updates on the team's work can be seen.

All seems highly satisfactory on the communication front, until a review of the initiative's progress at the end of the year. The actual implementation programme has gone well, meeting all its milestones, but the promised business benefits have not materialized. The problem is that, although the changes have been put in place, none of the behaviour changes, shifts in attitude, nor the re-engineering of processes has been delivered. This is partly, they now realize, because the communication of the changes has neither been wide enough nor has addressed the wider change management issues. Communication has focused on the announcement of changes, rather than enrolling those who need to change.

The communication approach treated all the constituencies as largely the same – giving each different relevant messages, but failing to under-stand that they had to go through different mental journeys and that different outcomes in terms of engagement and commitment would be required from each. Mass communication to all employees took place simultaneously with communication to managers, thereby treating managers as any other audience, rather than as the controllers of the gateways to communication.

The project team's communication focused on announcing the changes that they needed to meet their timescales, without signalling the implications or significance of those changes to the various constituencies throughout the organization. The adoption of a campaigning approach positioned the change as basically an IT project, run by 'techies', which would have few far-reaching implications. Those affected did not realize the implications of the change, and resisted making the changes once they did.

The adoption of an acronym, logos and newsletters signalled that this was only a 'flavour of the month' initiative and created the expectation that it would have a limited lifespan. Nor was there a signal to managers and employees about the relative importance and priority of the change initiative. Although the project was launched with the full commitment of the chief executive, the 'big bang approach' with little follow-up, meant that it came to be simply one other initiative on the list of initiatives being reviewed regularly by the board. It dropped down the order of priorities to join the other acronyms, regardless of their relative impact on the future of the business.

This is not an unusual case and it highlights some of the problems encountered in achieving the benefits of crucial projects.

Beginning on a major project is like getting the builders in. There is an initial resistance to, and inertia about, starting the job, but the vision of how beautiful it will all look when the work is completed is seductive. In organizations senior management stand on one side of a valley of change, gazing over to the far side, and to the sunlit uplands of the business benefits. Then the descent into the valley begins. As with building works, the day-to-day upheaval is underestimated. The sudden implications of making the change come forcibly home. Deep outrage is felt despite the project manager's claim that careful reading of the project plan would make it blindingly obvious, even to the uninitiated, that such steps were required. This is when the trouble begins. The optimistic commitment given at the outset is suddenly withdrawn. People claim that they did not understand the full implications and, had they known, they would not have committed.

This familiar descent into confusion, unrealized benefits and mutual frustration on all sides is often the result of poorly managed communication. Although good internal communication alone will not guarantee that a project delivers its anticipated benefits, poor internal communication alone can create a bumpy ride and ultimately derail the initiative.

Any organization, with a number of different change initiatives underway, should question its people's capacity to assimilate change. The Jensen Group's (1998) research into complexity in the workplace found that part of what drove an 85 per cent increase in work complexity was an average of over 35 separate change initiatives juggled by everyone in the workforce – on top of their regular, daily tasks. The same research showed that up to 80 per cent of the workforce could not make sense of the information they received. While almost the entire workforce have – by default – become knowledge workers, only a minority have the skills to use the information they receive in its existing format.

The pitfalls of project and initiative communication

Employee confusion and apparent management incoherence is not helped by a *laissez-faire* approach to internal communication, especially by those running initiatives and projects. Ironically these are usually highly important, with a high potential for success or disaster, and have large amounts of money at stake. They can command communication budgets which are only a minor proportion of promised benefits, but are nevertheless usually more generous than communication budgets in corporate communication departments. Such budgets allow communicators to use their purchasing power to get things done their way. Where enthusiastic 'gifted amateurs' have large chequebooks, they can quickly become loose cannons.

Where projects are managed separately from the line, the projects' approach to communication can create enough resistance to prevent the transferring of ownership to line managers. The way in which communication is managed can actually prevent the anticipated business benefits materializing. Companies tend to confuse selling with marketing in internal change communication. They use push communication to persuade people that the change is good, focusing only on creating awareness rather than translating awareness into action, or specifying the outcome that is needed.

During a study by the Jensen Group (1998), 38 companies shared detailed change management and change communication plans for driving new business strategies or major change efforts. All 38 plans concentrated on structuring coordinated messages through layered and timed use of media and events. Only one of the 38 plans provided an in-depth analysis of the audience's readiness for change in the form of specific behaviours for each stakeholder group that needed to change. Only two of the 38 plans detailed how the audience's behaviours would specifically change and be measured as a result of the planned communication.

The missing link

What is needed first in communicating an initiative is to create an initial understanding about why change is needed among the company's leaders and to fully enrol them in identifying what specifically should change. Communication of the initiative should not focus on the tools and means too quickly, but maintain concentration on the goal of change.

Project leaders can themselves be a source of confusion. If they are left to carry the burden of communication, without any link to a corporate communication effort, they can unwittingly cause confusion. Under pressure to deliver, and focused on their milestones and deliverables, the risk is that team leaders run their projects as separate stand-alone efforts.

Project managers tend to be passionate about their project and can lose sight of what is most relevant to the people they are addressing. The risk is them feeling that, even if people may not be that interested in the intricacies of what they are doing, they damn well ought to be.

The typical approach to selecting project communicators does not reduce the risk. A programme is established, containing individual project strands. Communication is seen to be critical to achieving the envisaged benefits, so each project within the overall programme has a communicator. They do the job part-time, along with their other responsibilities, and are selected for their enthusiasm and interest rather than any experience or skill. Together they form a communication group to coordinate their efforts. Communication is seen to be largely a matter of promoting the initiative and informing everyone about the changes to be made, so the communicator's job is seen as relatively straightforward requiring little specialist knowledge but a great deal of willingness and enthusiasm.

Once recruited, such communicators fall prey to 'logo mania', developing new identities and slogans for their project. If they have been selected for their experience in desktop publishing, a project newsletter is certain to follow, whether or not it is appropriate. When the only tool you have is a hammer, the solution is always a nail.

Initially, it is decided to coordinate communication and present a single face for the programme. But individual project teams begin to produce their own communications, in isolation. Although they know that this could cause confusion, project team leaders feel that they are being tasked to deliver on their own project and therefore have to organize communication for their project's benefit, not for that of the programme as a whole.

Project teams can see themselves as independent entities with no obligation to work alongside their colleagues in other teams. Their focus is on achieving their own objectives, sometimes in isolation. There is often no reporting line to corporate communication, human resources, or whoever is responsible for managing day-to-day communication. This means there is a greater danger of uncoordinated, and competing, communication, leading to incoherence.

Communication as implementation

Project leaders, selected for their project experience to drive change initiatives, concentrate on making things happen. They communicate only specific task-related information designed to help them achieve their timescale and milestones. This translates into a communication plan which is designed to announce implementation details. This can create misunderstanding and resistance, rather than creating widespread under-standing of the need for, and the implications of, change.

Failure to see the recipient's viewpoint

Project leaders create their own identity and promote themselves and their teams among senior management to gain recognition and advance their careers. Even when they are convinced champions of change, they can be seen as campaigning to push a solution for a problem which most employees either do not understand or do not recognize.

Initiative communicators can be caught in a double bind, when they try to promote their own initiative, and sell it to their internal customers like a product. The customers are presented with information about the product – the initiative – and asked what more they need to know about it. However, they are unable to make the link between what they might imagine the initiative involves and what their day-to-day needs and requirements are. Asking customers what they want to know about the product is unhelpful. Customers only have knowledge of, and familiarity with, their own needs. Internal customers do not know what they do not know, so initiative communicators go back to pushing their product.

Communication contamination

Consultants can contribute to the problem of poor communication inside organizations. Their terminology becomes others' jargon, and, as a result, contamination by jargon swiftly spreads to a limited number of managers who are keen to be seen to be 'in the know'. Those who work closely with consultants end up adopting their language, using their slides and imitating their presentation style. They become the carriers of the epidemic of half-understood and confusing language around the organization.

Who shall communicate with the communicators?

Where there are many uncoordinated communicators, they may not themselves fully understand the relationship between initiatives and therefore cannot clarify it for anyone else.

It is not uncommon for project team members to be unclear about their project's key messages, or to disagree fundamentally about the anticipated benefits. Yet, who else is going to be able to provide clarity for employees? The first place to create clarity is among the project leaders and team members themselves by getting them together at the outset to agree the central purpose and key messages of their project.

The success of any initiative depends on successful communication. One source of continual and credible communication is the project teams, in their daily contact with the organization. As research within companies continually shows, informal communication is more effective than formal. Project team members' informal daily contact with staff will have a greater influence than will formal communication.

Team members may be focused on getting the task done but are also affecting the climate of acceptance for the project. They are in regular contact with the rest of the organization, working out the details of implementation and often thinking aloud about the feasibility of different options. Without realizing it, they can contaminate communication and create concerns. However, since they have regular contact, understand the issues, and can spot problems early, they can be huge assets, well placed to exert considerable influence, if they are managed properly.

Day-to-day contact with user groups and members of departments which will be affected by change is likely to be more influential than occasional formal communication. Issues can often be identified early at grassroots level before they swell into serious concerns.

Using these assets depends on managing members of project teams as a network of formal and informal communicators.

Coordinating project team members: being on message

Project teams are both a key audience for communication and ambassadors for the project. As such, they need to be provided with common clear messages and to be equipped to communicate consistently with their contacts in the rest of the organization. To maintain consistency they also have to understand their roles and responsibilities, to commit time to identifying important issues and ensure feedback about those issues from their own teams.

Elements of an 'on message' discipline could, for example, include a standard slide pack for presentations, rather than each project team creating its own and increasing inconsistency, and a record of who has presented and said what, to which audiences, and at what point in the project life cycle.

Agreed key messages should be circulated for reinforcement by all team members. Project team leaders should spend time communicating with their own team members, with whom they should hold regular briefing and debriefing sessions.

When problems occur in initiatives, it is surprising how often the underlying issue was known about long before it came to light. Project leaders are close to the issues but are not always aware of the possible implications for employees. Those communicating the initiative can feel that they are flying blind without understanding the issues that lie beneath the project milestones. Developing the communication plan while so many project questions are still being explored can be like trying to assemble an airplane on the runway. Yet communication managers at least know what they do not know. Project leaders may not realize what they *do* know until the implications of an action taken as part of the project suddenly provokes a reaction from the rest of the organization. It is then that the project leaders confess that they had a passing suspicion about such a reaction, but had neglected to mention it.

An important strategy for avoiding communication crises and for improving forward planning is to encourage project leaders to describe the path ahead and speculate about possible impacts and implications. Getting a project team to think through some of the implications of their work means having them report back regularly not simply on their achievements, but on the benefits to the organization of those achievements. Telling employees that milestone number three has been successfully achieved means nothing unless it is spelled out why that is good news. Equally, project leaders need to include in their reports to communicators any alerts or possible reasons for concern they might have. Such concerns may not be for general communication but do help to share the leader's thinking and planning for contingencies.

An internal marketing approach to project communication

'Internal marketing' of an initiative is often misinterpreted as applying glossy sales promotion techniques to internal communication.

Initiatives are often communicated in a way which is more akin to product promotion than change communication. While their promotional communication is designed to create awareness of their presence and activity, it does not communicate the relevance, application or benefit to their internal customers.

Project teams can feel frustrated because they are unable to make effective headway while communicating in this way. They are perceived as self-promoting and removed from the business, and their communication effort is absorbed by having to explain the project's acronym.

Communication should aim to share the thinking from the broad concept down to the specifics. First, the whole organization has to be educated on the need for change and the rationale for the approach.

Without the right context, the initiative communicators find themselves at the sharp end trying to explain the specifics of their activity, but ensnared in debate about why change is needed in the first place – a symptom that the rationale for change was never established. Creating the right context depends on communicators at corporate and at business unit level consistently communicating supporting messages in their own areas.

In order to achieve the benefits of change, an organization has to ensure its various communication efforts are mutually reinforcing.

In external marketing, brand marketing and advertising create awareness of a product, preparing the ground for direct marketing and point of sale promotion. Finally, the salesperson, the customer service representative and aftersales support form the final links in the chain of marketing communication. Communication roles can be similarly shared in internal marketing:

- Corporate communication provides the overall direction and business priorities of the organization as a whole. On the principle that different types of leader have different levels of credibility, the broad picture of change can be communicated by the chief executive.
- Business unit communication talks specifically about challenges and day-to-day issues facing the business unit, the needs which the business has identified, and the gaps it needs to close. This responsibility can be taken on by the business unit leader.
- The project positions itself as the means of closing those gaps, and as a tool for addressing the business issues. This can be communicated by the project champion or initiative leader.

The business units are best placed to communicate the relevance and application of the work being done in the initiative. They can best make the link between the general need for change and the specific implications for the business unit.

The initiative communicators should therefore stop trying to sell change directly to employees, and instead provide the necessary information to the business unit communicators.

This approach shifts the traditional competition between communicators to one of collaboration. Each communicator plays to his strengths in terms of credibility, in a concerted internal marketing plan, to make the connection between the why, what and how of change.

Managing the communicators

If a project or initiative team wants to make change happen and integrate it into the day-to-day working of the business, it must first integrate its communication with the existing communication structure.

In a complex organization results may have to be delivered quickly so existing networks should be used, such as HR professionals, internal communicators, and marketing communicators.

It can make more sense for the initiative team to let the existing communicators use the existing infrastructure to speak to employees. This means that a project communicator can concentrate on enrolling the business's managers, and equipping existing communicators with the right information.

A better return on costs and more coherent communication can be achieved by limiting the number of communication channels. Project communicators often have the luxury of creating not just their project information and messages, but their own communication channels, too. This creates a confusion of roles in which project communicators act both as PR people – seeking coverage of their initiative or message – and media or channel owners, providing or inventing the channels to carry the message. These roles are better clearly separated into two – content providers and channel owners.

Content providers are those with information that they want to communicate; these may be the initiative communicators or senior managers who want to raise awareness about issues. They act primarily as authors, creating messages and information and giving this to the channel owners for distribution using existing communication channels.

Channel owners are responsible for providing robust communication channels that reach employees, and are accountable to content providers for ensuring that they get airtime for their initiative and project messages.

This separation of roles puts a greater emphasis on forward communication planning. It also requires content providers to provide easily translatable, well thought-through and clearly flagged information for channel owners. The onus is on them to ensure that their channels are sufficiently robust to deliver the promised reach to employees. If they do not, initiative communicators will start creating their own again.

Matrix complications

Collaboration between different communicators is particularly important in matrix organizations. Here, there is a danger of individual business unit communications having a knock-on impact on each other, especially where business units share locations and employees from different business units can find themselves, for example, eating in the same canteen. This leads to a situation where employees from different parts of the organization hear different things from outside. For example, there is a set of software applications called SAP, which enables users to access information about all aspects of their business. SAP is rapidly becoming the worldwide standard, and is used by over 15 000 companies across the world. In one organization implementing SAP, a manager in one business unit heard from an outside supplier which had done the same, that the letters SAP there had come to mean 'Stop All Production'. Another manager in a separate business unit in the same location learned from one of its suppliers that implementing SAP was the best thing they had ever done. Confusion set in between the two business units, as informal lunchtime chats undermined the formal communication.

These kinds of mixed message may well be inevitable, but they are exacerbated by different communication strategies and plans developed by different communicators who share the same location, but belong to different business units or departments. Communicators adopting different approaches and different timescales can make difficulties for each other as formal communication in one business unit is leaked as grapevine gossip in a neighbouring one. Employees are able to compare and contrast the messages, and tend to select the one that confirms their prejudice and suspicion. Because people's loyalty is often stronger to their location than to their business unit, they sift information not from a business unit perspective, but in terms of what it means for their location.

Communicators can make life easier for each other in these situations by integrating their efforts, agreeing common messages and timing, taking a united view on cross-business unit issues and keeping a calendar of upcoming events, likely developments and hot issues.

All of these highlight the need for a clear communication plan.

Developing a project communication plan

A communication plan allows you to smooth the path for change, allows people to put information into the right context, and increases their comfort with your initiative. It keeps key people who can present your case in the loop, and minimizes disruption and confusion.

There are four sets of questions that communication needs to answer:

■   What is the change? When will it happen? What will it entail?
■   Why is it happening? What are its intended business benefits? How

does it relate to other initiatives and the wider management agenda for change?

■ What are the specific implications and likely impacts of the changes? What issues does this create as it is rolled out? What is the process for gathering feedback and responding to it?

■ What lessons has the organization learned from other change efforts? How are these being incorporated in the latest proposal?

Developing a communication plan that will answer these questions involves six steps:

1 Analyse your audiences.
2 Set communication objectives.
3 Select the communication approach.
4 Develop key messages and themes.
5 Match communication vehicles to your approach.
6 Measure the outcome.

These are discussed below.

1 Analyse your audiences

Identify the different groups who either need to know about your initiative because it affects them, or who need to brief others about your initiative, or who can influence its success. You should think through how they will be affected by your initiative and what concerns you think they will have. Remember to include the people who can influence the success of your initiative, even though they may not be directly affected by it. These are your potential champions and ambassadors.

This analysis of stakeholders should include what their key concerns are, and what is the desired behaviour needed from them. Doing this well depends on two factors – the accuracy of your perception of the stakeholders' interests, and whether you can retain some objectivity, and not define stakeholders' concerns only in terms of their acceptance or rejection of the proposed changes. The danger is that communicators will aim for stakeholders' compliance, not their commitment. Project communicators can confuse achieving buy-in with 'closing the sale'. Overcoming employees' objections and rebutting their concerns may silence employees but not convince them.

Team members may disagree about the desired end point. One may be concerned to surface employees' real concerns and deal with them, another may want to identify the reservations to the proposed solution and rebut or downplay them.

To avoid analysing stakeholders from the viewpoint of whether or not they will 'buy' the change, a different approach is proposed, as shown in Figure 7.1. This approach looks at stakeholders in two ways – what impact the proposed change is likely to have on them and what their level of initial interest or concern is likely to be. It takes account not just of those stakeholders who might be concerned about, and object to, the change but also of those who are mistakenly feeling 'fat and happy' about the change. For each box in the grid there is a proposed focus to communication:

■ providing a 'wake up' call for those who need to realize that they will be affected
■ educating and informing those who will not be directly affected, and therefore do not need to be concerned
■ reassuring those who are needlessly concerned
■ engaging those who are concerned, and who have cause to be.

This allows communicators to direct precious face-to-face communication on to the two priority boxes – 'wake up' and 'engage'.

By way of example, an organization which was globalizing restructured its corporate head office. A shopfloor employee in the USA might

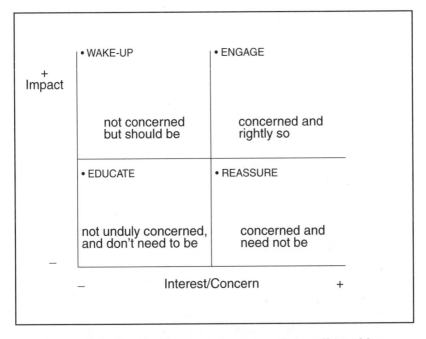

Figure 7.1   How different audiences will be affected by restructuring

be little affected by, and little interested in, the change. This would put him in the bottom left-hand box. However, the story would be different for a first-line supervisor, who might be equally uninterested, but *would* be affected. This placed him in the top left-hand box, needing a wake-up call. Despite his initial lack of interest, the organization needed that supervisor to understand the implications of being part of a global organization. Future business would rely on changing some local proced-ures, at which point this need for cooperation would affect his job. He therefore needed to understand how to balance local self-interest with the interest of the global network as a whole.

The top right-hand box includes those people who would be keenly interested and heavily affected – people at corporate headquarters and senior managers, all highly anxious about whether or not they still had a job. Areas of high anxiety demand more face-to-face communication, and more careful preparation on the part of those running communi-cation sessions.

Taking a senior manager through this grid makes it easier to identify where audiences with the greatest concerns are, and highlights what approach should be taken with different stakeholders and where time can best be invested.

2   Set communication objectives

Having identified your audiences, you should describe what you need from them for your initiative to succeed. This involves describing the outcomes you need from each audience in terms of specific, measurable behaviour and attitudes. For each group you should add a 'by when' date, linked to the milestones in your project plan.

3   Select the communication approach

Different initiatives need to be communicated in different ways. For example, the way in which a redundancy programme is communicated would be very different from that letting people know about a change to the car parking policy.

The communication of change in initiatives is often not a mass com-munication issue. It is more important to enrol managers who have to make things happen. Although most people should be kept informed of the likely implications, the successful communication of change initiat-ives depends on the successive enrolment of tiers of management, so that communication ripples, rather than rolls, out. Some organizations that have communicated directly to the workforce have found enthused employees returning to managers who do not know themselves how to handle the change appropriately.

Use both 'push' and 'pull'

'Push' is the favourable momentum created by senior managers, executives and key influencers. 'Pull' means the demand created by end-users who regard the change as something which can help them both professionally and personally. Key to achieving push is getting key players to buy in, commit to and sponsor the initiative. Creating pull depends on marketing the process so that it emphasizes benefits to users.

Impact must be measured so that senior managers can track progress and 'push' where necessary, and also to allow the target audiences to see the benefit of the initiative, thus creating more demand and 'pull'. However, the initiative will only be 'pushed' by senior executives if they see it as a solution to one of the problems at the top of their business agenda. This means finding the key business issues concerning senior executives currently, and demonstrating a clear link between them and the initiative.

Avoid staging a big launch followed by a sustained silence and few updates on developments. Avoid also the communication of an apparently complex programme; it needs to be simple and memorable. Create an umbrella brand for change or improvement programmes, with component initiatives sub-branded as members of the same family. This will create consistency and continuity as new elements are introduced, and flag a clear link between individual initiatives.

As well as formal channels of communication, look to the informal. A communication plan outlines the target audiences, issues, messages and the best match of media to objective. There is another side, however, to the equation – identifying which people are best placed to present communication and be involved in the face-to-face sessions. Given the power of informal communication and networking, communicators need to know who are the influencers and credible communicators who could be likely ambassadors for change for each stage of the project.

At each stage of a project – from initial concept to implementation – different peope have different levels of credibility and relevance. At the initial concept stage the leader is respected and believed for creating the vision and setting the direction. At the scoping and planning stage credibility is given to the more technical expert who understands some of the implications of the change, has some track record in making change happen, and combines both the will to push change through and the understanding to manage the implications. At implementation people are looking for their colleague, or local authority, to be able to talk to them not about the vision, not about the programme or project, but about the specifics of what they are likely to encounter at their desks or during their working shifts.

Avoid acronyms

What you call your initiative is important. Employees' complaints about initiative overload is as much a reflection of meaning underload. Employees report feeling deluged with an alphabet soup of three-letter acronyms. Selecting a three-word name for an initiative is a recipe for confusion. An initiative called, for example, 'Customer Improvement Initiative', is immediately collapsed into the shorthand of CII which goes into the alphabet soup with all the other three-letter acronyms.

Corporate identity experts always counsel companies when they change their name not to adopt three letters, such as ICI or IBM, because you either have to be very famous or spend a great deal of money explaining to people what those initials mean.

In one organization where employees reported confusion, some helpful soul compiled a glossary of three-letter acronyms which ran to 13 pages. This did not help; it merely highlighted the extent of the problem. However, the real problem is not the need for a glossary of three-letter acronyms, it's that acronyms convey little meaning. Managers trade three-letter acronyms, either pretending that they know what they mean or genuinely knowing what they mean but using them as terms which exclude the uninitiated. Then employees start guessing what the three letters actually stand for. One organization which had an initiative with the three-letter acronym 'ITP' ran an open competition about alternative meanings. While ITP actually stood for 'Innovation Through People', the favourite alternative meaning was 'Indiscriminate Termination of People'.

It is far better to choose a single word which is memorable and gives some sense of what the initiative is about. East of Scotland Water, for example, has a management development programme for their managers in the water industry. They call it Causeway, which gives some sense of a development path across water. Similarly Axa Sun Life's post-merger process for bringing together and uniting two disparate organizations is called 'Fusion'. This gives some sense of two things being bonded together, and gives you a clue as to what this initiative is about. While choosing a single word for an initiative reduces acronym confusion, you still have to choose carefully. One organization named its restructuring project with the biblically inspired 'Genesis', which brought the office wag's warning 'After Genesis comes Exodus'!

In an attempt to further increase clarity, some organizations have turned to using the branding principles applied to their external communication for their internal communication. The perception of initiative overload can be a direct result of not thinking through the branding and sub-branding issues, or explaining the interrelationship between different initiatives and their relative importance.

Brand guidelines and architecture are useful in external communication. They aim to explain the hierarchy and interrelationships of different products, and between brands and the organizations which own them. Brand disciplines are increasingly applied to initiative communication, since they are some of the few available tools for creating context and clarity amid complexity. They do, however, require discipline, which is often lacking in managers who would never risk messing with their company's brand image in the marketplace, but who believe they are gifted enough to turn their hand to communication inside the organization.

4   Develop key messages and themes

To develop the key messages for your initiative you need to understand what behaviours and attitudes you need from people and their current perceptions of your initiative.

Identify where audiences currently are, where they need to be and by what date. This gives you the rate at which the gap between the current and desired must be closed.

Even if people currently know nothing about your initiative, that does not mean they will listen to you neutrally. People will bring their own preconceptions to bear on whatever you have to say, so consider how they might react.

In addition to identifying what outcome you need from each key audience, identify the information each audience will need. This is likely to include the background to the initiative, its objectives and timescale, the rationale for the change and how it is likely to affect customers, suppliers and staff.

Messages should go beyond creating awareness to specifying what action employees need to take, as well as how they can get further information now, and what other information they can expect and by when. Motivating employees demands a realistic playback of their preoccupations. Messages must speak to their recipients concerns and preoccupations and present information from their viewpoint. Use 'hooks' – motivating, attention-getting statements which introduce the project in terms of the audience's need. Hooks are links between an individual's own agenda and the solution offered by the project or initiative. Different hooks need to be developed for each key audience.

The creation of hooks by 'leading with the need' is discussed in Chapter 11.

Weed out the management-speak
When employees are on the look-out for a hidden agenda, they can view management-speak as a cover for some terrible surprise. Every additional example of management-speak in communication merely compounds that impression. Do not allow anyone to send anything out without

having another pair of eyes review it, to guard against management-speak as well as misplaced assumptions about what employees already know or understand.

Research people's issues

Where there is a diverse range of audiences the needs and concerns of each audience must be clearly understood, met and addressed. Often communicators automatically assume that they already know what the issues and concerns are. It is often not information that managers lack, but perspective. They are willing to believe that employees will have substantial and serious worries, but are shocked to discover petty, but no less strongly held, concerns.

Initial research should be undertaken to identify the likely audiences issues and reactions. This will allow planners to work out what are the best outcomes for each audience group, to identify what the key messages are, and therefore to be able to track whether those outcomes have actually been achieved.

The Automobile Association wanted to introduce customer-driven rostering – basically a change to flexible working hours in order to be more available when customers needed help at the roadside. The organization declared that it would not introduce change before everyone affected had an opportunity to discuss the proposals and to fully understand the implications. The main benefit of its approach was that it communicated a proposal rather than announcing a *fait accompli*. There was still room for debate, and the purpose of communication meetings was to get reactions so that necessary amendments could be made to the proposal.

A further, and largely unforeseen, benefit was the extent to which, given the opportunity, employees discussed and fed back the detailed impact of the proposals on their day-to-day working and personal lives. What most concerned one individual was not the detail of the proposals but his realization that, with his mates on flexible rostering, getting them all together for their usual weekly football match could be an impossibility. For another, it was not the detail of the proposals but how he would be able to predict his regular finishing time so that his wife would know when to have his dinner ready. For yet another the question was when would there be any quiet time, which could be used for cleaning their vans?

This highlights the fact that, however well prepared the presenters of the proposal were, their audiences were preoccupied with very different issues, many of which were individual and personal, and often unpredictable. Early research before making presentations helps reduce unpredictability and allows communication to be more targeted and more specific about the 'what's in it for me?' for different audiences.

5 Match communication vehicles to your approach

Different communication processes achieve different objectives. If you are aiming to communicate with some audiences to create awareness and understanding, you may be able to use existing communication channels.

The most commonly used communication channels include e-mail, newsletters, memos, team briefings, noticeboards and video. These are media that are geared towards creating awareness and understanding. What the organization usually wants from its people is involvement and commitment, so extra time may need to be invested in creating additional communication channels that will deliver these objectives.

The more the organization needs an employee to move from awareness to commitment, the more face-to-face communication is needed and the more time is involved. If all the organization wants is awareness and understanding, the focus should be on the quality and the efficient distribution of information. If the requirement from employees is towards involvement and commitment, communication needs to concentrate on improving the quality of the relationships and interaction between people.

The following are a range of different communication objectives with the communication channels which can best help achieve them.

Awareness

Means of creating awareness will range from the corporate identity, press coverage, announcements on the bulletin board, internal and external advertising campaigns, to payslip inserts, memos, continuous strip displays, direct mail and employee annual reports. They may also include video, computer disk and e-mail. The focus of most channels like these is on the one-way distribution of information to a passive audience.

Understanding

The shift from awareness to understanding needs feedback and additional information, tailored to the needs of a more closely defined group of people. Communication is more face-to-face and more interactive. It will also be targeted on getting feedback to check for understanding.

Communication vehicles could include management conferences, roadshows, satellite broadcasting, videoconferencing and feedback forums. All of these allow more dialogue and face-to-face interaction.

Support

Creating support involves a significant shift in interaction. The aim is to elicit acceptance, if not of the change itself, then of the need for, and the rationale behind, it. Employees may not like what is happening, but they can accept why it is happening and support the logic.

Support can be created through business forums, training events and customer seminars. Presentations will be less formal, with continual discussion rather than set question-and-answer periods.

Involvement

The aim here is as much to encourage employees to share their pre-existing reactions, concerns and objections as it is to inform them about management thinking. There will be far more of a dialogue – sharing thinking, assessing implications, exploring alternatives and reviewing the best means of implementation. Here, the focus is more on listening.

Commitment

Commitment comes from a sense of ownership, and this comes from having participated in the process.

Gaining commitment entails a high degree of talking through the pressures affecting the business, and reviewing possible competitive scenarios and strategic options. The high levels of interaction and participation needed mean that this is a process that takes a good deal of time.

6   Measure the outcome

Impact can only be assessed if you know what to measure, so make sure that you identify observable outcomes and behaviours for each key audience.

Measure the relevance of the messages and changes in the level of people's understanding. Also, assess the communication process to find out which media are the most effective in getting the messages across, and measure the efficiency of planning, timing and execution of the communications. If, for example, a central helpline is provided, internal communicators should try to generate debate and encourage people to use it to get further detail. Use of the helpline would then become an indicator of how engaged and interested people are in the subject. What, for example, are the top ten questions being asked on the helpline?

Measuring impact and tracking results are discussed further in Chapter 11.

Plan for the unexpected

Finally, however good the communication plan, there are bound to be unexpected developments, unresolved issues and unexpected debate about messages and responses to employees' questions. Project communicators need to be in regular contact with each other and with colleagues responsible for communication across the business. They should be feeding back to each other on issues that are being raised and setting dates by which they can expect these issues to have been resolved.

The following chapter looks further at the need to manage and orchestrate communication.

Part IV
Pulling it Together

The management of communication

The preceding chapters have looked at how to achieve business ends via better internal communication. First, organizations, have to do the right thing and connect their internal communication to achieving their business strategy and, second, do things right – have efficient and effective processes. This chapter and those that follow are about doing things right.

So far, this book has listed a number of formidable tasks. Organizations need both to keep their people informed and create understanding and shared thinking. They must be able to tap into creative thinking and innovation. They need to align personal values and brand values to deliver value to customers. They need employees to feel part of a global network and collaborate in a matrix of teams while living and working in local communities. They need to do all this and cope with change and ambiguity too.

Achieving all this with existing communication practices is a tall order. It is like asking the crew of the *Starship Enterprise* to continue their five-year mission in time and space with only a Model T Ford to do so!

Chapter 2 warned how unclear, inconsistent and uncoordinated communication is causing confusion and wasting employees' time. Chapter 7 described how the change that organizations need to create is stymied by their own approach to communication, and stalled when 'big picture' information is not translated by managers into local implications. This chapter describes a fundamental shift in the way communication needs to be managed as an organizational process. It makes the connection between two of the key elements of good practice outlined in Chapter 2 – communication planning, which helps reduce the quantity of information, and channel management, which helps increase the productive capacity of communication channels.

It argues that communication management has lessons to learn from supply chain management, and that there are principles which can readily be applied in order to create greater value from internal communication.

It also proposes three main ways in which to bring greater coherence and improved quality to the communication that flows through the channels:

1 better management and coordination through board-level planning and communication 'air traffic control'
2 better quality of messages and information through communication supply chain management
3 better design and presentation of information.

Communication as overload

The limit to effective communication is not the number of trees left standing from which to produce newsletters or the number of e-mails that can be distributed in a single day. The limit is the extent to which people have the inclination, time and goodwill to engage with the communicator. Employees' mental capacity to absorb and process information is limited and this capacity has to be treated as a strategic resource.

Employees' willingness to consume all the messages aimed at them is shrinking, as is the time they are willing to give those competing for their attention. It is exacerbated by uncoordinated and inconsistent communication, and by poorly thought-through and badly presented information. Employees get half-baked information which they do not have the time to 'bake' any further. No time is given for employees to assimilate information, discuss key issues and their implications, and few channels exist for feedback so that improvements to information dissemination can be made.

Pulling communication together

Making communication coherent is a tough job in an increasingly complex environment. The problems that organizations are encountering highlight two issues – the limited capacity of organizations to organize and distribute information, and the limited capacity of individuals to process and turn information into something relevant and valuable.

Businesses must therefore more carefully manage access to communication channels, prioritize messages and manage the threat of information overload. There are three ways of improving communication management:

1 better management of the *capacity* of the communication channels through more selective coordinated use and greater linkage between them so that they reinforce each other

2   reduction of the *quantity* of messages through better planning and clearer prioritization and greater coordination of the communicators who produce them

3   better *quality* of messages and information by ensuring that suppliers of information provide higher-quality raw material, which makes it easier for employees to make sense of the information they receive.

All of these call for better planning by senior management, clear prioritization and the agreement of a limited number of key messages.

Regulating communication

Companies have a limited capacity to organize and distribute information, and individuals have a limited capacity and willingness to assimilate it. Where resources are scarce, companies have to be more intelligent in the way they use them. Facing a communication equivalent of the 1974 oil crisis, we have to learn to switch from the communication 'gas guzzlers' that are now too expensive to get organizations to their desired destinations.

Direct marketing companies have already learned this lesson. Customers grew weary of the deluge of junk mail, and incredulous that much of it was arriving simultaneously from the same company. Companies have now become better coordinated, more disciplined and more tightly targeted in their direct marketing. Some of these strategies are increasingly being applied to internal communication.

One of the companies which has done this is Post Office Counters. It has a turnover of £1.2 billion, a UK network of 19 300 offices, and 40 000 counter positions. There are 12 business units, producing 100 or so publications. In addition to the business unit newsletters, there is lateral communication across the business units coming from areas such as projects, business processes and functional departments.

With the unrestricted, and proliferating, number of channels, the board decided that a move towards greater central coordination was the only way to achieve consistency. They devised an internal communication strategy which depended on reducing the clutter of messages and channels. This was achieved by introducing licensing for communication, reducing the number of communication channels and publications, and introducing a common 'family appearance' for all their national communication channels.

Greater quality assurance of communication meant ensuring that projects each had their own communication plans, coordinated beneath an overall umbrella plan, and that all national communication channels were managed from the centre.

Under new licensing arrangements the 100 or so publications previously produced by different business units are now significantly reduced. Each business unit has one publication, in which they combine news on business issues, performance update and social news. Any other channels – whether electronic, paper, audio or video – that are intended to go out regularly must be approved and licensed by the central communication function. The business units can make proposals to introduce new channels, but these are submitted to a national publications manager for approval.

Any would-be communicators have to demonstrate that existing channels do not meet their needs, and that there is demand from internal customers for their proposed new communication channel.

However, behind any policy, there have to be some teeth to ensure conformance. Post Office Counters relies on the fact that every publication has to be distributed through the logistics business unit which is instructed to give early warning of any mavericks and deny them distribution. If the publication has no licence number in the corner, it is treated like unstamped external mail – no number, no mailout.

If recipients are sent pirate publications, which do not share the family look, they have two options – put it in the bin, or return to sender.

Such approaches reflect the lack of coordination of communication in any organization. There has always been a traditional rivalry between corporate centres and business units, between global headquarters and country operations, and between one country and another. Communicators have had to negotiate and cooperate to work across those tensions. Now life is becoming even trickier as organizations add to the mix the complexities of matrix structures, the decision to either centralize or decentralize, and the need consistently to manage the asset of a common brand. All this calls into play a new layer of communicators who operate along different lines of the matrix, whether in functional networks, product divisions, market sectors or key customer teams.

A matrix structure geometrically increases the amount of communication and multiplies the number of competing tribal loyalties. The more complex the matrix, the greater the number of communicators, the higher the level of competition for the employee's attention and the more jigsaw pieces the recipient has to assemble to produce a coherent picture.

Then, just as the organization realizes that it has created a loose affiliation of warring tribes of communicators, an additional group of communicators emerges to work on organizational initiatives, programmes and projects. Although these have finite lifespans, they are important to the success of the business and usually have a high profile.

All these communicators effectively compete for the time, attention and brainspace of employees. However, employees have different needs and concerns, and apply different groundrules to selecting and prioritizing information.

Within this matrix of communicators, each has a different preoccupation and a different offer. At the centre, they want to achieve a cohesive unity behind the brand name, and have common standards and processes, where it makes sense, across the business units. They also want a reasonable share of employee brainspace for corporate issues, and to add an identification with the organization as a whole to people's loyalty to their immediate business unit.

Within the business units communicators want to serve the management agenda of their immediate boss. That may be promoting the success of that business unit within the group as a whole, or directing employees towards specific objectives, even if that means blinkering them to the wider picture.

Corporate and business unit communicators can negotiate which corporate communication enters the business unit. However, their relationship with the initiative communicator is likely to be very different. Initiative communicators see their job as promoting their initiative, and compete for as much time and attention as possible. They are product-focused, and in campaign mode, aware of the importance of visibility not just to employees, but to the initiative owners, bosses and colleagues. Their communication runs laterally across the business units and can involve new communication channels that they develop themselves, such as videos, intranets, newsletters or roadshows.

As well as having different agendas, corporate, business unit and initiative communicators may actually have a different definition of how their communication is supposed to be adding value. In a number of organizations those at the corporate centre sees themselves as consultants, the business unit communicators see themselves as the efficient distributors of management messages, and initiative communicators see themselves as internal PR campaigners. This brings a further dimension of complexity, confusion, and possible trouble.

It is an old adage that too many cooks spoil the broth, especially when they each use a different recipe. Organizations pay for all the cooks, provide them all with the tools for the job, pay for all the ingredients and still end up with no broth.

This is not all the fault of the communicators – they have a difficult job intertwining a number of different strands of communication. They have to provide relevant information, create a common sense of identity across the business and build teamwork along different lines of the matrix.

Communication channels are limited but everyone's got a key message they want everyone else to remember. In today's organizations this is a complex task and can seem at times like playing three-dimensional chess. However, organizational communication is a team sport, in which coordinating all the players is the only way to score the goal. The rules of the game have to be set by the leaders, and there are six steps to better communication planning and the more effective management of channels:

1   Plan communication with senior management.
2   Agree a communication policy with the board.
3   Involve senior management in forward planning.
4   Ensure that change initiatives have communication plans.
5   Create greater coordination between internal communicators.
6   Practise 'air traffic control'.

1   Plan communication with senior management

There is a clear need for a more systematic and disciplined approach to communication planning. Research by Synopsis shows that only a third of boards actually approve the communication strategy and plan (Bloomfield et al., 1998). But 69 per cent of Fortune 1000 companies do not have a communication policy at all.

2   Agree a communication policy with the board

Too few businesses involve their top team in approving the internal communication strategy and plan. Businesses may say that they want their people to sing from the same songsheet, but they fail to ensure that the top team agrees the words. It is small wonder, then, that the result is mixed messages.

In one organization the failure of the top team to develop a prioritized communication plan left individual areas to do their own thing. Enthusiastic individuals unleashed their creativity on communication activities, competing to be louder, bigger and better than communicators elsewhere. Finally, like rival salesmen sabotaging each other's product displays, communicators ended up covertly tearing each other's posters down under cover of darkness.

Unresolved board-level disagreements translate into communication competition further down the organization. Although everyone can easily understand that coordination is needed for coherence, it does not mean that they will practise what they hear preached. For a senior manager charged with driving forward an initiative, for whom success is a career issue, altruism is likely to give way to self-interest, as they drive their communication ahead anyway. Prima donnas are generally reluctant to join a formation dancing team.

The only way of reducing the pressure is for senior managers at board level to commit to a more prudent management of that strategic asset, employee brainspace. That means having all the initiative owners, the business unit leaders and the chief executive all in one room, committing as a group to the common interest. Trying to tackle the issue individual by individual is likely simply to perpetuate the problem.

Different views on the role, value and purpose of internal communication need to be agreed by members of the board, including the best balance of openness, of sharing of information with managers and employees and the sensitivity of information. Consensus must be reached on the key messages and the amount of airtime they should receive, which messages need only go to specific managers or locations, and which initiatives should have greater emphasis and prominence. With an agreed overall picture for the jigsaw puzzle, employees will be better able to assemble their own picture from the pieces they receive.

3   Involve senior management in forward planning

Senior management should be involved in communication planning well in advance and should focus on business, rather than communication, objectives. They should develop an annual calendar of communication events and milestones, explicitly linked to the business plan, and review the communication plan quarterly. The emphasis should be on educating people about the rationale for change, rather than simply announcing conclusions. This will require involving communicators earlier in the planning process, rather than – as is frequently and unfortunately the case – when the implementation of a change begins and they are asked to make the announcements.

4   Ensure that change initiatives have communication plans

Without a common format it is that much harder to be clear on how and when different change initiatives will affect people in the organization. This results in change managers competing for communication time and resources, with the risk that change fails through initiative overload – too many changes hitting people too quickly. This may explain why employees keep experiencing sudden, apparently unexpected and uncoordinated change. This only serves to increase their anxiety, frustration and their perception that the management team does not have its collective act together.

Organizations need to think ahead, show clear linkages between different initiatives and give people the bigger picture of change. Initiatives should have individual communication plans that are linked to the business's umbrella strategy.

5   Create greater coordination between internal communicators

The number of communicators within organizations is increasing. Reasons for this include managers taking their communication responsibilities seriously, initiative leaders wanting to create support for their programmes and new divisions, departments and business units hiring their own communication specialists. If these communicators are not coordinated, they inevitably compete for time and attention, contribute to communication clutter and create inconsistency and mixed messages.

Different functions – human resources, corporate communications, IT, marketing, operations – own different pieces of the communication jigsaw which must all be assembled correctly for success. It is not enough for communicators to coordinate their diaries of events, they have to share their plans, priorities and thinking. Cooperation is not enough unless all plans are integrated.

Members of the communicators' network – wherever they are in the matrix – should work together to devise groundrules for sending messages down the communication channels, to map out who owns which communication channels, and to decide what the requirements are for each.

Organizations should differentiate between the roles of channel owners and content providers. Corporate communication, for example, can be responsible for managing communication channels, such as the corporate newsletter or the briefing process. It can also be responsible for providing corporate messages to other communication channels owned and managed by other parts of the business. One rule of engagement, for example, could be that the corporate centre provides the content to business units, leaving them responsible for disseminating it via their existing communication channels. Confining some would-be communicators to being exclusively content providers can reduce the problem of their inventing new channels and realize more value from the investment in the existing ones.

6   Practise 'air traffic control'

Communication will continue to be viewed as a soft area until leaders take a harder line. Unless business leaders insist that early planning, coordinated communication, and clear and consistent messages with identified actions, are agreed at the top of the organization, communication will continue to fail to deliver changed attitudes and behaviour.

Companies face the choice between self-regulation or confusing clutter. To reduce information overload organizations must adopt a more sophisticated approach to managing information and interaction via greater communication 'air traffic control'. They will have to shift from the current 'factory' model of communication, in which more and more messages are pumped down communication pipelines, to regulating the amount of information being circulated.

This raises the dilemma of being perceived as a communication 'policeman', standing between the information universe filtering out and depriving employees of information. Of course, some degree of editing is required, to reduce overload. Saul Thurman identified the 'information anxiety' syndrome – the fear that somewhere there is vital information you need but are lacking. What he didn't identify is that employees within organizations also suffer 'information paranoia' – the persistent suspicion that the truth is out there, and that vital information is being kept from you by a communication conspiracy.

The dilemma is that unless you show employees the complexity and extent of the information universe behind you, they cannot know what you are protecting them from, or what value you are adding.

The intranet allows people to access information for themselves. Perhaps in the future, using intelligent agents to alert individuals to relevant information might be a way of replacing filtering and editing, since a filter excludes and an adviser alerts. However, for the present, there is a need to reduce the complexity at source. It is not the job of communication managers to keep making rescue attempts on poorly thought-through planning and decisions, like throwing lifebelts to drowning men. They need to walk upstream and see who is throwing them off the bridge in the first place.

Communication has to be orchestrated carefully via an 'air traffic control' which has an overview of communication activities. This prevents mid-air collisions caused by would-be communicators taking to the air as and when they like.

The linkage between business strategy and communication planning at the centre and at business unit level should be more closely coordinated. Early planning and prioritization of messages is vital, even though this will inevitably cause some inconvenience to the senior management team.

An 'air traffic control' co-ordination group should be set up; this should comprise, for example, representatives from corporate communication, HR, marketing, change management, where it exists, and IT to prioritize and coordinate business-wide communication. It should assemble all proposed communication activity on a single Gantt chart or project plan to serve as a communication 'radar screen'.

An integrated communication plan should be prepared annually and reviewed quarterly. This should cover objectives, key messages, the use of communication channels, and outline how initiatives will be timetabled and coordinated. It should also identify the measures to be used in evaluating performance. The document should explicitly explain how action, messages and so on will be segmented by key audience. This should be approved, at least in summarized form, by the board, in order to ensure ownership by senior management and confirm that strategic objectives are being supported and sufficient resources and budgets are allocated.

Business units should have a similar local planning and coordination process, and their more detailed operational plans should connect to the integrated central plan.

These principles help put in place one of the two key elements of good practice – communication planning, which helps reduce the quantity of information and better utilize the capacity of communication channels. The other element is better quality of communication, and the following section looks at improving what actually flows through the communication channels.

Avoiding cacophony

Surveys consistently reveal a confusion between the volume of information and its value. Organizations need to focus more on the refinement of raw information into meaning and relevance.

We all think that we are good communicators. Anyone who has either the seniority to insist on being heard, or access to the right communication channels, can broadcast to the world. Unfortunately where there is no quality requirement for communication and where authors feel they are naturally good with the written or spoken word, high volumes of low-quality material result.

Organizations need a better understanding of the attitudes and outlooks of different audiences so that they can clearly link key messages from the centre with individuals' concerns and preoccupations. Where messages are mass-produced and distributed, there is little tailoring of information to the recipients' viewpoint, or awareness of the different requirements, mindsets or receptivity of different audiences. Making a stronger link between business direction and individuals' agendas has several advantages. For example, it allows for an earlier preparation for change and provides greater clarity of leadership. However, it requires more qualitative research to test managers' assumptions about their people, and better feedback channels to improve understanding of how employees decode the communication they receive.

Businesses need to get more out of their communication, in terms of cost, clarity and credibility. Some are beginning to realize that information overkill is consuming precious time, creating clutter, and creating mixed messages.

In an effort to reduce communication fatigue, IBM aims to reduce information and communication channels to the minimum. It has created an enforceable code of practice to reduce information to manageable levels. Its internal communication department acts as internal consultants and audits not only the amount of communication, but the effectiveness of channels. It also gauges the clarity of information as perceived by employees and whether or not communication has actually been effective in achieving the planned outcome.

IBM takes consistency and coherence even more seriously. To keep executives in harmony with corporate approaches, it provides a toolkit on the intranet, specifically for managers. This toolkit contains the five top-priority business issues for communication, together with the context and background information for each issue. Managers are therefore supplied with the means of communicating plus the means of adding value and context as they pass information on. The toolkit also contains guidelines for preparing material, and is intended to help managers think through the communication issues before putting pen to paper. From the communication department's point of view it is a framework for ensuring that managers who want to communicate provide them with higher-quality information, that communication planning will be better thought through and that managers will not appear unexpectedly in the department asking for a video to be made.

The interesting point about the IBM strategy is that the communication department effectively works with managers as partners in a supply chain, with the aim of producing an agreed outcome at the end of the chain.

Communication supply chain management

With more change, and more communication, being forced down limited-capacity channels to people who are filtering the information they receive, there is a need to squeeze more performance from the communication channels and to create more value from information.

Communication management has lessons to learn from supply chain management. The traditional debate between communicators, whether between corporate and business unit, or between initiative and project, has been based on two things: the communicator's right to address the internal audience and the communicator's assumptions about what audiences want and need. This is a production-led approach and is reminiscent of factories forcing products into their distribution channels and insisting that their salesforce offload them on to their customers.

The distribution of a message is too often mistaken for communication. It is frequently assumed that if information has been sent out, it has been received and assimilated. Fighter aircraft have 'fire and forget' missiles. Pilots can fire their missiles at a target, and then peel off, confident that the target will be hit. Managers have a similar, but misplaced, confidence about 'fire and forget' communication – information sent out without highlighting its significance and for whom it is intended, and without indicating why it has been sent or what action or response is expected as a result.

There are a number of disconnects between links in the communication chain. Messages are mistaken for communication, and success is defined only as the media's ability to deliver messages, with no regard for the final outcome. Competing communicators jealously guard the part of the communication chain they own, and managers are accused of filtering and blocking information, and disagreeing with its value. These disconnects are similar to those of another chain – that of supplier and customer.

For example, managers are currently used as a distribution channel to deliver information to an end-user. The distribution process is unreliable, not least because the information has not been designed for the use of either the manager or the end recipient. Both have to add the vital ingredients of meaning and relevance to make the information they receive valuable.

These are problems which organizations are already tackling and solving in their approaches to supply chain management. The problem faced by internal communication today is the problem confronting businesses with traditional supplier management – supply is divorced from the creation of customer value.

Squeezing more from the supply chain

The traditional communication cascade is a distribution channel that links a supplier to a final customer. The intention is that, as messages are passed down the chain, they will be localized, or sweetened with local information. The product being distributed is information, and there is a great deal of waste, confusion, discarding and frustration along the supply chain.

This problem is now greater because organizations have redefined the purpose of internal communication. In the past they wanted it to be a means of efficiently distributing information, but now they need it to be a process for creating understanding.

In the traditional cascade communication model, information is handed from link to link on the chain, without an understanding of how the whole chain works, what the different needs of each player in the chain are, or the desire to improve. Frequently, the information supplier creates problems for the customer by providing inferior material – written in obscure language, poorly presented, with no obvious point.

As the volume of information increases, the quality does not. Therefore, we have to make two changes simultaneously – identify what is the intended business value in communicating and design a better process to deliver that value. We need to see internal communication as a process of conversion rather than a process of distribution. Just as an assembly line worker converts or adds value to a component that he or she receives from up the line, so we have to convert information into meaning for ourselves so that we can make the right decision.

This process of conversion, outlined in Chapter 2 (page 22), has four elements:

■ content

- context
- conversation
- feedback.

The following section details how to provide the information content and allow the recipients to put it in context. Chapter 10 looks at conversation and the importance of interaction in creating understanding as well as the critical role of feedback in ensuring successful communication.

Content and context

If an assembly line worker receives a poor-quality component, he or she can stop the line and reject the component. There is no such facility for employees who are continually receiving poor-quality information which they find difficult or troublesome to translate. The worse the quality of the material, the longer the employee takes to arrive at the desired conclusion. Better-quality information would make the process easier, would waste less time and create less exasperation. To achieve this, quality must be built into the creation of information and those who author information must adopt a more thoughtful discipline.

Communication consultant and author Roger D'Aprix (1997) captures the point well:

... the analogy in our old manufacturing economy would be to have assembly line workers digging through piles of parts and raw materials to find the components for their products. No manufacturing plant manager would tolerate that situation for a minute. If we are going to use information as the raw material to build other products and services we need to treat it as carefully and as deliberately as a Toyota, a Motorola or a Sony treats its raw materials and its production processes.

As communicators, we have to make the same shift that companies such as Unipart have undertaken – from running a basic supply chain to running a supply partnership in which partners work together to increase the total benefit in the chain. The shift is from seeing the supply chain as merely a series of interconnected distribution channels to seeing it as interconnected partners who each have a responsibility to add value to what they receive and what they hand onwards – a value chain. A company's value chain is the whole string of activities – from procurement to aftersales service – in which it engages to create and deliver value to a customer.

The aim of partners in the chain is to remove steps that benefit nobody and eliminate procedures that add only difficulties and no value. They have a clear view of what value the final customer is intended to receive, and they understand the needs, constraints and capabilities of other partners along the chain. Furthermore, instead of accusing partners when the chain breaks down, they work to identify how things need to be improved.

Where is value best added?

Partners should not only improve the whole supply chain, they should also improve their own link in the chain.

The difference between this and the cascade approach is important. In a cascade the principle is to add local information to more distant information to make it more relevant. The problem is that the intention behind different pieces of information differs. For example, corporate communication's aim may be to give people a sense of identity with the whole organization and a wider picture – awareness and belonging. Local information may be designed by business unit communicators to involve people in contributing and improving. Different communications have different intended outcomes. Asking line managers to make the connection between the two sources of communication is less of a problem than the communicators agreeing the intended outcome.

By cooperating along the chain communicators became partners, orchestrating their efforts to maximize value and sharing know-how.

Internal communication has reached the same conclusion as supply chain management – quality along the chain is only as good as the weakest link. Car manufacturers, for example, have realized that final car quality cannot exceed the quality levels achieved by suppliers, so they have begun to share their quality know-how and training with their suppliers.

Taking such an approach to communication management connects communication suppliers in a process of value creation. It redefines the role of communication from the wholesaling and retailing of messages to ensuring understanding and sharing interpretation. The aim of this is to enable employees to deliver on the organization's value proposition to its customers.

Working in a supply chain means identifying what internal customers want and need. What are the customers' constraints and idiosyncrasies of customers, and how should communication processes and content be designed best to suit these?

Managing the supply chain is about how best to meet the requirements of the end customer, while also meeting the requirements and the agenda of intermediaries along the chain. Dumping half-baked information on intermediaries, such as business unit communicators, and asking them to distribute it simply transfers the problem. They are left with the problem of making the information more acceptable to their people – a task that involves time, effort and, potentially, loss of credibility.

Seeing internal communication as a process of converting information into meaning demands different rules. Partnership along the chain is vital, as is eliminating one party dumping a problem on the next party at all stages along the chain. For that to happen, the whole process not only has to be transparent to all, but also has to be managed by a process owner, from end to end.

Everything should be produced with the end customer in mind, with a common agreement about what value the final communication should produce. Finally, feedback from each point of the chain should be used to improve the process, and feedback from those at the end of the process should test whether the intended outcome was achieved.

Clarify the positioning of the communication department

Much of the pressure to pump messages into the organization is caused by senior managers insisting that communication specialists give them access to communication channels. Those specialists are often seen by their senior clients as simply part of the distribution process. This issue, and ways of dealing with it, is expanded in Chapter 9.

One of the difficulties encountered by the communication department is the way in which upstream and downstream customers perceive it as providing very different kinds of value. Senior managers want access to communication channels, and their downstream customers pray for a reduced flow of information and more clarity. Communicators have to provide a valuable service to both sets of customer. This means that the communication team has to provide value to its downstream customers in terms of reduced volume of information, and increased quality while also giving value to its upstream customers by helping them achieve their objectives via effective communication. This can all be accomplished by taking some of the following actions:

1 Focus on processes, not products.
2 Quality manage communication.
3 Reduce the number of messages and make them more memorable.
4 Design information with the recipient in mind.
5 Budget time not paper.
6 Measure the outcome.

1   Focus on processes, not products

Managers have to be educated away from an automatic demand for a communication product, especially when that product is yet another newsletter. Their real goal is usually to create awareness and under-standing, or create support and involvement or change. Working with communicators should enable them to identify what precisely they do want to achieve. Equally, communications specialists should help them identify the best process rather than the best product. For example, an article in a newsletter, a discussion in a team meeting, a reliable feedback process and a 'frequently asked questions' section on the company intranet could all be combined in a unified process to provide the desired outcome.

Reducing the volume of competing voices within the business means providing tools as well as rules. It is more acceptable to impose an 'air traffic control' structure if you also provide communicators with tools and processes that will still help them succeed.

Like IBM, Hewlett Packard and Microsoft give managers a planning tool to help them think through the communication needs of their project and to provide guidance on the effective use of communication channels. This allows to clarify their thinking, consider options and refine their messages. It also forces would-be communicators to specify more precisely the meaning and relevance of the information they want to distribute.

2   Quality manage communication

Increasing total benefit in the communication chain includes reducing the complexity of information and using clearer and more accessible language.

Communication is about the transfer of meaning from person to person, not simply the passing on of messages. The greater part of creating value – flagging the significance of information – should be done early in the supply chain, because those further down lack the context to do so. This frees managers and team leaders to add the value that only they can add – making the communication relevant to their team members whose issues and interests they know best.

All these steps help in the process of sharing, connecting and extracting meaning from information.

3   Reduce the number of messages and make them more memorable

There is only a certain amount of information that people will take in and remember. The more key points that are crammed in, the less chance there is to make information memorable. A survey among Church of England vicars spot-checked how many of the ten commandments they could recall unprompted. The average was two. If professionals can only retain a limited number of essential facts, what hope do the rest of us have in retaining the long list of key principles underlying the mission statement?

The less that managers put in, the more employees take out.

4   Design information with the recipient in mind

What the business really wants is to create meaning, significance and relevance for employees. However, companies practise a form of 'customer sacrifice' in which they push the burden of translating information into relevance on to the individual. This allows authors at the centre to mass-produce undifferentiated messages, with little concern for the needs of different individuals. Doing this may save time for the message senders, but takes up far more time elsewhere in the organization as recipients struggle to make sense of what they have received.

Just as mass marketing was replaced by segmentation marketing, so marketing to individuals will become the norm. The process of individualizing products and services to meet customers' requirements will be very different to making available only a standard off-the-shelf product. The same holds true for internal communication. Although the future ideal may be to communicate with individual employees as 'an audience of one', there is much that can be done now to move away from the current mass market approach to communication.

By presenting information with the end-user in mind and from the recipient's perspective, companies can simplify and improve their employees' quality of life. Relevance spells the difference between a welcome letter and junk mail. Messages that fail to register with recipients merely contribute to the clutter.

Organizations can no longer afford to allow almost anyone to write for general communication without guidelines or quality standards. With time being such a pressing resource, managers cannot be allowed to send out information that fails to make its point simply and clearly. Recipients need to know why they have received information and what, if anything, they are supposed to do as a result.

In the same way as the perception of initiative overload is exacerbated by the use of acronyms, as described in Chapter 7, so in 'information overload' the volume of information is less of a problem than its poor presentation. One way to tackle this is to adopt a quality approach to the creation of information, supplying templates that help authors send more immediately relevant messages. This is discussed in Chapter 10.

5   Budget time not paper

Written material should be easy to absorb and, if it is for use in face-to-face meetings, provide a springboard for discussion. Information provided for face-to-face communication is often written as though it were going to be read, rather than spoken. This can make it turgid, and also increases the amount of valuable meeting time it consumes. Instead, the material should be written and timed to be spoken, like a script for the radio, not a letter to the tax man. Information items should be allocated a time budget – how much of a meeting they will take up. This also helps identify whether an item should be included, and whether it is worth the time it takes up.

Better prepared and written information is one way to improve the return on time invested in face-to-face communication.

6   Measure the outcome

The acid test for the effectiveness of communication is how people rate, prioritize and consume information. Regular measurement is needed to test effectiveness. Without this feedback we could end up with a more efficient distribution system for messages which reduces the time and effort for the communicators' network, without actually producing the desired outcome.

Researching recipients' reactions to communication should be more than simply checking whether they have received it. It should also focus on how user-friendly they found it and what they concluded from it. Research by the Jensen Group (1998) showed that only 14 per cent of companies consistently ask the recipient how they would prefer to receive information. The measurement of communication's impact is the subject of Chapter 11.

In external marketing the effectiveness of rival media in delivering messages to target audiences is measured, as is the likelihood of the message recipients taking action. The same principle should apply in internal communication: the cost of getting information to employees, and the medium's effectiveness in encouraging them to convert information into understanding should be measured.

In surveys, employees invariably choose face-to-face communication as their preferred means of receiving communication, and their immediate boss is usually the preferred communicator. Why, then, do initiative communicators, for example, usually prefer the newsletter and the video, and now the intranet? Possibly because they represent a convenient way of exposing the greatest number of eyes to the greatest number of messages.

These channels have their place in the mix, but that place has to be earned. A decision as to whether a senior manager should produce a corporate video should only be made after comparing the cost of different methods delivering the message, its impact on the employee, the ability to recall key messages and the impact of the communication on likelihood to take action. This can help persuade would-be communicators that low-tech means can have more impact, and reduce the pressure on communication departments to create numerous communication products.

Conclusion

Business success depends on employees being able to make sense of information and turn it into appropriate decisions. Organizations can more valuably meet this goal by better management of their internal communication and by focusing more on the refinement of raw information into meaning and relevance. This requires the reduction of complexity, the simplification and integration of messages, and the use of the most appropriate communication channel.

It also involves managing the mix of information and interaction. Information involves the delivery and receipt of data and messages and concerns how best to share, structure and extract meaning. Interaction includes how people perceive and relate to each other, and involves issues of credibility, trust and collaboration.

Chapter 10 looks at the importance of interaction in helping convert information into understanding. Meanwhile, the following chapter discusses how the management of internal communication can be improved by repositioning the role of the internal communication department in the organization.

Repositioning the role of the internal communication function

Leaders know that communication is vital to change and want to use it as a strategic tool. How exactly they should use it to best advantage is less clear. Leaders want communication strategists but feel they get message writers and editors instead. Communicators want to fill the crucial role of communication strategists, but feel that they are being used more as writers and editors.

Chief executives want to get the best value from the business's tangible and intangible assets, especially the brands it owns. To do that they have to decide how should the organization be best structured, what is the role of the centre, and what is the best balance of corporate identity and branding.

Once the corporate body is designed, communicators have to provide the communication nervous system to make it live and breathe. How do they tailor communication structures to the type of organization and the strategy the business is pursuing, as well as ensure some flexibility for the next inevitable restructure? How do they resolve the tribal warfare between communicators worldwide, and how do they create clear rules of engagement between communicators?

There are four reasons why organizations need to improve their communication to add value for their businesses:

1 **The re-examination of the value of the corporate centre.** The increased emphasis on improving shareholder value has led organizations to focus more on corporate centre costs, and on the value it adds. This inevitably sparks a debate about the value of internal communication, and how the function should be structured, located and resourced to deliver what the organization needs.

2 **Restructuring and globalization.** There are many reasons for globalizing. Customers may demand global services, global consistency and a single point of contact for global purchasing. Companies may wish to take advantage of their experience and their expertise by creating global functional networks to standardize what they do. The spread

of global brands demands common worldwide approaches and consistency in marketing and manufacturing. These factors all put pressure on internal communication to help deliver these objectives.

3   **Brand discipline and the desire to protect the corporate reputation.** Companies whose value far exceeds their tangible assets are now commonplace, with a large part of this extra value coming from the value of brands and corporate reputation. To protect these assets, organizations are placing greater emphasis on ensuring that their employees' behaviour is consistent with their brand – yet another job for internal communication.

4   **The need to reduce information overload.** Making communication coherent and managing information overload is a tough job in an increasingly complex environment. Within an organization there may well be a raft of communicators, at the corporate centre, in the business units and dedicated to change initiatives who effectively compete for the time, attention and brainspace of employees.

In a world which is searching for value, this competition destroys it. To add value, communicators need to manage this complexity.

This chapter makes two important connections. First, it connects business leaders' need for strategic communication advice with communicators' aspirations to fill a strategic role. It looks at how communicators can place internal communication at the heart of the business and deliver greater value to senior management. Second, it describes how internal communication can be used as corporate glue to provide greater agility in shifting from one organization structure to another. It provides a framework for ensuring that communication architecture is matched to the business structure, its corporate identity and brands. This can be used for negotiating responsibilities between corporate and other communicators.

Finally, it highlights the importance of professional leadership and the development of skills in managing communication networks.

Valuing communication

The aim of internal communicators has been to alert senior management to the strategic importance of communication to the business. The real value of internal communication lies in its ability to help deliver business ends by enabling employees to turn strategy into action.

In organizations seeking a fundamental change in people's attitudes and behaviours to deliver on a strategy, people with experience in change management, or strategy and planning, are increasingly taking responsibility for communication. Where the need for change is high on the agenda, the internal communication function is usually close to those trying to make change happen. This acknowledges the importance of internal communications.

Now, just as communication finally finds a home, internal communicators may find themselves evicted, unless they can define their value to the organization and demonstrate a clearer return on investment. 'Nature abhors a vacuum' and, if internal communicators do not clarify their value proposition, the value vacuum will be filled by another department or outsourced.

There are areas of businesses which are quietly getting on with harnessing communication to change cultures, re-engineer processes, restructure their organizations and align behaviours with the promise of their brand. It is just that the internal communication departments are often busy elsewhere, either missing the action or being kept out of it.

Leaders are wasting communicators' expertise and experience by not making best use of them. Internal communicators are typically overloaded and frustrated as they try to focus on the strategic while having to deal with the tactics of drafting and crafting, managing logistics and producing events. The danger is that, despite good intentions, internal communication will be dragged down by leadership's outdated perception that communication is about newsletters and awaydays. In trying to fulfil a range of different expectations, communication departments may end up having to deliver at the lowest common denominator – distributing other people's messages.

Before trying to add value, define it

Businesses are learning a simple lesson – the solution they provided yesterday is taken for granted today. If you stand still you go backwards as your product or service becomes a commodity. The problem you evolved to solve may no longer be such an issue – and your solutions no longer seen as valuable.

Internal communicators need to do internally what their own organizations do externally – define a clear value proposition which their internal customers will value. They have to communicate that proposition clearly to manage expectations, and then they organize themselves and acquire the skills to deliver it.

Positioning the communicators

Organizations need to organize their communication departments to suit their strategy and their structure, and for better management of communication. Communication professionals need to be networked, coordinated and of a high standard.

Internal communication departments are often prevented from adding value by lack of access to decision-makers and by their internal customers' perception of them as messengers. This is exacerbated by their own narrow focus on internal communication, rather than business, objectives. Finally, communicators do themselves no favours by measuring how efficiently messages are distributed and neglecting to measure how well the communication process produces the intended business outcome.

Part of the pressure comes from internal clients' expectations, spoken or unspoken, of what service they will receive. Internal clients tend to think through their problem, decide on a solution and then look for someone to supply the solution. However, they often ask for what they believe the department can provide, not what is actually needed. And what they believe can be provided depends on their perception of the department, and the skills and abilities of the people within it.

If, for example, a senior manager, who is responsible for a major initiative, wants to raise awareness of it, he or she might well feel entitled to some internal PR support. Faced with the demands of a powerful senior manager, it would not be surprising for communicators to jump to it and provide it – whether or not it is appropriate.

In order to reduce the pressure on communicators, and avoid disappointed expectations, their role must be clear, and the service they provide clearly defined. A lack of clarity in these two issues explains why internal communicators are not being involved closely enough with the functions which typically plan and drive change – strategy and planning, marketing and IT.

By any other name

Internal communication exists under a variety of different names in different organizations, such as employee relations, internal marketing and organizational communication. Although some organizations see these as interchangeable terms for the same thing, they reflect different expectations of the value to be gained from internal communication, and an unclear positioning of the department's role.

The position of internal communication depends on a number of factors: the structure of the organization; whether it is centralized or decentralized; what industry it is in; and whether branding and marketing is important to its competitive strategy. It also depends on where the business is located – unit, country, corporate, global – and the split between corporate and operational communication.

Yesterday's communication today

The position of internal communication is largely driven by history. In some cases it has been seen as a hygiene factor and parked somewhere – such as with the company secretary. In other cases it has been put in a department where it was seen to be providing some value. In organizations whose focus is on manufacturing, for example, and for which unions and industrial relations are vital, internal communications may be positioned within employee relations, industrial relations and personnel. On the other hand, in highly regulated industries, such as the pharmaceutical business, internal communications can be the responsibility of the financial and legal department.

Over time, however, competitive strategy changes, and the role of internal communication needs to change with it. If it does not, the internal communicators can be left high and dry, working in a no longer valued role. To be an ace industrial relations negotiator in, for example, an organization which is no longer unionized is to fall from grace. The ideal role is as the communication champion, bridging human resources and the external marketing and public relations functions. For this, internal communication needs to be coordinated as part of a bigger communication picture.

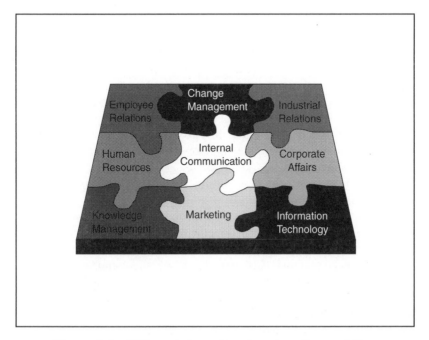

Figure 9.1   Different departments own pieces of the communication jigsaw

In some organizations the internal communication function has developed along an evolutionary path. Internal communication does not have to move from department to department since, whatever its location, it merely needs to form links with other departments. However, that does not stop organizations moving it around.

The value of internal communication to the business changes as what the business needs from its employees changes. Over the years, this may shift from happy compliance to empowered innovation.

If it started life as part of personnel or industrial relations, the communication function may move to corporate affairs. This happens when the organization promises employees that they will hear news from the management before they hear it from the media. One of the reasons why internal communication becomes part of corporate affairs is the importance of consistently integrating internal and external messages, and getting a better return on marketing investment by using external marketing and advertising for internal audiences.

Corporate communications is often the natural home for internal communication, particularly for organizations which have learned the importance of good communication with their external stakeholders, via investor relations or coping with a crisis.

Once internal and external messages are coordinated, internal communication may be moved into human resources. This happens when the organization discovers that the managers' skills, and the way employees interact with each other, is critical to delivering on the brand promise. Training, management competencies, appraisal, measurement and reward are all part of human resources' remit and exert a powerful influence on communication behaviour.

For those organizations in which delivering on the brand promise and increasing customer focus is vital to success, internal communication may become part of marketing. In Parcelforce, for example, internal communication reports to the director of marketing and sales. The function was included in marketing quite deliberately, as part of creating greater commercial awareness during the culture change from civil service to the competitive market.

The Body Shop's internal communication is part of corporate communications and reports to the director of communications. Because of its focus on retail business and its brand, there would have been a logical connection with marketing. However, the company's policy of not advertising, its history of campaigning for causes and a necessary focus on investor relations and the share price put corporate communications at the heart of the business.

Hewlett Packard also has internal communication as part of corporate communications. The business imperative is to create customer loyalty, which, they say, 'comes from moments of truth, delivering brand values, through people'. So internal communication's role is to support the translation of brand values into appropriate employee behaviours.

At Tesco, internal communication used to report to the HR director. With the growing emphasis on employees delivering on the promise of the brand, it increasingly worked with corporate affairs and with corporate marketing. From there, it was a small step to becoming part of corporate affairs.

Home is where the heart is

For internal communication to bring the business value it has to have a home close to the heart of the business. It has to be positioned where it can support the way in which value is created for customers, and where the money is made – sales in a sales organization, quality in a product organization, knowledge-sharing in a professional services business.

In Xerox the emphasis on product quality and customer satisfaction as a competitive edge is reflected in the grouping of employee communications with external communication, under a director who also heads human resources, development and training, quality and customer satisfaction.

Halifax believes in the marketing advantage of how its people deliver customer service. This is reflected in the fact that internal communication is grouped with corporate affairs, corporate marketing and personnel.

It is useful to be housed within a function that the business values and respects. Marketing is only a safe haven if the business understands and values marketing. If marketing is seen as glorified sales promotion, internal communication's role will be writing the wording to put on the tee-shirts. If human resources is seen as a euphemism for collating sick notes, internal communication will be seen as policing the health and safety noticeboards.

When an organization redefines its strategy, the heart of the business moves. Redefining its offer to the customer, or changing its target market, also redefines what attitudes and behaviours are needed from employees. This in turn redefines what information they will now need to do the job, and redefines the role of the internal communication function.

Putting the internal communication department within employee relations may make sense in a manufacturing company which depends on smooth industrial relations. When such a business redefines itself from being a manufacturing business to being a brand-owning, market-led business, the internal communication department needs to redefine what value it will bring to the party.

Relevance and value

The single most important factor in the success of the communication department is the personality of whoever leads and champions it. The most successful communicators operate at board level with a director, of whatever function, who is close to the heart of the business. This person has street credibility, is seen to add value and understands communication and its importance. Moving the responsibility for internal communication around departments is often a disguised quest for just such a personality.

Whoever is managing the communication function needs to understand the business strategy, the obstacles to achieving it and the sources of frustration at the top of senior management's agenda. They have to be able to develop communication solutions to the business's problems. To do this, they must have access to the chief executive and become involved early in planning and prioritization. Ultimately, they must be able to use internal communication to help the business deliver on its differentiating customer proposition. If they do not address these issues, internal communicators risk being without a home in their own organization.

The communication supply partnership

Chapter 8 outlined the need for a clear internal communication process that provides relevant information, with the clearest possible meaning. This requires integrating the chain of communicators from strategic thinker to front-line decision-taker.

Internal communication has to be treated as an end-to-end process, with reduced complexity, greater cooperation among those communicators who feed into the supply chain of information, and clear roles and accountabilities. Internal communication departments need to manage, not control, the end-to-end process, ensuring that it is transparent and tracking any breakdowns. To do this they need close links with other departments who communicate within the organization such as human resources, since communication style, interpersonal skills, appraisal and reward are critical to the process of turning messages into meaning.

Companies that want maximum value out of their investment in internal communication should be using it to help them achieve strategic objectives.

The job of a communication specialist is to diagnose business problems and propose a communication solution. While this includes supplying solutions proposed by internal customers, internal communication specialists have to be the doctor, not just the pharmacist. Some education of senior management in different approaches to communication may be necessary. However, rather than trying to push communication up the management agenda, it is more effective to link communication with what is already at the top of it.

Points of pain

As communication is a means to an end, it is better to start at the end – what is the business trying to achieve and what obstacles are causing it pain? Depending on the strategy, points of pain can include:

- low retention of customers
- high cost of customer acquisition
- high cost base
- lack of internal cooperation
- falling market share
- increased cost of administration
- low retention of staff.

Finding the points of pain for senior management and using communication to reduce the pain is central to creating value. Getting the opportunity and permission to explore those points of pain is the first step.

Value is in the eye of the client

Internal communicators can help solve business problems, but they have to find problems which concern the internal client. Value, like beauty, is in the eye of the beholder. If the internal client does not recognize the problem, nothing that is done for him will look like a solution.

Whether, for example, internal communication can valuably increase staff retention depends on whether staff turnover is a problem for the business. High employee turnover may be a key concern for IT departments and management consultancies because of skill shortages, but be a matter of some indifference to a retailer who accepts the seasonal migration of young shop assistants.

If the business has any aspirations, there will inevitably be barriers to achieving them. If it is happy where it is there will be opportunities for improving what it currently does. Either way, some element of communication will be involved. The internal client may be unaware of the problem, or unaware of the link between their problem and a communication solution. Or they may be aware of both but not see the internal communication department as the place to go for help.

To be recognized as a source of help and value, communicators have to develop a problem-seeking mentality.

Permission depends on perception, perception depends on positioning

Internal communicators must clarify their role and how it adds value to the business. Their ability to do this depends on how they are perceived within the company. Mismatched perceptions between departments and internal customers create frustrations for both. These frustrations are inevitable unless the service being offered is clear to both sides.

Communicators want to reposition themselves in the eyes of their organization, to take a more strategic role and to provide advice and support. However, communication department staff may be viewed as skilled craftspeople and wordsmiths who can turn out beautifully crafted messages and then distribute them efficiently. While communicators often perceive themselves as facilitators and consultants, their time is frequently consumed in producing. It is easy to become preoccupied with tasks that *you* believe to be valuable but are not actually valued by your internal customers – for example, developing strategy when they are desperate for a video, or publishing newsletters when what's needed is a major change in employees' attitudes.

More often, communicators complain about being deluged with requests for immediate tactical help that divert them from taking a longer strategic view. The job that communicators feel they should be doing may not be the one that the rest of the organization expects of them. Internal customers may therefore turn to other departments when looking for strategic help.

It does not have to be that way. Internal communication in Andersen Consulting reports to the worldwide director of marketing, and its role is defined as change management. Ernst & Young puts communication at the nucleus of the firm, combining management consulting and change management.

It is not only consultancies that see internal communication more strategically. Post Office Counters treats it as an extension of change management, and the Royal Mail's director of communication also has a strategy and planning background.

The positioning of internal communication

The department has to be clear about what it offers to the business. It may combine a number of roles, such as:

- **Messenger:** providing an efficient message delivery service for management, getting the right messages to the right people at the right time using the right channels.
- **Innovator:** developing communication tools, and new channels for communication, maximizing the use of new technology and developing new ways of monitoring and tracking performance.
- **Problem solver:** diagnosing problems and providing solutions, making the connection between communication strategy and business results, understanding the internal culture and adapting communication to match it.

Each of these roles is a different value proposition – ways in which internal communication can add value to the business. Each one of these demands a different set of skills, and the department needs to be organized differently to deliver on each.

As shown by Figure 9.2, the internal communication manager may have to fulfil a number of roles:

- facilitator/consultant
- planner
- technical adviser
- craftsman
- distributor.

Working in internal communication demands the full range of these roles. A powerful strategy can be derailed by the inability to string simple words together to communicate it. The internal communication manager will have to work with internal clients at three levels:

1 **Strategy:** involved in the development of strategies, policies and frameworks; involved with the high-level alignment of communication strategies with business objectives and plans.

2 **Management:** planning and managing the implementation of communication strategies; managing communication resources.

3 **Execution:** designing events and newsletters, distributing materials and coordinating activities.

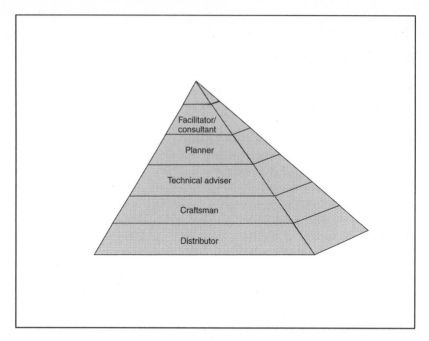

Figure 9.2   The variety of roles to be mastered by professional communicators

With luck, a communicator will be able to operate at all three levels. However, sometimes communicators are expected by the business to operate at one level while being restricted to another – expected to deliver change while only being allowed to deliver messages.

Structuring the function to mirror the organization structure

The number of communicators in organizations is increasing as management recognizes their importance, and as organizations shift their structures. The greater the move to a matrix, for example, the more the need to communicate along its different lines and the more likely that each line will hire its own communicator. An increasing number of organizations are now asking how this network of communicators should be structured and managed, and how they should relate to each other.

Chapter 4 included a discussion of the relationship between restructuring and internal communication. Communicators were advised to do six things. The first four of these were:

- Calculate where the 'centre of gravity' for employees' identification and loyalty should be.
- Understand how the business has balanced business structure and brand structure to create best value.
- Identify how the structure/brand balance might change.
- Match communication 'wiring' to structure and brand.

The following sections continue that discussion into the remaining tasks:

- Identify how communication can add value by greater consistency, coordination, and accountability.
- Identify how communication should be managed to add most value.

Figure 9.3, first seen in Chapter 4, matches the management of corporate identity and brand against how centralized, decentralized or centrally coordinated the business is. On the chart are mapped how different organizations combine their approaches to management and brand.

The value of looking at how these relate is that it gives you an idea of how best to develop rules of engagement for internal communicators, both at the centre and in business units.

In looking at how different businesses approach and structure their internal communication, some clear principles emerge:

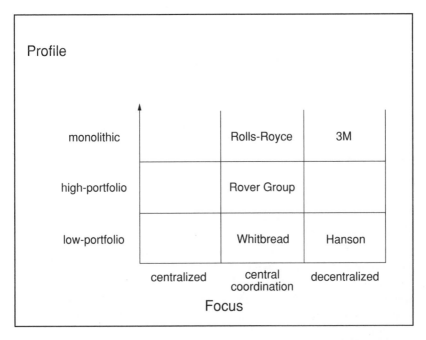

Figure 9.3 **How companies balance structure and identity**

- There is a clear definition of the role of the internal communication department.
- Internal communicators form a professional network, which has professional leadership and development.
- There are clear roles and responsibilities between communicators.
- There are clear accountabilities, which are measured regularly.

Adding value by greater consistency, coordination and accountability

The migratory path

Most organizations are on a migratory path which may take them from decentralized low-profile portfolio to centralized monolith.

Shakespeare's King Lear is a textbook case of a leader who decides to shift from a strongly centralized kingdom with a monolithic identity. Lear decides to restructure, and divides his kingdom into two dukedoms, each with its own strong leader. He also decides to do away with a central head office location, travelling instead to each dukedom in turn with his retinue of knights.

King Lear's tragedy begins when his visits to the dukedoms prompt questions about the number of knights he needs to have with him – clearly, an allegory of the reviews of the value of the corporate centre and the trend towards headcount reduction at the centre. Lear's tragedy is that having decentralized power and reduced the role of the centre, no one pays much attention to him when he decides he would rather like to reverse the process and centralize power beneath his crown again.

While this should not conjure up a picture of a corporate strategist going mad in a storm on the heath, it gives a clear warning. For organizations trying to recentralize under a single monolithic brand, reversing decentralization is not an easy option.

Profile versus focus

In order to reverse decentralization organizations need to understand, in communication terms, where the levers are, which of them they need to pull and in what direction. There are four areas which help create the best architecture for internal communication to fit an organization's structure and identity:

1   the requirement for consistency

2   the need for coordination
3   the need to set accountability
4   how the three levels of communication management – strategy/plan-
    ning/execution – are divided and located.

Figure 9.4 illustrates the varying importance of consistency, coordination
and accountability in different organization structures.

Consistency

The more an organization raises its profile from low-profile portfolio
owner to monolith, the more important consistency becomes. With businesses drawing on the assets of brand and reputation, sticking to brand
values and protecting the corporate reputation become more important
as the number of people using the brands increases.

The tools that help create consistency include communication templates, delivery guidelines and toolkits and shared communication
processes.

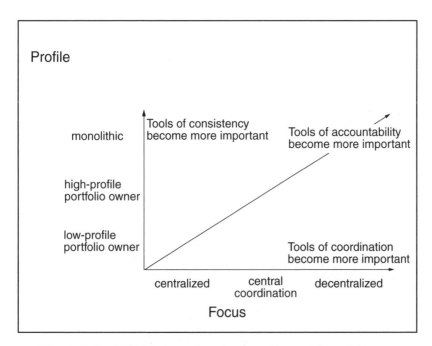

**Figure 9.4   Shifting brand and structure requires different
management of communication**

Coordination

If an organization, other than a federal one, shifts from centralization to decentralization, the need for coordination increases. Individual businesses will still have some degree of corporate family membership to balance with local priorities, and coordination will help avoid duplication and get the most from resources.

Tools for helping create greater coordination include a communication 'air traffic control' discipline, a standard communication planning framework, planning and communication toolkits, an internal communicators' network with professional leadership and skills development.

Accountability

As both the profile rises, and the business decentralizes, the need for accountability increases. Businesses are able to take advantage of the brand and have greater freedom to do what they see fit. To balance freedom and responsibility, business units are required to work within strategic and financial frameworks, and are accountable for producing results. The same holds true for communication. Tools which allow freedom while ensuring accountability include shared communication standards and clear measures, regular tracking and measurement, and linking communication competencies to appraisal and reward.

Dividing communication responsibilities

This section identifies what is the best mix of roles and skills, and how consistency, coordination and accountability can best be used for organizations at different stages in structure and identity.

If organizations are to win the game, they have to ensure that their internal communication is match fit – it has to fit their structure and fit their brand. As the strategic goalposts shift, so too should the way communication is managed.

Figure 9.5 labels different options for structuring and managing communication. In each of the boxes we are looking at three aspects:

1   the best location of the roles of strategy/management/execution
2   the mix of tools of consistency, coordination and accountability
3   the range of communicators' roles – distributor/craftsman/technical adviser/consultant – and where these should be located.

The individual options, indicated in the boxes, are discussed below.

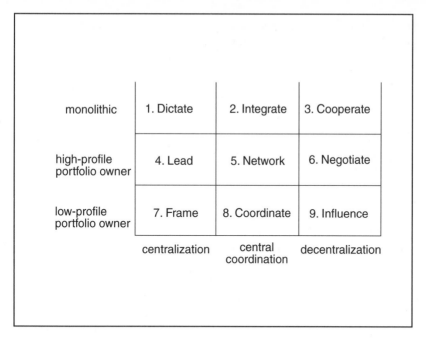

	centralization	central coordination	decentralization
monolithic	1. Dictate	2. Integrate	3. Cooperate
high-profile portfolio owner	4. Lead	5. Network	6. Negotiate
low-profile portfolio owner	7. Frame	8. Coordinate	9. Influence

Figure 9.5 Different options for managing internal communication

1 Dictate

In a centralized organization with a monolithic brand, communication is likely to be run on the Roman Empire model. There may be few organizations which are actually structured as centralized monoliths, but there are certainly a number of organizations who run their communication as if they were!

In this option, strategy and planning are carried out at the centre, with execution and delivery of prepackaged messages done locally with minimal change. This is like being the McDonald's of communication – trying to ensure consistent delivery of a centrally developed communication product at all locations around the world.

The problem is ensuring that what is dictated is actually delivered locally, since there is a danger that local business units may feel the communication material they receive is so unresponsive to local differences that they substitute their own. This makes the tools of consistency more important, so the organization has to provide clear guidelines for what is mandatory for communication and what is optional. Preprepared packs are also needed to allow that to happen with maximum consistency.

This option demands that the consulting and planning roles have to be at the centre, together with the communication craft skills to develop messages and package them appropriately. At the local level all that is required is some degree of craft skills, to translate and tailor messages minimally, and the skills for distributing them to people locally.

Since the centre is likely to feel it has best practice, and that there is little need for transfer of skills to local communicators, there are unlikely to be communication networks or training and development events.

2   Integrate

In this option, local business unit freedom needs to be balanced with the consistency of the brand. With the complexity of matrices in the organization and a growing number of communicators, there is a need for a far stronger discipline than mere cooperation – integration.

In organizations with monolithic brands the accountability to deliver a result consistent with the brand is high. While communication planning and execution will be devolved more to business units, it is at the centre that strategy will be set.

For an organization which is shifting to central coordination, it will be important to have 'air traffic control', a communicators' network with shared quality standards and strong professional leadership.

Strategic skills will be needed at the centre, as will the ability both to set up planning frameworks and facilitate members of the 'air traffic control' group. BT and Barclays Bank have both shifted towards integration, as have Motorola and AT&T.

In the business units there will be a need for able communication managers who can interpret the overall strategy in the light of their business unit needs and can carry out sound planning, working alongside the local management team. The business unit will also need good craft and execution skills to turn the plan into effective messages and guaranteed distribution.

3   Cooperate

When monolithic brand organizations decentralize, communication management has to include managing the risk to the corporate reputation.

While the need to maintain consistency of the brand and integrate communication remains high, the ability of the centre to command obedience, and the inclination of the business units to obey, is low.

In this situation quality standards, and frameworks have to be used to create an 'eggshell of excellence' that prevents inconsistencies undermining the brand. Therefore, strong strategic and planning skills are needed at the centre to develop frameworks and toolkits which are suited to a wide range of different business units and reflect their different markets. At the business unit level strong strategic, planning and executional ability is needed.

Organizations in this situation are most vulnerable to incoherence.

There is therefore a need for strong 'air traffic control', as well as strong local skills development. Also necessary is a well integrated network of good-quality communicators across the organization, with clearly defined competencies and job descriptions.

Finally there should be a strong reporting line between local communicators and the central communication function to ensure the quality and professional development of the network.

However, this option is labelled 'cooperate' because it relies for its success on the centre's sensitivity to the needs of the business units. It also depends upon the business units' ability to recognize the need for consistency to ensure a coherent brand and consistent delivery to their shared customers.

In terms of roles, those at the centre will largely be consultants and planners, with few craft or execution skills. The business units – especially the larger ones – will need the full range of communication roles in their departments.

3M is a good example of a decentralized network of 35 businesses, sharing a monolithic brand. It ensures cooperation between communicators through shared messages and tools across its different regions worldwide. The role of internal communication at the centre is to act as consultant and supporter, with the individual businesses focusing on their own internal communication strategies and plans.

The role of the centre is to help create cross-business communication, to supply corporate messages in common format, which will be tailored at local level. The responsibility for local external and internal communication is held in the individual businesses and organized by the relevant European Business Centre.

The marketing communications manager, and the corporate communications manager act as the 'professional leaders' for all the communication people in the region. The marketing communications manager acts as consultant and adviser and brings marketing communication people together from those units which overlap in terms of products or share similar customer bases, such as face masks and sandpaper.

4 Lead

In a centralized, high-profile portfolio owner, where both the corporate owner and the businesses it owns are strongly branded, there is likely to be a network of marketing and communication professionals. They will have strong views on communication issues, as well as proven expertise in brand management.

Communicators may have the power to dictate but they recognize that success depends on enrolling fellow communicators. This calls for leading the way, not dictating the rules. Developing new ideas, sharing approaches, importing leading practice from outside and providing professional leadership builds a functional network and ensures more consistent approaches.

5 Network

A business which is a high-profile portfolio owner and centrally coordinated wants the advantages of scale and synergies wherever possible. However, it also respects the individual brands' power over issues that directly affect the customer, and the delivery of the product or service.

Communicators have to create 'dual citizenship' so that employees both identify with the portfolio owner and are loyal to their own brand. This means that corporate communicators at the centre will have some reach into the individual businesses. They will work in cooperation with the local business unit communicator to strike the best balance of corporate and local information and the best emphasis on corporate and local brands.

There will be a strong overall corporate strategy set at the centre with a planning framework within which the individually branded businesses develop their own local communication strategy and plan. This means that both strategists and consultants are needed at the centre. Since the centre is also likely to provide corporate content via a corporate newsletter, a corporate video and information into the business-wide briefing process, it will also need craftsmen, such as writers and editors. It might also be providing a corporate intranet, with pages dedicated to the individual businesses. For this, and to provide advice to the business units on the best use of media, the centre is also likely to require a technical adviser.

The business units, meanwhile, will require strong planners and executors, and sound communication channels. Since the units will have a wide range of communicators, there will be a need for strong 'air traffic control', a strong network of internal communicators, and professional leadership from the communication department at the centre. Because they have to work within the overall corporate framework, the business units will also require strong communication managers, working at the same level as the business unit management team.

The relationship between the communicators at the centre and those in the business units will be a collegiate one of equals. Their roles will be similar, although their focuses may differ – one focusing on a corporate brand, the other focusing on the business unit brand. While the high need for coordination to ensure coherence will be recognized, the business units will be given sufficient leeway to concentrate on satisfying their individual markets and to act in line with their individual brands be acknowledged.

This option is called network because it entails shifting from occasional networking between communicators – meeting to exchange ideas – to a formal network of interconnected responsibilities.

In a network the relationship is not primarily between the centre and the business units, but between the business units themselves. Resources and expertise in one business unit should be available to all the others in the network. Business unit communicators with specialist expertise act as lead managers for particular areas such as face-to-face communication, intranet, measurement and training. Measurement of communication takes place across the network, with common standards and measures.

The network provides more flexibility for shifting to another structure, whether that is a move to greater centralization, reducing the number of brands in the portfolio or a shift towards a single monolithic brand.

The Rover Group, as discussed in Chapter 4, is a high-profile portfolio owner which has become more centrally coordinated.

There is no external communication at business unit level; corporate issues relating to a brand or a location are managed centrally. Internal communication is devolved to business units and is focused on industrial relations, union partnership and changes in working practices.

Given the complexities of balancing corporate reputation, product brands, industrial relations and community relations at their various locations, there are inevitably a large number of communicators involved. These come from marketing, corporate affairs and personnel. This calls for careful networking, clear rules of engagement and shared processes, quality standards and frameworks.

Business units and the centre are linked together by a communicators' network which is closely coordinated. Communicators report to their business unit personnel director who have regular meetings on employee relations which allows further coordination.

6 Negotiate

In a high-profile portfolio owner which has a number of different brands, and where the business is decentralized, the branded business units' management teams will feel autonomous. The inclination of the local management team will be simply to get on with the job and to target communication on their own local agenda. There will thus be a healthy scepticism about whether employees within a business unit need to feel like members of the corporate family – however high-profile its owner.

In these types of organization local brand loyalty tends to be strong, and pride in the business is based on its location, its product or the service it provides. Communicators at the centre and in the business units will continually be negotiating about their mutual rights and responsibilities and how great a share of voice within the business unit the corporate centre should have.

This negotiation can be more difficult when some of the businesses are perceived to be more important than others, and where some business units feel they are second-class citizens. While the 'favoured children' feel that they can get away with doing their own thing, the others feel they are forced to toe the line. On the other hand, where the high-profile portfolio owner is seen to be a benign parent, bringing strength and lustre to the individual business units, business unit communicators will feel more willing to wrap themselves in the corporate flag.

In this option, there need to be strong consultants and strategists at the centre who command respect, and can deal with local communicators who are likely already to command respect as part of their business unit management team. The corporate centre is likely to be staffed by the same kind of people as the business units – strong communication managers and able strategists, with good communication planning skills. Good craftspeople will be required both at the centre and in the business units, as there will probably be corporate newsletter and business unit newsletters which will need to complement each other rather than compete for the same employees' time and attention.

At the centre, communicators will need to have a view across all the business units and be able to deliver to the business unit managers added-value business information to which gives them a wider perspective outside their own unit. However, the balance of power lies with the business unit, and the central communicators are likely to seek, rather than demand, their help. They will negotiate for a share of voice and for compliance to corporate standards.

At this stage the tools of coordination are important. An internal communicators' network will be needed, so that communicators from business units get together to share best practice. There they can identify how one business unit's solutions can be transferred to others and discuss how corporate approaches need to be tailored to business unit needs.

The centre needs to develop a communication framework to ensure consistency, aid best practice exchange and avoid the reinvention of communication wheels in all the business units. Communication toolkits, which allow for consistent planning across all the business units, need to be developed and shared, together with a communication skills development programme. These enable communicators to come to the centre in order to learn consistent approaches which can be adapted locally, and also to spend time and network with each other. In addition, it allows them to build some sense of dual citizenship, which will aid later negotiation between the centre and business unit, and also between business units.

7   Frame

A low-profile portfolio owner which is centralized, like a Procter and Gamble, wants both employees and customers to identify more with the individual brands and less with the corporate owner. Communicators in the centre provide strong frameworks, quality standards and clear processes for measurement. Those in the business units tailor the specifics to both the requirements of their own brand values and their business unit's approach.

Such organizations can allow the local communicators to tailor and repackage in a way that they feel is appropriate, in the knowledge that the power they hold at the centre will ensure that the framework will be followed. Such a structure calls for a central communication department with consultants and planners who can create frameworks which will apply across the business, without creating a straitjacket for communicators in the business units.

Business units, on the other hand, will require people at the planning and execution level since, once the strategic framework is set, their job is to reinterpret it and translate it in the light of their own brand values and market.

The relationship between the business unit and central communicators will be that of internal client to consultants. While the business units will not be expected to set their strategy alone, they will be expected to draw on some of the expertise at the centre, and to get advice on how the corporate framework can best be adapted to their business's needs.

8   Coordinate

A low-profile portfolio owner which is centrally coordinating wants 'back of house' synergies, while allowing the branded businesses to respond to their individual markets.

Whitbread Plc is a good example of this kind of organization and is also a good example of the coordination option.

In addition to brewing and retailing premium lager, like Stella Artois, and specialist drinks, Whitbread owns a range of branded outlets: TGI Friday, Pizza Hut, Marriott, David Lloyd Leisure, Brewers Fayre and Costa premium coffee shops. Whitbread employs some 90 000 people and serves 10 million customers per week.

The company combines high-quality 'front of house' customer service with the exploitation of 'back of house' economies of scale in purchasing, property and IT. The 'front of house' is managed by branded businesses in ways appropriate to its target markets.

Although Whitbread Plc sees its business as being brand-led, the Whitbread endorsement is not put on all brands. There are few benefits in being part of Whitbread – customers do not buy from one brand to the other simply because they are part of the Whitbread portfolio.

The brands tend to have separate cultures, with employees identifying with those brands. Employees tend to be largely uninterested in Whitbread Plc as a whole. The vivacious Italians staffing Costa coffee houses need to feel part of Costa – that is where their centre of gravity is.

However, managers need to understand the whole Whitbread picture, so that they can understand the reasons for some decisions being taken, and appreciate the trade-offs that need to be made. A sense of Whitbread among managers also helps to share resources, take advantage of size, and to share best practice.

While it aims to achieve the benefits of synergies where they exist, the centre allows the branded businesses to get on with the job. Each business has its own internal communication person who has similar leeway. In this decentralized approach to internal communication, the central internal communication function acts as a corporate message supplier, manages a professional network and acts as a consultant.

The central internal communication department communicates with the top 2500 managers, supporting them in communicating to their people, stimulating communication between the business units, and creating a feeling of 'dual citizenship' – of both their own business and of the wider Whitbread business. As a provider of content, it creates and sends out briefings to the top 2500 managers and provides a central news service into the brands' own newsletters. As an equipper and consultant it helps managers in the divisions translate corporate values and information into communication appropriate to their brand, and provides skills training.

Since it is a low-profile portfolio there is no common brand 'exo-skeleton' to keep the business hanging together. The relationship between business unit communicators is therefore an important corporate glue. Communication quality has to be maintained by close networking within the internal communication network. The head of communications therefore provides professional leadership for the communication network of 14 local communicators in nine business areas.

In this kind of organization, not having a strong corporate brand puts the corporate centre in a weaker position to achieve its aims. It cannot create the goodwill to help cooperation that a shared identity fosters, and it cannot invoke the need for business-wide consistency that a monolithic brand provides. This can create a stand-off. On the one hand, the corporate strategy demands finding and exploiting those areas where cooperation makes sense for the business. On the other, each business unit has a strong and distinct brand and claims it has to do things differently and therefore cannot cooperate as much as it would like.

The danger here is of increasing frustration between the centre and the business units, as areas of cooperation, cost saving and best practice exchange are slowly and painfully wrung from internal negotiations. Internal communication will be expected to help accelerate cooperation, but the communicators themselves will first have to learn to coordinate.

The key issue for this stage is that levels of skill should be high both at the centre and in the business unit, since the best way to achieve success is by planning and coordination. Communicators at the corporate centre will need to act as consultants and planners, while those in the business units are likely to fulfil all the communication roles from consultant to distributor. Moreover, communicators will meet regularly for planning and exchange of best practice.

This option places a great onus on the corporate communicators. They have to demonstrate their value if they are credibly to lead the network. This can entail providing opportunities for professional development, hosting events to enable best practice exchange between all members of the network and providing communication tools, processes and approaches to measurement which save business units effort and avoid duplication.

9   Influence

An organization which is a decentralized portfolio of individually branded businesses owned by a lower-profile corporate brand is the exact opposite of a centralized monolith.

Being decentralized and with no shared brand, there are few other sources of corporate glue than communication. Monolithic brands have an advantage that everyone at least salutes the same flag and feels similar tribal loyalties. Whereas the centralized monolith can dictate, and the corporate centre can be very 'hands-on', this type of organization has a corporate centre which has to be 'hands-off'. However, there is still some need for balancing the eagerness of the decentralized and branded business units to follow their own priorities with the need for some corporate membership of, and loyalty to, their wider family. This is because the portfolio owner is likely to make investment decisions and trade-offs between the businesses which, without understanding the wider context, can seem perplexing and frustrating for those in the business units. So, there is a need to maintain a wider view of business issues across all the businesses.

Bearing in mind King Lear's abortive attempt to recentralize, it is important to maintain corporate glue and lines of communication. This is because, at some point in the future, there may be a need again to shift the structure. It is easier to make that change if the glue and the communication lines already exist.

Only the top management tiers of the business units will need to feel a broader loyalty and dual citizenship. The relationship between communicators at the corporate centre and those in the business units is one of influence rather than command.

Since there may be no need for business units to stick to an overall corporate strategy, there is unlikely to be a need for communication planners at the corporate centre. Each business unit will be expected to develop its own communication strategy to suit its market and its brand proposition. Where the corporate centre does not provide newsletters or videos or briefing processes to all employees, there may be no need for any craftspeople to produce them. However, at the centre there will be a need for communicators who can create understanding of a wider business context among business unit managers. This will require a communication strategist who understands the business and can integrate communication to all stakeholders, both internal and external.

One of the cardinal dangers in decentralized, individually branded businesses is the variability of the communicators they hire. Despite the fact that so much rides on the shoulders of good and competent communicators, the experience and expertise of communicators tends to vary widely. In addition to lacking skills, they can also lack status with their local management team. Even where they have the same job title, they may be doing quite different jobs and may be expected to provide very different services.

A powerful source of corporate glue will be the internal communicators' network. Rather than focusing on the corporate strategy, and on planning, meetings are likely to concentrate on agreeing common standards and common approaches.

The point of all these boxes is this: ask yourself which box you think your organization is in. Then ask yourself whether the way you currently run your internal communication fits that box. Ask your counterpart in another part of the business the same question. Chances are, where you should be, where you are, and how you manage need to be realigned. Communication either adds value or destroys it. If it is not aligned then it is destroying value.

Managing communication structure to add most value

The preceding descriptions of options emphasize the importance of networks of communicators working closely together. The more important organizations consider communication, the greater the number of communication specialists, and the greater the need for close alignment between them.

In addition to full-time communication managers, there are two other kinds of communicators' network which organizations use effectively. The first is a network of part-time managers who work with local management and advise them on best practice and provide local support. The second comprises employees, with part-time communication roles, who are used as an information distribution channel and for gathering feedback. Body Shop, for example, uses staff on the ground, trained to act as conduits for vertical and lateral communication. Such networks have common problems. Members tend to vary in terms of skills, motivation and status. Communication professionals at the centre cannot depend on them if they are perceived too differently in terms of role and service. Part-time communication managers, for example, may work closely with local senior management but will have varying abilities in terms of discussing business issues with them or identifying business needs and appropriate communication solutions.

This can be a greater problem when the agenda of the local client differs from that of the business as a whole. It has been known for the local baron to instruct his communication manager to steal the best bits from corporate media and insert them into local videos and newsletters prominently featuring the baron.

Whatever the role internal communicators may take at the centre, other communicators in the organization have to adopt complementary roles. It is pointless for the centre to provide strategic frameworks, while members of the network are not providing a basic service. This means that a development path for network members has to be put in place.

One company that has realized the need for this is Ernst & Young. As a professional services company, Ernst & Young focuses on increasing value to their external clients. In order to do this, they need to be able to capture and re-use their knowledge, which means having well thought-through internal communication. Having an effective network of internal communication managers is an important part of this.

Each Ernst & Young office has a nominated, part-time, internal communication manager, working on the task for about 300 hours a year. They are usually fee-earning, credible and able, and their communication job is seen as part of their development. This makes a communication network of 45 people, who the company uses as distribution channels for information and as facilitators of communication and providers of local support.

The first part of the internal communication manager's role is to ensure that necessary information from the centre is available in local offices. The second, and more important part is working with the local office manager to identify the local impact of strategic decisions. For instance, the overall strategy may require the organization to target a particular market sector or service line. How this will affect individuals in an office is considered by local management. Then, the most appropriate means of communication are agreed within the office, with input and guidance from the internal communication manager. This part of the role requires an understanding of communication planning, including being able to identify the different potential audiences for specific messages and how to establish feedback channels.

Making this system work and providing this understanding requires investing in the network. Several times a year managers are brought together both for training in communication techniques and to exchange ideas, experience and best practice. The network also uses a Lotus Notes discussion database to exchange ideas and information between meetings.

The role is now recognized as valuable and high-profile, and is used both by the firm and the individual to add to personal development. Internal communication managers have appropriate performance measures added to their annual business and development objectives. This helps raise the profile of the role, as well as acknowledging its value. Typically, an individual spends 12–18 months in the role, then hands over to their successor. This rotation also ensures that the organization has a growing population of 'communication-literate' managers within the organization.

Professional leadership

Internal communication is still evolving as a discipline, and communicators' networks need professional leadership and development to bring them to maturity. That leadership has to include equipping, coaching, developing, and evaluating, if the value to the business is to be realized.

Corporate communication departments should be helping communicators across the organization grow professionally and encouraging internal clients to value and use them appropriately.

Repositioning the role of the communication function: a summary

1 **Define the value communication should add.** Internal communicators need to do internally what their own organizations do externally – define a clear value proposition to advance the business strategy. They must communicate that proposition clearly to manage expectations and then organize themselves and develop the skills to deliver it.

2 **Use communication to solve problems.** In order to be convincing, internal communicators must understand the business issues facing the organization and be expert in using communication to help remove barriers to success. Senior managers are interested in their business problems, not communication problems. While they may agree that communication is important, and genuinely feel it ranks among their priorities, they are more likely to be interested in solving their own operational problems – increasing market share or reducing waste. Rather than trying to push communication further up senior management's agenda, the internal communicator should try to link communication with issues that are already at the top of that agenda. Measuring the return on investment can then focus not

on how efficient the distribution of communication has been, but on its effectiveness in helping remove obstacles to the business.

3   **Link communication architecture to the brand, identity and structure.** An internal communication strategy should support the business strategy, and should help an organization compete more effectively.

Organizations need to structure their communication department to suit their strategy and their organizational structure, their corporate identity and their brands. For better management of communication, to eliminate confusion and to coordinate messages, they will need to reorganize their communication departments. Communication professionals must be networked, coordinated and of a high standard.

4   **Apply process improvement to communication.** The drive to identify and improve key processes has forced organizations to re-examine their basic assumptions about the communication process. Process improvement is based on a continual cycle of planning, doing, checking via feedback and then revising. The same disciplines should be adopted for internal communication – track feedback from employees, and then respond, revise and improve.

5   **Educate the senior managers.** Few senior managers have thought through the implications of changing communication internally. Commitment without understanding risks unexpected surprises and recrimination.

To bring all the different issues, agendas and values to the surface, debate is necessary. Managers are more likely to enter such as debate if it starts with a business problem than if someone launches into the complaint that 'your communication is poor'.

6   **Agree the remit.** To escape from the dilemma of having to be strategic while overloaded with the tactical, communicators need explicitly to agree with the top team where their time and effort can most valuably be spent. This 'value proposition' states how internal communication will add value to the business and frees communicators to deliver against it. This does, however, require the right people with the necessary skills.

The structure of the communication network should also mirror that of the organization and how it manages its brands. In addition, clear roles and responsibilities between different members of the network must be established to avoid duplication and confusion. If this is not done, local implementers will see themselves as consultants and begin to offer something different.

Communicators' roles should be defined to ensure a match of

expectations, so that those with only executional abilities are not expected to deliver a culture change. Managing the expectations and demands of local clients should be done through discussion and by establishing an informal service-level agreement and providing clarity about professional development.

7 **Build networks and alliances.** The internal communication function should connect with human resources, information technology, change management and knowledge management departments, and with the external marketing and public relations functions.

8 **Learn from others in the business.** Lessons learned in other areas of the business – that value is created through careful management of assets, efficiencies in supply chain management, applying a customer focus and continuous process improvement – should be applied.

Information into interaction

This chapter looks at two fundamental issues that undermine organizations' ability to make change happen – the lack of shared context and the flawed nature of language in communicating.

In a rapidly changing world, employees' understanding of the commercial context is increasingly important. However the first casualty of communication is often context. This chapter argues that if organizations want to create understanding, they need to turn information into meaning. To do that people need to explore, test and understand the implications of the information they receive. This happens best through conversation, which enables them to develop a shared understanding by sharing views and perceptions.

Conversation is important not simply because it creates understanding, but also because it creates value. As the proverb reminds us 'as iron sharpens iron, so one man sharpens another'. People prompt each other to think, build on each other's ideas and, together, discover new ways of doing things which alone they would have missed. By the way in which they interact with each other individuals can open up each other's thinking or close it down. Organizations that want innovation in their people should begin by looking at how they interact with each other. The quality of people's interrelationships makes a fundamental difference in communication. It is this quality which organizations need in their communication – not the quantity that technology on its own creates.

The moment of truth for communication is in conversation, whether this is in formal meetings or around the coffee machine.

Formal communication is outgunned by the informal. The most influential communication happens day-to-day, informally and in passing. Its effectiveness is most affected by the manager's style in dealing with his or her team. Time is one of an organization's scarcest resources, and face-to-face meetings represent a significant investment of time – 50 per cent of working time is spent in meetings, many of which are badly managed. Improving face-to-face communication is critical to increasing the return on that investment. The impact and effectiveness of communication can most easily be improved by widening the skills of the manager and increasing the ability to build relationships with his or her people. Therefore, this chapter concludes by looking at the role of the manager and the skills that will be needed in future.

The chain of meaning

Increasingly, companies want their people to have a better understanding of the economic environment and how they are doing within it. They want them to understand the issues the organization is facing as a consequence, and to focus on how best to tackle those issues. Finally, they want them to be clear what they are expected to do as a result.

In short, what businesses want from their communication is an unbroken chain of shared meaning. They want the ability to transfer significance and to create the right action. They also want to avoid having to keep spelling out the issues. They want their people educated enough to spot them for themselves, so that, to borrow a phrase, they won't 'need a weatherman to know which way the wind blows'.

Mistaking the menu for the meal

However, the information that companies produce and distribute does not always help create that understanding. Information makes sense in context. Without the same context, it doesn't make the same sense – like issuing a menu to evoke the impact and experience of an enjoyable meal. Information and context fit together like a lock and key. Either without the other is useless. Sending information without context is sending the lock without the key.

For example, consider the dilemma of the finance director of a successful multinational company. He is passionate on the subject of internal communication and feels that there should be daily bulletins alerting all employees to the fact that the company's share price on the Nikkei has shifted. For him, that information is crucially significant. It will have a major impact on the business – an impact that he can already foresee. It will have repercussions that will extend to the lowest level of the business – repercussions that he can already predict. For him, seeing the share price shift is like a valley dweller hearing the dam burst. His overwhelming urge is to be an organizational Paul Revere riding through the darkened corporate corridors, alerting the slumbering natives to the imminent danger – with the clarion call 'The Nikkei has shifted, the Nikkei has shifted'.

Unfortunately, what is clear to him is not so clear for others. Most of the 'slumbering natives' he sees working in his organization would not understand what a Nikkei is, or the significance of it having shifted.

They would resettle themselves at their desks, muttering about the excitability and typical lack of consideration of finance directors.

Paul Revere may have had the original communication roadshow, but no matter how often the finance director takes to the road, unless he finds another way of speaking to his employees, he is never going to get them to that 'Aha!' moment of discovery where they share his urgency and understand the implications.

The finance director therefore has to find another way of communicating that urgency to his people. However, for him, the need to do this is as difficult to contemplate as explaining in detail and at great length the phrase 'this building is on fire'.

The significance which the finance director attaches to the information needs to be translated into other people's contexts. As a first step he has to realize that doing that is a trickier process than he thinks.

Misunderstanding is endemic, and conversation is its cure

Misunderstanding costs all organizations time and money and is due to the basic nature of language. All words have multiple meanings, but these meanings are narrowed down by the context in which the words are used.

The meaning of words is not a simple equation; a word does not have a single meaning, it has a large number of possible, and very different, meanings. Unless the speaker tells us explicitly which definition she or he intends, we must work it out from the context of the talk.

Consider the unsuspecting tourist in the USA looking for some place to park and joyfully finding a sign saying 'Fine for parking'. Does this mean that the space is allocated to parking, or the opposite, that parking there will be penalized?

Because words take their meaning from the context in which they are used, and because the context is created by each one of us making our own interpretation, there is always the possibility of misunderstanding.

People expect us to make sense of what they say even when they do not say it clearly or precisely. They assume we already have enough background knowledge to understand much more than they actually say. Nor do people expect to be asked what they mean, even if those who hear them do not precisely understand. When we ask people to be more precise about what they are saying, they can become annoyed and defensive, partly because such a question implies that they are not expressing themselves clearly. Questions can be perceived as reflecting badly on the speaker.

However, we cannot use one-way communication to tell people what to do, or what we think and want, and expect them to understand. One-way communication does not allow us to discover whether there is a shared context for understanding. Unless there is opportunity for conversation, we have no way of checking.

Conversation and shared context make understanding each other possible. Conversation turns information into understanding. We give explicit information that the listener might not have, and we ask questions to make sure what we have said is understood. But the more complicated the communication, the more depends on extensive shared context. And when clear communication is important, we cannot afford to assume that we share a context.

Asking questions in business

So, questions are necessary to check understanding, and any situation in which we are discouraged from asking questions risks creating misunderstanding.

The bad news is that, in business, we are routinely discouraged from asking questions or limited by the organization's culture as to the questions we can comfortably ask. Coupled with that, there is a cultural reluctance to speak up. Typically, Synopsis's survey research shows that 69 per cent of employees do not feel they can speak up without being perceived as negative (Bloomfield *et al.*, 1998).

However, more insidious is the fact that, asking questions can be difficult simply because people think language is basically clear and unambiguous and expect us to understand them the first time. We also believe that asking questions exposes some failing in the speaker or the listener. Therefore, if we ask questions, it is our fault for not listening properly or, worse, we are implying that the speaker was not clear.

Across most organizations there are topics and areas of concern that people feel they could never talk about with their boss. Believing that words are normally clear and unambiguous, they are afraid that they are at fault for not clearly understanding. This belief hinders people making sense of each other and leads to managers sitting in company conference, determined not to admit that they have lost the plot.

Added to this comedy of errors is the negative effect that communication media can have. Whatever aspirations managers may have for two-way communication, most presentation media are one-way and are not designed to encourage conversation. Worse, room layouts are often unwittingly designed to signal to participants in meetings that they should be passively accepting presentations from the performer at the front and not engaging in conversation. Organizing groups in sizes that expose the maximum number of eyeballs to corporate messages suppresses conversation. Furthermore, managers are routinely trained in presentation skills that relegate conversation to a question-and-answer session at the end. This led in one organization to the chief executive passionately appealing for feedback and tough questions at a management meeting whose slick professional staging and theatre-style seating guaranteed no such feedback would be forthcoming.

Finally, employee feedback is usually solicited to check whether there are any problems. Exploration of understanding is superficial. If employees seem happy, the communicator's job is done.

Misunderstanding between people is normal and highly likely because talk is routinely vague and ambiguous, and you cannot eliminate the in-built ambiguity of language. You reduce the problem of misunderstanding by creating a shared context for understanding through conversation and checking on feedback. Inconsistency is inevitable without feedback, and understanding is unlikely without conversation.

Most face-to-face cascade briefing processes are based on the belief that everyone is entitled to receive information on the company's direction and progress, and that each should receive a single consistent message. This pursuit of consistency can, however, become a production-line approach to communication. The desire for uniform standards means a single core brief has to be read out, with some local tailoring and some local addition.

While minimizing mixed messages by agreeing core information is sensible, inconsistency is almost unavoidable. It makes more sense to encourage conversation in meetings to check interpretations and then to fine-tune the communication in response to feedback. Unfortunately, current approaches to communication in organizations do not encourage conversation.

Approaches to writing information further undermine the imperfect face-to-face systems we have. Poor planning and coordination and poorly written communication increase the barriers to effective face-to-face interaction.

Information into interaction

Since organizations now appreciate the need for employees to understand, what becomes crucial is interaction between a manager and his team. Therefore, communication has to be managed for the best chance of creating understanding during that interaction.

This means removing the barriers which currently exist to interaction, and reorganizing the information to frame it for understanding. This calls for restraint and coordination among information and message providers, and the investment of time, use of better skills and greater accountability among managers.

As first outlined in Chapter 2 (page 22), effective communication is a four-step process of conversion:

1   providing content
2   creating context
3   having conversations
4   gathering feedback.

All four steps are needed, and each is a vital link in the chain of communication (see Figure 10.1).

In a classic team briefing the manager adds value to the process by adding in local items of information. This is not enough for the future. The manager has to add value by turning information into meaning, and highlighting the implications and significance of information for his or her people.

The manager has to be able to make the link between the organization's agenda and that of his or her people. This means seeing the significance of information from their viewpoint and then being able to make the connection between the intended meaning of the information and employees' needs and concerns.

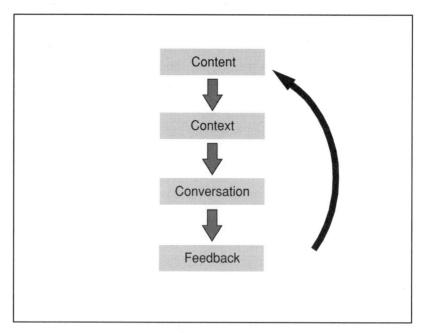

Figure 10.1   The communication process

What breaks the connection?

Although this may be the ideal, the internal communication process is often managed as a series of discrete and disconnected elements. Each has its own problems and is managed by different people with different definitions of what they are doing. For each of the four ideal stages of the communication process, there are characteristic barriers to success which undermine the intended outcome:

- **Content.** Information is provided in non-user-friendly fashion with unclear meaning and intent.
- **Context.** People with different background contexts and mixed perceptions of each other's credibility are unable to relate to each others' contexts, and use information that is unclear.
- **Conversation.** The format of meetings prevents interaction, skills are lacking and the mode is one of presentation, not discussion. There is not enough time or opportunity for dialogue between people to digest and assimilate information, with the result that the more they are force-fed with it, the less they make of it.
- **Feedback.** Organizations are unclear what feedback they actually want – acknowledgement of receipt of messages, satisfaction with the way the meeting was conducted, or innovative ideas for improvements? Managers can filter out feedback or feed all the unresolved issues up the organization where they clog up senior managers' time.

The number of people in the room directly affects the degree of interaction in a meeting, as does room layout. The volume and clarity of corporate information has an impact, as does uncertainty about its intended purpose, what feedback is expected and what will be done with it. Much therefore depends on enough time being available and the manager's skills in making the best use of it.

What is needed at each step of the process?

The challenge is to manage communication as a process that gives managers the best chance of converting information into meaning for their people in conversation.

Content
In terms of infrastructure, organizations need distribution processes that can efficiently deliver information to identified audiences. In terms of information they need to have clear messages, well articulated in plain

language and presented in a familiar and recognizable format, with the intended meaning clearly highlighted.

Context

The value of the manager is in adding context, painting a clear picture and creating understanding. For managers to put information in context, they need to have the context themselves. This means giving them an opportunity to discuss information, unpack its significance and challenge its rationale before they are asked to go and do the same with their people.

Managers should be provided with key messages and user-friendly information, with clear meaning that gives them a reasonable chance of being able to translate it into local significance.

Conversation

Managers and team leaders should be provided with the appropriate skills to prepare information, breathe life into it and engage in a conversation with their own people to create clear understanding. Given the low level of communication skills of managers, and their focus on presentation skills alone, communication coaching and skills training is vital.

Feedback

There should be upward channels for response, together with clear guidelines for managers in prioritizing areas for feedback, with timescales for reporting back on actions taken as a result.

As a minimum, feedback should be used to test understanding, not simply to report exceptional complaints. Managers should feed back to authors on how their information was interpreted, what employees made of the information and what action this has created. Feedback should be treated not as a check on employees' happiness with the message but as a means of continuing the conversation and providing input to the next round of communication.

Greater forward planning

All this, like so much else discussed so far, demands a more disciplined approach to communication and forward planning. Managers want to be able to add value, so there should be no sudden shocks, surprises or inconsistencies which they would find difficult to explain. This means that the top management team has to agree a limited number of prioritized messages and be able to present them in a unified picture.

Losing context

The cascade process of communication is well designed as a means of distributing information in a stable organization, undergoing little change. However, when organizations move the goalposts, and redefine what their communication should deliver, the cascade process can be left behind.

In a cascade process, managers further down the chain become successively less able to add meaning to information. They lose more and more sight of what was the original impulse behind the information and have less and less shared understanding of the context which gave rise to it. The absence of any translation and setting of context means that, when those messages do reach the bottom of the organization, they often have little meaning or relevance. This inevitably reduces people's ability to make any useful contribution to the team meeting and results in a lack of upward feedback.

Such a situation arose when Lyons Tetley, now the Tetley Group, conducted a root and branch review of its face-to-face communication. It was focusing on product innovation as a way of increasing its share of the beverage sector. After a restructuring of senior management responsibilities, an announcement that the two most senior jobs in the UK and in the US had been restructured was disseminated through the team briefing process.

This was duly briefed down through the workforce who received it either with apathy or with resentment. Why on earth should they be interested in the senior promotions? Wasn't this just fat cats dividing the cake up differently amongst themselves? Would they now be receiving higher salaries for their new responsibilities? What about the workers? Why was it that the senior people could get more money while the workers were still demanding air-conditioning in the factories?

This was a classic comedy of errors. There was actually very good news and great significance in the announcement. However, that meaning had been successively extracted from the communication as it was passed down the cascade process.

So, why had these two senior jobs been restructured, and why had responsibilities been changed? The focus for the business was on product innovation. Resources for the research and development of products had to be tightly allocated to make sure that the business was not diverted into fruitless areas. From being production-focused, Tetley changed the business culture to become much more customer-focused and market-led. The company was looking outside to the market, identifying different consumer trends, spotlighting those areas for product development and organizing their leadership in order to direct resources on areas with the best chances of pay-off.

In the UK, tea drinking was in slow decline, while coffee drinking was on the increase. In mainland Europe, the opposite was true. Coffee drinking, long since traditional, was in slow decline, while tea drinking was becoming more fashionable. In Europe, tea is drunk hot. In the USA, tea is drunk cold, as iced tea, and there are even tea-flavoured popsicles.

The reorganization of responsibilities between the UK and the USA was therefore a reflection of consumer trends – a way of organizing around products which different consumers preferred hot or cold. It should have been a positive signal to the workforce about the future of the business, the extent of investment in new product development, and about where the opportunities for extra jobs, interesting work, and exciting marketing activity were likely to be.

All of this began life as a one-page brief, but briefers headlined the announcements of the different chief executives' roles and titles and dropped the context and the explanation.

It is easy to get the wrong end of the stick when that is the end being presented to you. This example is not at all unusual. Many organizations which have put basic team meetings in place are frustrated by the outcomes.

A telecoms company introduced a regular face-to-face communication meeting they call 'Face 2 Face'. This involved staff getting together for between half an hour and an hour on a regular basis – usually monthly. The leaders at each level talked to their team and updated them on how the company and their own area were doing. This meant that all employees were kept informed by their immediate boss on what was relevant to them. This should have been a winning formula because, in most communication surveys, employees rate their line manager as the most important channel of communication. People also say that they prefer face-to-face communication, and they like to get information in groups, so that everyone hears the same messages and gets to hear each other's comments and questions.

The instructions for managers for Face 2 Face stated that it was the manager's responsibility to create discussion. The aim behind Face 2 Face was to generate conversation, in the belief that conversation creates greater understanding, greater ownership and greater impact of information.

However, things started to slide when managers found it difficult to follow the instruction to create discussion. They agreed with the principle that creating discussion might be useful, but the teams were unclear why they should be discussing anything.

The number of people in the meetings tended to vary, and it was difficult to create any real discussion among groups of 20 people or more. Even if managers succeeded in provoking discussion, the some of their questions remained unanswered. What's the intended outcome and response? Who is interested in the outcome of the discussion, and what sort of response or reaction will there be as a result?

The teams appreciated the time together but wanted to use the time to discuss team issues and performance, and there was a limited amount of patience for other items.

Items that were included in the Face 2 Face briefing notes were far removed from the team's circle of interest and its day-to-day focus. Issues which were too corporate with no apparent impact seemed irrelevant and a waste of time, so it was difficult to raise anything beyond a token discussion of them, that soon petered out. This was because the principle that underlay the process was being defeated by the practice.

This company had invested heavily in face-to-face communication in the belief that it was important, but they were not getting the results they wanted. While the initial aim of the process was to create understanding and conversation, Face 2 Face had come to be used as a catch-all for distributing all manner of information. Different senior managers could insist that they have their item included in the session, whether it was operational information, the discussion of a large-scale change programme or a change to the stationery requisition form.

This reflected the different perceptions of the purpose and role of Face 2 Face. Some senior managers believed that it was intended to give employees a fuller understanding of business context so that they would be able to embrace change better. Other senior managers believed that it needed only tell employees what was necessary to carry out their jobs.

This difference of outlook translated into practical difficulties, as both groups of managers simultaneously used the process for different purposes. Some senior managers happily provided information for disseminating via the Face 2 Face process which they saw as an efficient means to distribute instructions; others added information on changes to car policy, for example, because it was a convenient way of getting the information out.

This resulted in poor-quality briefing material, unfit for the intended purpose of discussion and engagement and designed with a very different purpose in mind. Information was provided, which might not be of interest to the team but which senior management believed staff should welcome. Consequently, managers found themselves asked to lead lively discussions on such subjects as changes to the car policy, which did little for their own credibility and produced little value for the team.

Common problems and how to resolve them

This organization is not alone – many organizations are finding that face-to-face communication in teams shares some common problems:

- **Lack of clarity at the top.** The 'management-speak' used to formulate the messages in the core brief can be misunderstood by those putting it together. If these people do not fully understand the brief, by the time the messages reach the end of the management chain, they can be impenetrable.
- **Lack of translation.** The failure of local managers to set corporate messages in a local context often results in the core brief being seen as both remote and irrelevant to the local job.
- **Management style.** Various forms of heavy-handed 'management style' can inhibit the team and prevent them becoming engaged and involved.
- **Disowning the brief.** Managers can be guilty of distancing themselves from the information they are presenting. The 'do not blame me, this is what they have told me to tell you' approach immediately undermines the credibility of the messages. It also means that the manager will not bother to set the core brief in a local context or add any local information.

Gaining value from face-to-face communication and improving the quality of interaction require the simple groundrules described below.

1   Be clear why you are doing it

There are often confused and different perceptions about the purpose of face-to-face communication. At board level, for example, the aim behind team meetings might be to create a flow of creative ideas for improvements within the business. At business unit level, senior managers may ee its value in creating a greater focus on customers. Within a team, however, the purpose may be to swap updates on day-to-day activities.

A problem arises when at each level in the organization there is a different perception of the value and the purpose of communication. If the corporate centre sees the role of communication as the dissemination of corporate information, if the business units use it to create a sense of identification within the business unit, and if local managers see it as a means of engaging employee enthusiasm and empowering them to solve problems, then there will be conflict and confusion. Communication from one level to another should form a chain of shared meaning, not a cascade of confusion.

Unless there is a common understanding all along the chain – between all parties – on the purpose, intended value of communication, the links will not be forged and time, effort and energy will be wasted.

In the past face-to-face communication has been seen as a distribution channel for giving instructions, reminding people of procedures and regulations and alerting them to issues and complaints. Now it is more likely to be used more valuably in stimulating discussion, creating greater understanding of issues affecting the business and fostering greater support for the business strategy. Engaging team members in problem-solving and seeking their responses to particular issues uses managers' and employees' time better and produces more value both for them and for the business.

Nowadays, meetings are also more likely to be used to put previously distributed information into context, and for creating discussion and prompting feedback. This does, however, rely on people actually reading the information beforehand which may not always happen.

2   Agree what information face-to-face meetings will contain

The aim of the process should not be to deliver efficiently a series of messages tailored to different audiences. There are more effective ways to distribute information, via more neutral media – electronically or in print. The aim should be to use team meetings to strengthen the relationship between team leaders and their teams. Making managers translate information helps connect managers' and their teams' agendas, and forces leaders to consider carefully what the messages they receive actually mean.

3   Avoid overload

Employees will tolerate some non-local messages, if the rest of the meeting is useful in addressing their local problems. Interest in wider issues depends on creating discussion and interest in their immediate issues. The core brief rides on the back of local issues – too heavy a core brief and the horse dies beneath the jockey.

One of the general principles of team briefing is that 70–80 per cent of the information should be 'local' items, with the remaining 20–30 per cent being the information passed down from above. This emphasizes the importance of allowing time at each level to discuss and understand information. More importantly, it demands preparation time on the part of line managers as their ability to translate corporate information into local significance will be vital.

4   Prioritize a limited amount of information

When it comes to communication channels, clutter kills. Avoiding clutter requires prioritizing issues, and only using face-to-face meetings for information which requires context and is worthy of discussion.

Linking employees' and the business agenda is easier if the core brief is not developed as a mere summary of discussions at board level. It is better to develop it as a combination of what the business needs to tell people, and the preoccupations and responses to concerns fed back by employees.

Senior management need to understand that their employees' have limited capacity for absorbing information, and that information coming from management will not have the highest credibility. They need to concentrate on a limited number of key issues and messages, and adjust these in response to feedback which they should actively seek.

5   Do not overload the time

Creating conversation takes much more time than announcing an item of information. The capacity of meetings to carry corporate information is radically diminished by using the process to create understanding. That means switching information that does not need putting in context, or discussion, into other channels.

Local team leaders have to understand that it is in the team's interest to include both local and business-wide issues. Equally, the board has to understand that only by creating interesting local meetings can they generate interest in wider issues. They cannot afford to overload them with non-local information, since this will kill interest, create boredom and ultimately ensure that no-one attends.

Advertisers know that they attract attention by siting their advertisements alongside interesting editorial. They also understand the necessity of an advertising/editorial ratio to retain readers and prevent an offputting advertising overload. The same principle applies to internal communication.

If the focus of the session is the team's issues, there is likely to be room for only two or three additional information items. This demands restraint from would-be authors and a 'local to corporate' ratio that leaves most of the time for the local team to talk.

6   Raise the energy

People enjoy meetings when they gain something from them – either solving a problem that annoys them or being able to air their views. Rarely does corporate information excite them – it is usually the team leader's ability to maintain energy levels and involve people, and the cross-conversations between team members, that make the session worthwhile. This puts a premium on the team leader's style and skills.

7   If you want discussion, make the information discussable

In face-to-face meetings, teams are usually more comfortable talking about specific task-related items close to their experience. Thus there will be a greater interest in local items and their implications. People will be able to discuss them because they have experience and understand the issues.

If a mix of corporate and local issues is included, there is a danger of a breakdown. Any meeting takes time to warm up, and putting the corporate information first risks it being passed over without discussion or interest during the warm-up period. This is a particular danger when people have no relevant experience to draw on and few opinions to volunteer. Discussion cannot be jump-started with items that have low mileage for discussion. Such items should be reserved for later in the session.

8   Make it a cycle, not a cascade

Team briefings cascade communication monthly over a period of 48 hours. Although feedback channels usually exist, cascading information can be like dropping a stone down a well and hearing no splash. Spreading information around the business requires more frequent and more active contact to keep communication moving. Feedback from communication meetings should form the agenda for the next round so that people can see a cycle of continuing conversation, not a monthly offloading of corporate information.

9   Build in time for discussion

Time for discussion should be built in between tiers of managers. Briefers can only sell what they own, and ownership grows from discussion and understanding – which takes time at all levels. The chain of communication usually breaks because not enough effort has been put into forging the links at the top.

To get the most from the meeting team leaders need to be able to create a sense of common purpose as a basis for addressing real areas of disagreement and resolving conflict. That means focusing on issues of common interest and finding a link between business issues and issues at the top of the employees' agenda. Finding that common ground, and speaking to the needs of the team, is a key skill that managers need.

Good intentions to create discussion and interaction can be thwarted by the information provided. Information and interaction are inextricably intertwined. Creating better interaction demands a thoughtful approach to developing the information.

For communicators, the biggest challenge in aligning the business and the employees' agenda is to close the gap between the language spoken by senior management and the language that employees speak and understand. We use words to denote categories of similar things, and help make the world manageable. We speak in generalities, emphasizing the common traits and ignoring the specific individual differences of things. However, while people may speak in generalities, they tend to think in specifics – discussing the abstract while fearing the concrete. This is what makes the use of 'management-speak' such a danger. It trades in generalities and abstractions so that the specific point underlying the generality is not brought home. Language is a tool, and when employees do not get the point it is often because management has blunted its edge.

Words have multiple meanings, all occupying what is called a word's semantic field – its range of possible meanings. Generalized language raises the likelihood of two people conversing without ever making a meaningful connection. We all take refuge in abstract language, especially when it lends significance or helps us avoid discomfort. This may explain why for one maintenance company 'vegetation management' turns out to mean cutting the grass and, for another, 'multi modal logistics transfer' means taking a parcel off a truck and putting it in a van. Similarly, managers making employees redundant are often masters of the euphemism because the plain facts are so painful.

In the same way that Dr Johnson rewrote parts of Shakespeare because he thought his choice of words was too plain and basic, so managers take plain speaking and inflate it with management-speak until all edges and outline are lost. Give them generalized terms and business abstractions to discuss with their people, and the danger is that they will start from the abstract and work outwards, making it all indistinct.

Language and trading labels

The process of achieving change is often confused because the terms we use, such as 'professionalism', are so broad, and therefore so easy to misinterpret, that they lead to misunderstanding. While 'professionalism' is often quoted as one of the core values which organizations are trying to put in place, it is only one step removed from words like 'proper' or 'appropriate' behaviour. The use of the word 'professional' signals that the speaker has a clear perception of what is permissible behaviour. This is largely undetectable by the listener, who brings to the conversation a completely different set of meanings for the word 'professional'.

In one organization, there was a complaint about the failure of employees to live up to one of their key values of being 'fast-acting and helpful'. While some complained about a certain individual being anything but fast-acting and helpful, it quickly became apparent that the individual in question saw himself as the epitome of this description. What, then, was the explanation for his apparent slowness or refusal to cooperate speedily?

While he saw himself as fast-acting and helpful, he also saw himself as careful and prudent. He would not simply react in a knee-jerk fashion to requests but rather considered them against a longer timeframe and within a broader context. While, to others, he seemed slow and reluctant, from his own perspective he was being thorough and responsible.

It was clear that his mental picture of the statement 'fast-acting and helpful' differed from that of his colleagues. When he heard the phrase in the mission statement 'fast acting and helpful' he mentally added the words 'within reason'. When he heard the phrase, what was his mental picture of the appropriate behaviour? Without holding a conversation with him it would have been impossible to tell, and, without conversation, he may never have realized himself that he was adding an automatic and unsuspected caveat to his commitment.

Key to effective communication is turning abstractions into concrete examples. Without this translation into specifics, without getting feedback and exploring what meaning the other person has selected from the field of options, we are not communicating but simply trading labels.

Although successful communication relies on translating the abstract nouns into concrete examples, people's impulses can be in the opposite direction. In one engineering organization, a project manager felt increasingly frustrated by the lack of enthusiasm that teams in other areas expressed about his initiative. Being close to the project and well aware of its potential, he was disappointed by his colleagues' failure to become engaged in the subject, and infuriated when presentations to them fell victim to the 'MEGO' syndrome – 'my eyes glaze over'.

Following in the tradition of acronym soup, described in Chapter 7, the project was called FMA – a three-letter acronym. This name conveyed little meaning but signalled that it was vaguely technical and yet another initiative. Few people understood its purpose, and fewer still were interested in finding out more. Referring to the initiative by its three-letter acronym extinguished any flicker of interest.

Pressed to explain the original idea behind the project, the manager explained why he was so enthusiastic. FMA stood for Failure Mode Analysis. So what was that? It was the term used to refer to the new practice: 'We're only going to service equipment when it's actually needed, not just because the service book tells us to do so. We've got some clever ways of monitoring the state of equipment so we can predict and anticipate when it really is going to require servicing. This way we put our efforts into where they are needed, avoid wasting money on equipment that doesn't need it, and stop hampering our own people by taking their equipment away unnecessarily.'

An original, vivid and compelling idea had been turned into a generalization, and then abbreviated to a three-letter acronym. The original inspiration had been like a lightbulb being switched on over someone's head but the communication of the idea had turned the dimmer switch down on it.

Teams which had been deprived of equipment they needed when it was removed for totally unnecessary servicing could immediately identify the benefits of such an approach. Finally, someone had the good sense to tackle the issue in a practical way.

Talking about FMA was an immediately effective way of killing interest and hiding the project's light under a bushel. By referring to his colleagues' frustration about being deprived of vital equipment the manager quickly got his team's attention. That is because he followed the principle of 'lead with their need' – framing communication from the recipient's perspective, not from the communicator's viewpoint.

Hooking people's interests and relating information to their preoccupation can be done by 'leading with their need'. When the chain of meaning from seeing the big picture to taking the right action is broken, people lose the plot and do not see any reason or urgency to take the action that's being urged upon them. They do not see how the action – apparently part of management's agenda – relates to their personal agenda. One of the tenets of communication with employees is that it should always spell out 'what's in it for me' – the implication or benefit for the individual. This is a step that is often missed. To answer the question 'So what?' the communicator has to shift from communicating to a generalized mass of people to nailing down the specific implications for a single individual.

Ironically, however, the chain of meaning is often broken not at the 'What's in it for me?' stage but at the 'what exactly is it?' stage. It is impossible to get commitment and compliance if there is not first clarity. One of the most common failings in communicating an initiative like the earlier example of FMA is never quite making clear what is its point and what it entails.

Information and interaction

In conversation information is processed into understanding. This depends on the clarity and relevance of the information and the quality of the interaction. Information and interaction are the Yin and Yang of communication.

If companies want to use communication more effectively to create understanding, they will need to raise the quality threshold of information. Clear standards and formats for producing information for communication reduce the amount of gibberish inflicted on recipients. There must be clear guidelines for producing higher-quality information which is written in plain English, from the recipient's viewpoint, with a clear emphasis on the purpose of the communication, whether for information, consultation or action.

For employees to be clear about what, specifically, the organization wants them to do, information must be integrated. Focusing on individual initiatives one after another, for example, gives a distorted view and, more importantly, unbalances employees' pursuit of objectives.

Organizations tend to ask employees to take a balanced view of shareholder value, customer focus, productivity efficiencies and cost savings. However, if they keep sending them individual bits of the jigsaw, with no labels for assembly, and no picture, it is no surprise that people swing from one focus to another and fail to see any coherence.

Many managers are often unclear exactly why they are communicating some information or what is its intended purpose. As one manager said, 'I spend a disproportionate amount of my time repackaging information I receive to make sense of it.' Managers can therefore feel that they are being forced to create their own framework to integrate the information they receive.

Assembling the jigsaw

The lack of prepackaged and pre-assembled pictures creates inconsistency and confusion in organizations. Managers at local level trying to create their own general picture – like primitive tribes developing myths and legends to explain the natural phenomena they see around them – add to this confusion. While locally created pictures provide some consistency and explanation, they differ from that of the neighbouring department and do not always accommodate new developments. Consequently, lateral communication between departments and business units can create confusion, as they both argue from different jigsaw pictures.

Traditionally, internal communication followed the rules of mass communication, with a limited number of messages targeted at a relatively undifferentiated mass of employees. In external marketing the aim has been to translate general messages into individual significance so that customers will take action. In this area there is a chain of communication which takes a broad message and translates it into individual significance. The advertising and the public relations campaigns create an awareness of the company, its service or product, which is followed up by a sales promotion, and by the sales force.

The same approach can be applied to internal communication. The art of a salesperson is being able to link the specific needs of a prospective customer to the capabilities of the product or service they are offering. Managers have to learn the same skill to make the link between information and implication. They have to make the final important connection to the individual's agenda because, from their daily contact with their own people, they are best placed to know what their issues and concerns are likely to be. Managers have to understand the individual hooks and interests of their people; they are best placed to 'lead with the need' – to connect individuals' agendas to that of the organization.

To make the connection between the organization's agenda and that of their team members, managers must do two things with information:

- start with the hook – whatever is at the top of the employee's agenda, and in which they are most interested – in order to lead with their need
- make the connection to the 'so what?', and translate the significance of a message into the implications for the employee.

To make these connections they have to understand their teams' preoccupations and the underlying point in any news or information they are expected to communicate.

To do this, managers have to be able to review the information they receive and tease out the connections – which items are capable of discussion, how information relates to their team, and what implications need to be spelled out. They have to follow the first rule of face-to-face communication – start from where your people are, not where you would like them to be. In other words, they should start with the team's express needs, talk about the underlying issues and show the link to a proposed solution. This can only be accomplished by describing an unbroken chain of logic between context and action, with the links answering the question 'So what?'. For example, an instruction to car manufacturing workers to cover up personal jewellery prompted suspicion and annoyance. Would management next insist on covering up tattoos? Then the line of logic was shared with supervisors.

■ Competition is increasingly fierce in low-cost economies such as Malaysia.
■ Consumers are more demanding, and able to demand higher levels of quality for lower cost.
■ So we have to find ways of reducing cost, and raising our quality to meet their standards.
■ So we have to be rigorous not just about quality of build, but absolute unblemished perfection of paint finish.
■ Therefore we are going to be all the more careful to avoid the smallest of blemishes.
■ The most frequent form of blemishes is inadvertent scratching from personal jewellery.
■ So we are going to ask you to tape up belt buckles, rings and watches at the beginning of each shift.

In this way, it was explained, they could make sure that inadvertent blemishes did not cost the company its reputation for quality. It would also reduce their workload in vehicle preparation, because they would not be putting time and effort into rectifying inadvertent mistakes.

The provision of this line of logic did not mean that supervisors had to take their own people through the whole rationale, although they could if they wanted to. As a minimum, they could follow a short form of making the connection – 'Why? What? So':

■ *Why?* The most frequent form of quality blemish is a scratch from personal jewellery.
■ *What?* We're asking associates to tape up rings, watches and belt buckles to avoid inadvertent scratches.

■ *So* – we'll reduce the workload in vehicle preparation, and free them up to do work we currently pay dealers for.

The changing role of the manager

As people work more in teams, dealing in ideas and information, managers and team leaders will need to facilitate and explain. They will have to create understanding of different parts of the system and how they fit together. Managing will be less about exercising power and directing, and more about making interconnections clear, and engaging and enrolling colleagues to identify issues and work together to solve them.

Middle managers: the missing link

Scarcity of time requires managers to learn how to make better use of time spent in face-to-face communication. The middle manager has always acted as a distribution channel for information through team briefings, for example, and there has always been a suspicion that they block and hold back information. Technology is now being used to bypass middle managers thereby removing from the communication chain the one person who is best placed to turn information into meaning for the employee.

However, Tesco, for example, have used managers to educate its people. Tesco's retail business involves frequent day-to-day communication on detail and logistics. Traditionally, employees have been told only the essentials needed for operating the store.

Now the company has shifted from communicating purely operational information to communicating the broader view, so that its people know the business plan, understand the local implications for them, and are able to take specific local actions. Tesco has learnt that communicating down to the shopfloor means talking in simple terms, with a focus on customers. Sessions are run in-store by managers using desktop presenters, which reflect the external advertising and sales promotion material. Tesco found it more effective to communicate simply, in plain language, face-to-face via the manager whose role is to help staff understand the whole picture and to coach them in playing their part better.

Making the link

The role of the middle manager has changed for good. No longer needed as a conduit for the dissemination of information, managers should be adding value to communication, by acting as coaches and advisers to their people, and providing the wider context. However, filling these roles requires training in the right skills. Management style and skills are a key to success, but communication skills are often seen as 'nice to have' rather than 'necessary to have'.

To change communication style from presentation to conversation requires the ability to present information from the recipients' viewpoint, to put information in context and to engage employees in discussion. The abilities to write succinctly, to chart up information, present clearly and use audiovisual equipment are necessary when the purpose of the meeting is primarily on passing information. If the purpose is to involve team members in innovative problem-solving, more advanced skills are needed, such as understanding group dynamics, how groups interact and how what you say affects the group. This understanding of the mental and emotional currents that underlie communication will become increasingly important to opening up employees' thinking and expanding what they believe to be possible.

Launching out on face-to-face communication without preparation and training does not work. Deciding to use team meetings for creative idea generation or problem-solving, and then only providing team leaders with a three-hour module on the use of an overhead projector is not a formula for success.

In a 1998 survey of chief executives, carried out by the University of Sheffield, 94 per cent of them identified communication skills as a key management attribute for the year 2010. Communication skills for the twenty-first century will include the personal communication skills of listening, influencing and eliciting feedback. Facilitation skills are as fundamental today as presentation skills were yesterday, and there will be a greater need for coaching colleagues on their personal communication skills.

An alarming number of managers do not possess basic written communication skills. This prompted one chief executive to decide not to invest in the intranet until managers could first get words clearly down on paper. Added to these basics, managers will need an understanding of the best use of media – for example, when to use e-mail versus face-to-face communication – a subject discussed in Chapter 7.

Managers and team leaders need training in assembling information, preparing and putting it into context, leading discussion, stimulating and handling questions, and feeding back. Professional communicators – including HR managers and internal communicators, initiative and project leaders – will need training in planning and preparation, how to assemble the big picture information, creating key messages, assessing the communication needs of their internal customers, and skills for influencing and negotiating.

However, managers are as keen to accept that they are not good communicators as they are to agree that they need remedial lessons in driving or lovemaking! Before managers learn new skills, they need to realize that they lack them. This calls for holding the mirror up in front of them by means of tools such as 360-degree appraisal. This is designed to demonstrate to managers where the views of others converge, to identify areas for development and improvement.

Tracking the outcome of communication, and using measurement to improve, is the final link in the chain. The following chapter looks more closely at measuring impact and improving the return on investment in face-to-face communication.

Measuring impact

In Chapter 2 the advice was to regard internal communication as a process and to manage it as a cycle. The cycle of communication is completed by measuring impact. Make sure that the circuit is unbroken – without measurement, a communication strategy becomes like a computer that is not plugged into the electricity supply.

The bottom line for internal communication is its contribution to the bottom line. This chapter covers the final link in the chain, and makes the connection between investment in internal communication and its pay-off in the changed attitudes and behaviour of people.

Measurement is not new, and there is an accepted management truism that what gets measured gets done. The patchiness of face-to-face com-

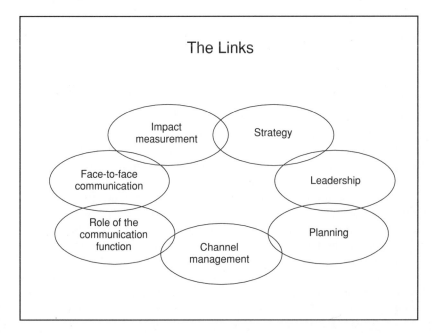

Figure 11.1 Measurement is the final link in the chain

munication inside organizations and the frustration on all sides testifies to the fact that internal communication is not being done well, partly because it is not being measured effectively.

In principle, measurement is attractive to managers, but in practice, when it comes to communication they are unsure about how best to apply it. Many organizations are moving towards an integrated, balanced approach to measuring their business performance, such as using a balanced business scorecard. This acknowledges that no single measure can provide a clear performance target or focus employees' attention on all the critical areas of the business – things are too complex for that.

A balanced scorecard is an attempt to integrate the different factors against which a business needs to deliver into a single scorecard which gives an 'at a glance' understanding of how a business is performing.

Such approaches to business measurement, which acknowledge the importance of employees' contribution, inevitably highlight the need for effective measurement of internal communication. This means that organizations need to understand quickly how best to improve current approaches to measuring communication.

This chapter argues for the need to change the basis for measurement in two ways – first, away from employee satisfaction to successful business outcomes and, second, away from the efficiency of message distribution and creating awareness to testing whether communication has succeeded in converting information into action. Making these changes requires businesses to be clear, at the outset, about desired outcomes. After all, if you do not know where you are going, any road will take you there.

The chapter goes on to recommend that research be used with the intention of changing employee behaviour and should be conducted more frequently than the usual two-yearly survey. Ways of getting greater value from research are given, as well as ways of assessing the impact of communication at a number of levels. This chapter also argues that, if communication is to improve continuously, information about the whole process, as well as the final outcome, has to be gathered – measuring impact at each link in the communication supply chain from raw messages through to action and feedback.

Internal communicators need to measure the impact of what they do, and use measurement to help bring about change and increase communication competence. To support this, reasons why impact should be measured and a description of some of the barriers to doing it effectively are set out.

Finally, it is proposed that measurement should focus on outcomes and be linked to contribution to the bottom line. This is backed up by some practical advice on how to set standards for communication and how to measure impact.

Introduction

At the beginning of the 1990s companies began to use employee attitude surveys more extensively to track employees' satisfaction with communication. Then, the concern was to identify employees' needs and improve communication to satisfy them. Companies that have religiously continued measurement ever since have won high ratings both for their communication and for employees' satisfaction. However, what they have often not won are the business results they need. They can get good survey results and bad business results – a sign that their communication, however satisfactory, lacks impact. To get the impact they want, organizations need to shift their focus.

Communicators readily agree that communication is a means to an end. Yet all too often that end is either ill-defined or unmeasured. Rather than measuring how many people boarded the train and got off at the right stop, communication measurement too often limits itself to whether or not people liked the colour of the engine and found the ticket easy to read.

Communicators can be vague about what changes in attitudes and behaviour their communication is designed to bring about, or measuring its effectiveness in achieving those changes. Nor are their internal customers any better. If they see the role of internal communication as delivering their messages, they are likely to define success as the arrival of the message at its destination. Being asked what their communication is designed to achieve would be as alien as the postman asking what objective their postcard was designed to achieve.

Why measure impact?

Effective research into the impact of communication brings a range of benefits. The value of conducting internal research is that it brings people to an awareness without triggering their defences – it gives an opportunity for education not accusation.

Companies need to know what their people's concerns are and how they get their communication. Without this information they might as well be broadcasting into outer space. Internal research allows you to target your communication more effectively, to set benchmarks and to measure performance and return on investment. *PR Week* advises that 15 per cent of a communication budget should be allocated to measuring impact and effectiveness.

Measurement helps replace opinion with fact, tracks progress towards objectives and can help change behaviour by focusing people's attention on what they need to do differently. It signals what is important to the business and shows that management is serious about change – especially when leaders offer to be measured and accountable first. It also forces both the management team and employees, to clarify their expectations and helps keep communication visible and on the management radar screen.

The results of measurement can be used to acknowledge good performers, demonstrate the value that internal communication is adding to the business and improve the communication process by highlighting inefficiencies.

Barriers to effective impact measurement

If the benefits of measurement are so manifold, why do businesses experience so few of them? There are a number of obstacles – namely:

- measuring efficiency, not effectiveness
- not measuring at all, or too infrequently
- not using feedback to change attitudes and behaviour
- measuring only part of the process
- not using measurement to drive improvement
- not connecting measurement to outcomes which benefit the business.

The following sections expand on these barriers.

Measuring efficiency, not effectiveness

Because organizations are spending time and money on communication – whether on formal communication or behind closed doors as gossip – they usually want to know whether their communication is effective. Each time there is an off-site meeting or a senior manager has lunch with employees, poor communication will be an inevitable subject for discussion. However, it is almost impossible to answer the question 'What is the company gaining from its communication budget?' without pulling back and looking at the wider issues that have an impact on communication. Without doing this, organizations will only be able to look at whether their communication activities are efficient – for example, how much it costs to produce briefing packs, how well the newspaper is distributed, what is its readership, whether employees have the opportunity to view a video, and whether they attended and liked the management conference.

It is quite possible to get high scores in all of these measures of communication efficiency and yet see no sign of its effectiveness in creating attitudes and behaviours needed to make the business succeed. This is like measuring the efficiency of a car engine, without ever discovering whether the engine is taking the vehicle any distance in the right direction.

Not measuring at all, or too infrequently

Measurement provides feedback on progress towards a goal. Regular measurement is important to keeping efforts on track. A person who weighs himself on New Year's Day and resolves to diet, but does not weigh himself until the next New Year's Eve is unlikely to achieve his or her goal. Measurement against the intended target is the only way to ensure that what is planned actually happens.

Research by Synopsis shows that businesses are not doing enough to measure and track the progress and impact of their communication efforts. In a survey of 123 UK and US companies, only a third fully assessed the effectiveness of their communication (Bloomfield *et al.*, 1998).

Not using feedback to change attitudes and behaviour

Without feedback, an organization is likely to keep on doing what it traditionally believed is important. Managers may feel that communication is valuable but, short of time, it may be something they never quite get round to. Guilty though they may feel about this, it does not improve their priorities or their performance. Publishing the results of research is more likely to embarrass them into improving their performance. Unless they research to change managers' behaviour in this way, organizations face a long road of well intentioned surveys that fail to deliver the necessary changes that they want.

Measuring only part of the process

Nothing can measure a process where the outcome is not clear, where the process is disconnected or where expectations are undefined and conflicting. Communication involves a chain of interconnected activities, from the person who writes information, to the person who distributes it, to the person who receives, interprets and explains it. Any one of these can fail, and measuring only the final link in the chain does not help identify where the problem lies.

Not using measurement to drive improvement

Research into communication effectiveness has shown that, although many senior managers in the UK now have specific communication targets and are measured against them, the measure is mostly private to the individual being assessed. Performance against standards is rarely published internally.

In measuring how communications is performing, there are two options – keep the measurement private – only the guilty manager knows how he has done – or make it public by publishing scores. Embarrassment is more effective than guilt in motivating managers to change. Good companies do regular surveys and measurement, include communication competencies in appraisals, track managers' performance and publish the results.

Not connecting measurement to outcomes which benefit the business

Although senior management may believe that effective communication is fundamental to effective change they do not routinely put that belief to a practical test.

The Jensen Group asked over 70 companies in the USA to show how they tracked the connection between communication and successful change. They found almost no benchmarks or measures specifically linking communication effectiveness to change effectiveness. Although most of these companies tracked – precisely – the impact of training on plant safety, the impact of advertising on sales and the impact of investment on growth, they tracked the success of change communication intuitively.

How to get value from research

If the above are some of the barriers to effective measurement, what are some of the ways of getting value from research? Figure 11.2 outlines the typical steps in conducting research via a questionnaire survey.

Research is more than simply a backward-looking 'How did we do?' assessment. It is a feedback mechanism for those setting strategy, enabling them to change tack and respond to changing situations. Effec-

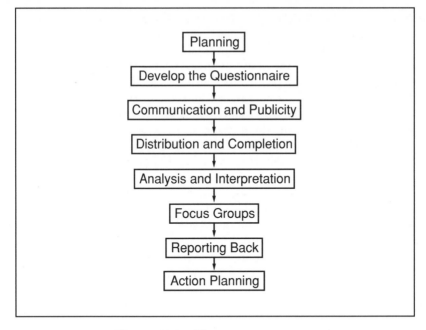

Figure 11.2   The survey process

tive communication comprises three elements. First, it is based on business objectives. Second, it is based on a clear set of expectations about what will change as a result of communicating. Third, it is focused on the conversion of information into understanding and then into action. Measurement has to reflect these three elements.

The following subsections describe the key elements of successful research and provide guidelines on using internal research effectively.

Specifically, successful impact measurement:

■ assesses the impact of communication at a range of levels
■ measures the process from start to finish
■ measures outcomes – changed attitudes and behaviours
■ measures drivers – things that contribute to successful change
■ links to accountability and measurement systems
■ measures success and makes a link to the bottom line
■ is based on a clear set of communication standards.

Assessing communication impact

Typical measures of communication are based on one of two approaches – checking whether employees are satisfied with what they get, or checking whether they received the messages. Both of these are hangovers from an outmoded model of internal communication that is based on delivering messages to employees in a way they like.

In training and development, organizations have moved further forward in measuring the return on investment of their training budgets.

Trainers who receive post-course evaluations call them 'happy sheets' because they can only test trainees' immediate reactions to a training event. Even where these are ecstatic, companies have learned that a good course experience is only the first step to successful training. The other, more important, issues are whether the skills that are taught actually transfer back to day-to-day work, whether they meet the needs identified by the business and whether they cause a measurable change in key business outcomes, such as sales or customer service. Achieving a return on the investment depends on whether the training need was correctly identified, whether the training addressed the need, and whether the learning was transferred to on-the-job practice.

A similar set of issues applies to communication. Like training managers, internal communicators have options about the level at which they measure communication. They can use surveys as 'happy sheets' which may allow them to test employees' satisfaction with the efficiency of their communication channels. After all, without a sound foundation of communication channels, communication is unlikely to achieve anything. However, when finance directors raise questions about the return on investment in communication, they are not asking about its efficiency, they are questioning its value – what does internal communication actually do for the business, and is it not effectively a corporate tax – an unfortunate necessity, like the statutory audit, with no real value in itself?

If communicators intend to fulfil a strategic role, they have to be able to measure at two levels: first, the communication process – how healthy are the communication channels and processes – and, second, communication outcomes – how communication is contributing to the business's success (see Figure 11.3).

Measuring the process

The first step consists of measuring the process – the communication supply chain – tracking the efficiency of channels and evaluating the distribution of information and messages.

Questions about the communication channels might include:

- How effective is this medium in getting the message across?
- What is its cost-effectiveness?
- What is the take-up of new channels – for example, websites and helplines?

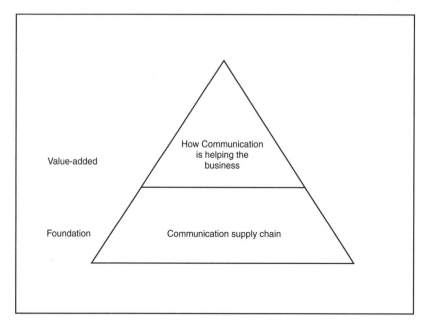

Figure 11.3 Measuring foundations and value

- How often are team briefings actually held?
- What percentage of employees receive a publication?
- What percentage read it?
- What proportion of the distribution is wasted?

Measures applying to messages and information could include the relevance of messages, and how readable, understandable and user-friendly do customers find information they receive? Are information and messages being effectively distributed, and are they targeted at the right audience? Were messages received, and if so, did people understand, and then believe, them?

Although focused on the communication process, these measures can demonstrate the value of internal communication to the business by identifying the percentage of employees who know and understand the corporate direction and objectives, the volume of usable suggestions contributed by employees, the average financial value of suggestions, and the average spend per employee on internal communication versus the value of those suggestions.

These measures all concern the efficiency of communication processes and channels. While they are important indicators of the health of the communication circulatory system, they say nothing about whether or not the body is moving in the right direction. Efficient processes are needed to distribute information, and channels need to be used effectively for communication. But these are means to an end, and that end is changed behaviour that benefits the business.

Figure 11.4 shows how efficient and effective communication processes are the foundations of successful communication, but that the added value to the business consists in using these processes to change attitudes and behaviour.

Measuring outcomes

Measuring outcomes is focused on increased knowledge, changes in attitudes and changes in behaviour that have an impact on the bottom line. These measures assess whether or not internal communication has achieved its objectives. Questions are therefore about changes in the level of people's understanding and changes in their attitudes and behaviour.

Communicators can demonstrate the intangible value they add through such measures as the percentage of employees who say they are motivated by what they read, or who believe management to be a credible and trustworthy source of information. Other measures might be the percentage of people who feel that they can identify with the company's vision and values and who feel that their suggestions are listened to and valued, as well as the extent to which they respect and trust their leaders. Questions might explore whether the target audiences

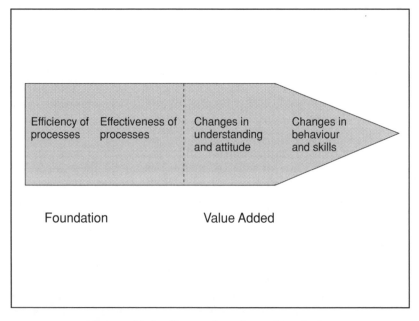

Figure 11.4 Measuring the value chain

have a greater understanding of the business priorities as a result of communication and whether they modified their opinions or behaviour as a result. Did enough people take action such as signing up for a specific programme, taking voluntary redundancy or relocating, or joining the voluntary Employee Share Save scheme? Have employees identified improvements to provide better customer care or service quality, and have they identified savings as part of a cost reduction exercise?

The key is to specify the outcome you desire. For example, one morning you wake up with spots and you do not want them. You go to the doctor, he gives you a prescription, you take the medicine and the spots disappear. You are happy with the outcome. If the spots do not disappear, no matter how well the doctor dealt with you, or how legible his handwriting, how courteous the pharmacist or how tasty the medicine, if you do not get the desired outcome you will not be satisfied.

First, you need to identify the behaviours and attitudes which you require of people if your business is to be successful. Second, you need to assess the effectiveness of different communication vehicles in causing those attitudes and behaviours to come about. This should include identifying how people select and prioritize information, the length of time it takes them to assimilate information, and the recall of key messages compared to the cost of messages and the credibility of the message source. Barclays Bank, for example, calculates that it costs £65 000 in employees' time to watch a 12-minute video. Any communicator wanting to use a video therefore has to demonstrate a return on investment not just on the video's production cost, but also on its 'consumption cost'.

Matching research to communication objectives

Communication can be seen as a process of conversion of information into meaning and then into action. If the channels and processes are efficient, and the messages are clear and well crafted, but the outcomes are not as intended, the conversion process has broken down. Somewhere, links in the communication chain have become disconnected. Measurement should therefore track the process of conversion as well as the final outcome.

Measurement at each stage of the communication process (see Figure 11.5) allows you to find where the process breaks down and why. Different questions are needed for each stage of the process.

■ **Content**
- How effective are communication channels?
- How well is information distributed?
- Do the intended recipients actually receive it?
- How accessible is the format in which information is presented?
- How clear is the language?

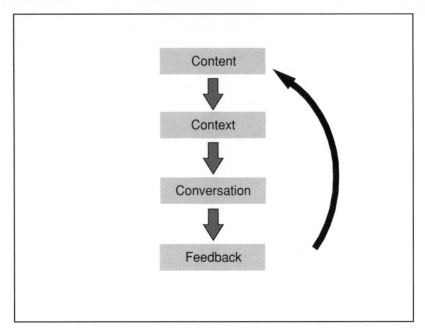

Figure 11.5   The communication process

- How relevant is the information?
- How well are key messages recalled?

■ **Context**
- How well was the team leader able to make the link between the general business context and specific commercial issues?
- How clear was the relationship between general points and local implications?
- How well were the issues presented?

■ **Conversation**
- How well did the leader stimulate conversation?
- How involved did people feel in the conversation?
- How safe did they feel to raise difficult questions?
- How well do they feel they understand the rationales for decisions?
- What opportunities were there to contribute?
- What channels exist to put forward comments and get feedback on suggestions?

■ **Feedback**
- Were questions raised?
- Were questions answered?
- How long did it take to get responses?
- How credible were the replies?
- What action was taken?

Linking to accountability and measurement systems

If communication is about making change happen, then changes need to be reinforced so that they take root. A powerful way of reinforcing is to link reward systems with desired behaviours.

Competency frameworks, appraisal systems and 360-degree feedback all provide ways to make this link. Where human resource departments are responsible for both management development and employee research, they should ensure that the communication competencies are included in appraisals, and that the competencies being measured via appraisal are the same as those tracked by employee surveys. Surprisingly, they are often different.

Measuring success and making a link to the bottom line

To demonstrate value, communicators need to make their communication objectives specific. One company had a key goal of improving its Return On Net Assets (RONA). To most staff, RONA meant nothing. Communication would only help improve RONA if people could understand what it was, why it was important and how they could affect it. The communication department set itself the objectives of helping:

- reduce costs by 5 per cent by eliminating scrap
- reduce cycle time by a factor of 4.

Within 18 months, these outcomes were achieved. These had only been achieved because people understood specifically what management was trying to do. While the communication department was only expected to communicate the new RONA initiative it opted as well to 'gain a 10 per cent increase in demonstrated employee understanding of the new approach'. It educated employees about what RONA meant, why it was important, how it affected them locally, and what action they could take to improve matters. Their follow-up research could determine what actions, if any, employees took once the message was understood, and so measure the contribution of the communications to reduction in cycle time and costs.

Making a direct link between communication and the bottom line is the Holy Grail of most communicators, perhaps because it is so difficult to do.

While it is difficult to demonstrate the direct return on investment in communication, it is possible to show the links between communication and any improvement in the business. This is easier when communication is treated as a process that begins with creating awareness and ends in action being taken.

Business goals and measures need to be broken down for employees so that functions, departments and teams are clear about what they need to do to contribute to business success.

One example is a telecoms organization that was suffering from excessive customer loss and wanted higher levels of retention. Simply communicating the urgent need to employees to reverse the trend might have created urgency but would not help them do much about it. However, once they had been alerted to the issue, the company's employees were asked to identify those 'moments of truth' that often determined whether a customer stayed or left. One of these was how well the customer service department was able to resolve billing queries. This, in turn, depended on how quickly the finance department responded to customer service's calls and provided relevant information. Employees in each department were able to identify how they could work better together, which in turn improved the level of service to customers, reducing the irritation that caused some customers to leave.

While internal communication could be measured initially on how aware it made employees of the issue of retention, its real contribution was in educating employees to identify moments of truth and then concentrate on those they could affect. Improvements in the level of service between finance and customer service could be measured, demonstrating a strong link between internal communication and customer retention. However, did this show a direct cause-and-effect relationship between communication and retention? No, but it did reveal a chain of consequences that linked the two. In other words, it demonstrated a correlation.

Showing correlations

Correlations show a relationship between two factors. A strong correlation does not necessarily show that one thing causes another. There is a strong correlation between having tattoos and having a criminal record, but that does not mean having a tattoo makes you commit crime. However, correlations do enable those in communication to demonstrate a relationship between effective communication and better business performance.

A survey by the Institute of Work Psychology at Sheffield University (1998) shows a strong correlation of job satisfaction and feeling committed to one's employer with higher profit and greater productivity. So, if communicators can show that they have helped raise job satisfaction and loyalty, then they have made a link to bottom-line performance.

These figures are backed up by a Gallup Poll (Caffman and Harter,

1998) which indicated that four staff attitudes correlate with higher profits:

1 Staff feel they can do their best every day.
2 Staff believe their opinions count.
3 Staff see a commitment to quality.
4 Staff see that their teamwork clearly links to the company mission.

A computer organization analysed results of its staff opinion survey against measures of productivity and staff retention. It found that employees who rated communication positively and were satisfied with how their supervisor communicated with them were more likely to be highly productive and less likely to be looking for a new job. The opposite was also true: employees who rated communication as poor had low productivity and were often actively looking for another job.

Similarly, a Xerox's analysis of their staff attitude survey found that those sites where employees rated communication highly were the most profitable, and employees there experienced high job satisfaction.

Beware benchmarks

Because correlations are so important, it is vital to avoid confusion in measuring communication's impact. Some organizations have regular surveys which include broad comparisons with other companies, against benchmarks. These benchworks provide a useful starting point for investigating areas that could be improved. However, using benchmarks brings its own problems. Using a benchmark with other organizations demands that questions are sufficiently general to be comparable. This works against a company being specific enough to identify what its unique problems are. There is also a danger in companies comparing themselves to others, instead of focusing on what they need for their own future. Some benchmarks are not that high, and some organizations will need to exceed the norm to meet their business aims, regardless of how they compare to other organizations.

Those companies which set the benchmarks, and are leaders in their internal communication, are usually the first to declare they have not yet got it right. They caution other companies against believing that equalling their scores means that their business problems are over.

Internal communication needs to be aligned to business strategy, and different companies in the same industry can have different strategies. It is useful to benchmark not just against companies in the same industry but also against companies with similar strategies from different industries. For example, internal communication in a customer service call centre in a financial services business could usefully compare itself to one in the water utility business.

Measurement is vital, but surveys are deceptive

Surveys are a useful tool, but they need to be used carefully. Results should be scrutinized, rather than taken at face value. Surveys contain questions which are usually answered in the same way, no matter which company is being surveyed. For example, working relationships within an organization are almost always rated as very positive. Job satisfaction scores are also typically fairly high. Questions about pay usually prompt employees to say that they are unhappy, since they quickly realize that it is not in their best interest to tell their employer otherwise.

Reactions to one's immediate boss are usually more favourable than reactions to company management. This favourability is driven by visibility. Where an employee is more familiar with his boss, and has a relationship, rating is likely to be positive. The boss may not be rated highly in terms of power or ability to actually get anything done, but they are seen to be nice.

First-level supervisors tend to be rated more highly because they are seen to take their people's side. When times are hard, and when the management message is likely to be an unpopular one, reactions to the immediate boss are artificially favourable because it is this individual who allows the company to be seen more as the 'villain'. This can be the result of the company failing to equip managers with the means to put hard news in context. This makes it easy for them to protect their relationship with their team by acting merely as messengers.

Attitudes are affected by the national climate. ISR, a leading company in employee surveys, notes that employees in the UK are the most negative in Europe (International Survey Research Ltd, 1998). UK employees have the lowest or second lowest favourable response in ten out of 15 categories in the survey among countries across Europe. They also show the most marked decline in satisfaction levels since 1994. Feelings of employment security and company identification among UK employees have also deteriorated since 1994, and UK management are now rated less favourably by their people than management in any other European country.

Employee attitudes change over time, and also fluctuate with changes in the national economy. The period 1977–87 saw a sustained improvement in employees' perception of the competence, credibility and caring qualities of management. This was based on the optimistic expectation that all the delayering and redundancies had been completed once and for all, and the future would now be leaner but rosier. Organizations surveying employees during this period would have seen continuing improvement in attitudes of employees – buoyed up on a wider wave of change which was perceived positively at the time.

Since 1987 there has been a dramatic decline in these areas, together with a decline in perception of employment security – downsizing and delayering are a way of life, not a passing phase. Organizations surveying

employees since 1987 would have done well if their employees' perceptions of management had simply remained constant, with no
deterioration.

If you are benchmarking with other organizations, you need to take
into account their ratio of males to females in the workforce, as well as
the proportion of managers to non-managers. Female employees respond
significantly more favourably than the national average towards most
issues. Managers are almost always more positive than non-managers.
Similarly, length of service is a factor. Satisfaction levels are affected by
length of service. The groups with the highest morale are those who
have been in the company for the shortest period of time and those
who have been there longest. Those with length of service between these
two extremes have lower levels of satisfaction. This may be because
morale is highest in starters, who have high expectations and for whom
reality has not yet set in, and in long stayers who have either found their
niche or have adapted themselves to the organization.

Communication is usually rated somewhat unfavourably. Employees
rarely feel that they receive all the information they require in a form
and at a time which meets their needs. The more employees are told,
the more they realize what they previously did not know and therefore
the more they presume that there is still to learn.

The rating of communication is profoundly affected by expectations
– the UK's employees are least satisfied with communication whereas
those in Mexico, South Africa and Brazil are most satisfied. This does
not imply that Mexico is proficient at communication and the UK is
poor. It is more likely that Mexican employees expect less and are more
grateful for what they receive.

This means that we have to be very clear about what we are promising
in terms of communication, since satisfaction is so directly linked to
expectations.

Communication standards

Employee dissatisfaction with communication is inevitable unless the
promise the company is making is clear. Without an agreed set of expectations, people will judge effectiveness against their own set of criteria,
and it will be impossible to satisfy everyone's needs. A further risk is
that, without clear standards, employees' expectations grow as internal
communication improves. Meeting expectations actually raises them,
since the better internal communication becomes, the better employees
expect it to be.

This is one of the reasons that communication surveys almost always
report that communication is poor inside a company. Those companies
that run regular surveys can find that the poor scores their communi-

cation received in the first year's survey improves in the second year as employees see the fruits of managers' commitment to communication. Employees' expectations then rise and, in the third year's survey, scores go down. This is not because the communication improvements have disappeared, but because employees are now applying different criteria. Internal communication is poor, they say, but now for a different reason.

Some organizations have asked whether chasing employees' expectations is like trying to reach an ever receding horizon. If employees are never going to be happy with communication, why waste time and energy trying to improve it? The answer is that internal communication has to be improved for the business's success, not for employees' happiness. Customers are equally demanding, and their expectations – particularly of levels of service – keep rising. However tempting it is to stop raising the company's game to meet their expectations, most companies know that they have no other option.

Measurement should be based on what the business needs, not what the employee wants. Setting clear standards, and objectives for communication reduces the risk of dissatisfaction and lets employees know what will, and will not, be available.

The senior management team have to agree among themselves what their standards are, so that performance against them can be measured and tracked. The key is to identify what is realistic and acceptable and what senior management are willing to back. It is pointless for the top team to declare that their communication will be open and honest, if they then clam up when times become tough. The top team needs to make clear, and commit to, these standards. This will itself demonstrate their importance and will, in turn, increase their effectiveness.

Meeting employees' expectations for communication raises those expectations, so communicators will periodically need to revisit and clarify standards. Regular reviews, either quarterly or six-monthly, will be required to monitor and assess how well these standards are being met. The most time-efficient way of doing this is to survey a sample of the workforce with a combination of questionnaires and focus groups. Some organizations, like Shell and Oracle, use regular web-based surveys continually to monitor performance.

Measures should closely reflect standards. If one of the standards is that team meetings will be held regularly to improve face-to-face communication, then it is not enough to measure whether they actually happen; their quality also has to be checked.

When companies set standards for their communication they effectively make a promise to their people. To increase the chances of keeping that promise, organizations must look ahead over the next two years and anticipate the impact of upcoming changes on staff attitudes. In the light of these, communicators can then identify which issues they can affect, what promise they can realistically make, and what measures they should therefore be applying. For example, if a significant restructuring is likely, a company might be well aware that its communication can do little to make employees' feel safe and secure. While the company cannot promise good news, it can promise early warning and clear information. This means that communication standards would be based on a promise of speed and clarity, for example:

■ 'Employees hear about decisions well before they are implemented.'
■ 'Employees hear about future plans and management explains why they are making changes.'
■ 'The rationale behind reorganizations is clearly explained to employees.'

By setting clear standards, companies avoid simply asking staff to assess communication, while leaving each employee to apply different criteria. Instead, a company should specify which criteria staff should apply.

Figure 11.6 shows a number of communication standards, together with the means by which each is measured. This provides a communication scorecard against which performance can be monitored and regularly reported.

The results from tracking performance should be broken down by grade and level and data should be analysed on length of service, grade and location to identify which issues are critical for which groups of

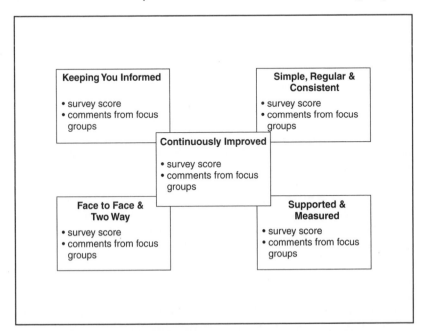

Figure 11.6 An example of a communication scorecard

employees and for which functions of the business. This allows greater targeting of solutions to specific problems – for example, clerical and secretarial staff may want better distilled information, while middle management may want more context to decisions.

Measuring impact in practice

There are a number of simple steps which can be taken to improve how the impact of communication is measured. These are detailed under the following headings:

- Flexibility and responsiveness
- Coordinating different measurement systems
- Matching research to business strategy
- Assessing the appetite for research
- Understanding the context
- Focus on the points of pain
- Managing expectations
- Managing your response rate.

One problem that besets effective measurement is the proliferation of questionnaires, with every department using them to gather responses. If the knee-jerk solution to a communication problem is a newsletter, the knee-jerk reaction to wanting feedback is a questionnaire. As waves of questionnaires pester employees they become devalued as tools, and response rates drop as employees tire of filling them in.

This problem is compounded by poorly designed and confusing questions. These create problems for interpretation and, worse, difficulty in defending any interpretation to senior managers who suddenly become statistical experts when the survey results are presented.

For example, a typical question is 'The company does an excellent job of keeping us informed about matters affecting us.' This question collapses together a number of issues – the excellence of the job, the degree of keeping staff informed and whether or not the information is about relevant matters. Another question frequently used in surveys is: 'My manager communicates effectively.' Answering this question depends on your perception of what job you believe your manager is supposed to be doing and what you believe constitutes effective communication.

These kinds of question can produce few clear indications of what action needs to be taken as a result. This compounds the lack of managers' ability, or time, to make sense of what survey data is telling them, so that they have little chance of converting the survey results into appropriate action. This does not mean no action will be taken since, usually, organizations invest heavily in feedback and action planning. What it does mean is that the action taken may not solve the company's communication problems, effort will be wasted, and frustration all sides will increase. This frustration can be avoided by approaching surveys differently.

Flexibility and responsiveness

In the past the employee research survey has been seen primarily as a means of letting employees 'have their say'. Now there is a move toward using internal research to track how employees are delivering the organization's strategy.

Traditional research into communication channels, commissioned every two years as a way of keeping a finger on the pulse, may be a useful health check for an organization in a stable market. For any organization in a changing market, however, the tracking process is likely to be more urgent. Companies are unlikely to be able to afford the luxury of only checking communication every two years – the equivalent of MOT testing the communication vehicles. Research has to be used more frequently to help the business successfully achieve its aims.

Organizations want more frequent and less cumbersome ways of keeping up-to-date with issues and attitudes, and this increase in frequency has led to more flexible ways of assessment than the questionnaire survey. Nowadays, research is seen not as the biennial inspection of the dipstick, but as an instrument for the corporate dashboard, providing continual feedback that allows greater responsiveness.

One approach is to use user groups as feedback channels, much as market research companies maintain focus groups to track changes in consumer attitudes. Xerox, for example, uses three tools to assess communications impact:

- their employee motivation and satisfaction survey
- a leadership survey
- a communication needs analysis.

Halifax Plc have a range of mechanisms in place to gather feedback and assess the impact of communication:

- qualitative research
- quarterly tracking questionnaires
- two-yearly staff opinion survey
- staff suggestion scheme
- live feedback from roadshows.

Coordinating different measurement systems

There are often a range of different and discrete measurement activities within an organization, each owned by a different department and measuring different aspects of the business. For example, the marketing department may be measuring the health of the brand, the human resources department may be using appraisals to track management competency, and the internal communication department may be running a staff attitude survey.

In a world where employees are bombarded by questionnaires seeking their views on everything from the company's strategic direction to the usefulness of the vending machine, consolidating research is vital. If different types of research, run by different departments, use complementary measures, they can provide different pieces of the jigsaw that fit together to give a clearer picture. Marketing, for example, can still track the health of the brand, while the internal communication survey measures how well brand values are conveyed and understood. Finally, the human resources department can appraise managers' ability to open and lead discussion about converting brand values into appropriate action.

Matching research to business strategy

In delivering business strategy different things are needed from different people. For example, customer-facing staff may need a deep understanding of customer preferences and profiles, a wide knowledge of a range of different products and knowledge of cross-selling opportunities. Research should therefore be targeted on assessing how well equipped people feel, their knowledge of customers, and their familiarity with the product range.

If your strategy is to differentiate yourself through excellent customer service, it is not enough to measure whether employees are aware of the strategy – you have to test for knowledge of the customer. Questions should reflect the company's competitive differentiation, testing, for example, the understanding of different customer types, and whether some are more important than others. They could also test knowledge of product range, typical customer needs and knowledge of the competition.

Assessing the appetite for research

Because conducting any form of research raises employees' expectations that things will change, you have to be certain that managers have the will to make changes. One issue to consider, therefore, is how managers might react to the results.

It is worth thinking through how bad the results might be, as managers rarely come out of surveys covered in glory. Therefore imagine a poor set of results and consider how managers might respond. Talk through with them what the results might be, and consider how to move things forward should your predictions come true.

Understanding the context

Research findings in themselves tell you almost nothing about the organization's state of health. You need to understand the context in which the survey has been undertaken and in which your business is operating.

For example, one organization's survey results showed that employees were highly satisfied with the benefits they received and very satisfied with their jobs generally. They believed they received enough information, and were very proud of being part of the company. Out of context, these responses suggested a highly satisfied and aligned workforce. However, the organization was about to enter a period of rapid change which would generate high levels of uncertainty among the workforce and a requirement to move from long to short production runs. The survey results showed therefore a 'fat and happy' workforce who were not well placed to respond to the challenges of change that they were about to face.

Focus on the points of pain

Use surveys sparingly, and do not use questionnaires to trawl for a wide range of issues when you have a specific problem. If there are poor levels of customer retention, inadequate cross selling, poor quality, or high staff turnover, for example, then focus research on what is driving these poor outcomes. In these instances you need rapid results, so design short questionnaires and use interviews and group discussions to get answers quickly.

Managing expectations

Since conducting research raises expectations that you will do something with the answers, only ask about issues you are willing to change. Ask if people are satisfied with their pay or their physical working environments if you have the budget and desire to do something if they say they are not. Direct the research questions on to issues about which you can do something, and on which you can afford to take action.

A good way to uncover managers' expectations is to ask them to predict likely employee responses and to consider what actions they would take if their predictions proved correct.

Managing your response rate

There are a range of factors which can encourage a high response rate to a questionnaire survey.

First, ensure confidentiality and reassure employees that their responses will remain anonymous by guaranteeing that no results will be broken down for subgroups of less than ten people. If confidentiality has been broken on previous surveys, this will inevitably reduce the response rate.

In addition, use advance publicity to let people know what is going to happen and when. They need to know why the survey is being undertaken, what they need to do and why they should take part. Questionnaires tend to end up in the bottom of in-trays, so publicize it by means of articles in the staff newsletter or posters on the noticeboard to keep it at the front of people's minds.

Inevitably staff will ask their managers whether it is worth taking part, so make sure that line managers are briefed to answer any questions that their staff have. Getting line managers bought into the survey process goes a long way to ensuring its success.

In times of turbulence and uncertainty people may well read sinister motives into being asked their views. You therefore need to have a compelling reason for why the survey is happening and a sound business rationale for conducting it.

Inevitably, any survey has its minor problems. You can minimize these by piloting the survey on a small group of people. This allows you to debug it, check that the language is appropriate and find out how long it takes to complete. Piloting helps you put the survey into the respondents' own language, therefore making it easier for them to complete it.

People need to be given the time to complete a survey, and that time should not be too long. People are busy at work, and are probably aware of the importance of productivity. Sending them a questionnaire that will take 40 minutes to complete will therefore ensure it goes straight into the wastebin. Anything much longer than 20 minutes is stretching people's goodwill too far. A survey that takes much longer than 30 minutes probably means that your aim is too wide and that you do not really know why you are doing it.

One of the key factors in getting people to complete a questionnaire is an easy-to-use design and layout. The question flow should be clearly signposted, the ordering of questions should be logical, and there should be plenty of white space between questions so that it does not look too lengthy. You should aim for consistency in question layout, but have some variation to prevent the appearance of monotony. You may want to conclude the questionnaire by asking people to write their own additional comments. The value from these 'open ended' questions varies, but it does give people the opportunity to 'have their say'. When respondents fill all the space available, and then continue their comments on additional pages that have been stapled to the questionnaire, you know that the company has problems.

Revisiting the circle

Impact measurement has to be continuous for two reasons: first, because its purpose is to help keep communication aligned with business needs and, second, because people and their expectations keep changing. John Lennon said, 'Life is what happens when you're busy making plans.' If you have reached the end of this book, and carefully thought through how each link in the communication chain should work for your organization, life has probably moved on again while you were reading.

One of the key lessons that this book has emphasized is that good communication is a means to an end. That end is often receding. Good communication is a vehicle, not a destination. Once businesses raise their communication game, the market's goalposts usually move and the rules are rewritten. As John F. Kennedy said, 'The only unchangeable certainty is that nothing is certain or unchangeable'. As the business context shifts, business issues and strategy will change. Communication strategy will need to be realigned, and a new wave of measurement and tracking put in place. When I was growing up I measured my height; now as I grow out I measure my weight.

The requirement for business success is good communication, and the price of good communication is, if not eternal vigilance, then regular revisiting and review. A final word from George Bernard Shaw that increasingly appears on the pinboards of communication directors makes the point: *'The greatest problem with communication is the illusion that it has been accomplished.'*

References and bibliography

Chapter 1

Bloomfield, Richard, Lamb, Alyson and Quirke, Bill (1998), *Talking Business – New Rules for Putting Communication to Work*, London: Synopsis Communication Consulting.

Deekeling, Egbert and Fiebig, Norbert (1999), *Interne Kommunikation*, Frankfurt: Frankfurter Allgemeine Zeitung Gabler.

Deloitte and Touche (1996), *Information Management Survey*, London: Deloitte and Touche.

Pitney Bowes (1998), 'Managing Corporate Communications Study', conducted by the Institute for the Future (IFTF), with research from the Gallup Organization and San José State University, 2 March.

Chapter 2

Bennis, W.G. (1989), 'Managing the Dream: Leadership in the 21st Century', *Journal of Organizational Change Management*, 2(1).

Farkas, C. and Wetlaufer, S. (1996), 'The Way CEOs Lead', *Harvard Business Review*, May.

Chapter 3

Doyle, P. (1997), 'Management Section', The *Guardian*, 14 June.

The Economist (1999), 'We're Going to have a Revolution', 9 January.

Hopton, C., Bain & Co. (1994), 'Measuring and Maximising Customer Retention' Conference, March.

Institute of Management (1994), *Survival of the Fittest*, London: Institute of Management.

Knox, S. and Maklan, S. (1998), *Competing on Value – Bridging the Gap Between Brand and Customer Value*, London: FT Pitman Publishing.

Mitchell, A. (1999), 'How Brands Touch the Parts Others Can't Reach', *Marketing Week*, 18 March.

Reicheld, Frederick (1996), *The Loyalty Effect – The Hidden Force Behind Growth, Profits and Lasting Value*, Boston: Harvard Business School Press.

RSA Inquiry (1995), 'Tomorrow's Company: The Role of Business in a Changing World', Aldershot: Gower, 6 June.

Torrington, Derek and Hall, Laura (1991), *Personnel Management – A New Approach*, (2nd edn), Hemel Hempstead: Prentice Hall Publishing.

Vandermerwe, S. (1993), *From Tin Soldiers to Russian Dolls*, London: Butterworth Heinemann.

Chapter 4

Financial Times (1998), Jackson, Tony, 'Inside Track', 13 May.

Overell, S. (1998), *Highs and Lows of the Modern Working Week*, London: Institute of Management.

Torrington, Derek and Hall, Laura (1991), *Personnel Management – A New Approach*, (2nd edn), Hemel Hempstead: Prentice Hall Publishing.

Towers Perrin (1999), *The Role and Effectiveness of the Corporate Centre*, London: Towers Perrin.

Olins, Wolff (1995), *The New Guide to Identity – How to Create and Sustain Change through Managing Identity*, Aldershot: The Design Council and Gower Publishing.

Chapter 5

Business Intelligence (1997), *Creating the Knowledge-Based Business*, London: Business Intelligence Unit.

de Geus, Arie (1997), *The Living Company*, London: Nicholas Brealy.

Deloitte and Touche (1996), *Information Management Survey*, London: Deloitte and Touche.

Després and Chauvel (1999), 'Mastering Information Management', *Financial Times*, 15 March.

Hammer, M. and Champy, J. (1993), *Reengineering the Corporation*, London: HarperCollins.

Handy, C. (1995), 'Trust and Virtual Organizations', *Harvard Business Review*, May–June.

Hansen, M.T., Nohria, N. and Tierney, T. (1999), 'What's Your Strategy for Managing Knowledge?', *Harvard Business Review*, March–April.

Larkin, T.J. and Larkin, S. (1994), *Communicating Change, Winning Employee Support for New Business Goals*, New York: McGraw-Hill.

Pascabella, P. (1997), 'Harnessing Knowledge', *Management Review*, October.

Pitney Bowes (1998), 'Managing Corporate Communications Study', conducted

by the Institute for the Future (IFTF), with research from the Gallup Organization and San José State University, 2 March.

Stephenson, K. (1998), 'What Knowledge Tears Apart, Networks Make Whole'.
Internal Communication Focus, (36), June.

Stewart, T. (1997), *Intellectual Capital. The New Wealth of Organizations*, New
York: Doubleday.

Chapter 6

American Electronics Association (1991), *Survey*.

Bloomfield, R., Lamb, A. and Quirke, B. (1997), *The Human Factor – New Rules
for the Digital Workplace*, London: Synopsis Communication Consulting.

Kotter, J.P. (1995), 'Leading Change: Why Transformation Efforts Fail', *Harvard
Business Review*, March–April.

Kotter, J.P. and Heskett, J.L. (1992), *Corporate Culture and Performance*, New
York: The Free Press.

Larkin, T.J. and Larkin, S. (1994), *Communicating Change. Winning Employee
Support for New Business Goals*, New York: McGraw-Hill.

Pascale, R., Millemann, M. and Gioja, L. (1997), 'Changing the Way We
Change', *Harvard Business Review*, November.

Quirke, Bill (1996), *Communicating Corporate Change*, London: McGraw-Hill.

Schaffer, R.H. and Thompson, H.A. (1992), 'Successful Change Programs Begin
with Results', *Harvard Business Review*, January–February.

Scholes, Eileen (1997), *Handbook of Internal Communication*, Aldershot:
Gower.

Chapter 7

Heeren, E. and Lewis, R. (1997), 'Selected Communication Media for Distributed Communities', *Journal of Computer Assisted Learning*, **13** (2), June.

The Jensen Group (1998), *Changing the Way We Work: The Search for a Simpler
Way*, London: The Jensen Group.

Scholes, Eileen (1997), *Handbook of Internal Communication*, Aldershot:
Gower.

Chapter 8

Bloomfield, R., Lamb, A. and Quirke, B. (1998). *Talking Business – New Rules
for Putting Communication to Work*, London: Synopsis Communication Consulting.

D'Aprix, R. (1997), 'Partner or Perish', *Strategic Communication Management*,
(3), April–May.

Deloitte and Touche (1996), *Information Management Survey*, London: Deloitte and Touche.

The Jensen Group (1998), *Changing the Way We Work: The Search for a Simpler Way*, London: The Jensen Group.

Pitney Bowes (1998), 'Managing Corporate Communications in the Information Age', London: Pitney Bowes.

Tufte, E. (1989), *Envisioning Information*, Cheshire, CT: Graphics Press.

Chapter 9

Bloomfield, R., Lamb, A. and Quirke, B. (1998), *Talking Business – New Rules for Putting Communication to Work*, London: Synopsis Communication Consulting.

Chapter 10

Economic Intelligence Unit quoted in *Marketing* magazine (1998), Institute of Work.

Mellor, V. (1997), *Strategic Communication Management*, (6).

Chapter 11

Bloomfield, R., Lamb, A. and Quirke, B. (1998), *Talking Business – New Rules for Putting Communication to Work*, London: Synopsis Communication Consulting.

Caffman, C. and Harter, J. (1998), *A Hard Look at Soft Numbers*. London: Gallup Organization.

Dauphinais, B. and Bailey, G. (1994). *Reengineering for Revenue: New Perspectives on Creating Shareholder Value*, New York: Price Waterhouse.

Institute of Work Psychology (1998), *Survey*, Sheffield: University of Sheffield.

The Jensen Group (1998), *Changing the Way We Work: The Search for a Simpler Way*, London: The Jensen Group.

International Survey Research Limited (1998), *The Rise and Fall of Employee Morale: Attitudes of UK Employees*, London.

Index